Unity in Process

Unity in Process

Reflections on Ecumenism

Edited by Clive Barrett

DARTON · LONGMAN + TODD

First published in 2012 by Darton, Longman and Todd Ltd
1 Spencer Court
140 – 142 Wandsworth High Street
London SW18 4JJ

ISBN: 978-0-232-52943-2

A catalogue record for this book is available from the British Library.

Phototypeset by Kerrypress Ltd, Luton, Bedfordshire
Printed and bound by CPI Group (UK) Ltd, CR0 4YY

Contents

I By Way of Introduction

1 *An Invitation*

Alison Tomlin

Well, God, here I am again, trying to respond to your invitation. I really want to – with all my heart and mind and soul. Whenever I pray my desire is to become more the person I am called to be.

But when I look at the invitation to be one with you and with others, and pay attention to that very complex chapter 17 of John's Gospel, I become more confused, not more whole. At least, that is how it feels.

Reflecting on where we belong;

> on truth;
> on being sanctified;
> on being protected and guarded, but sent out;
> on being glorified;
> above all on what your word really is and means;
> then I get lost

It should be really simple. We are called to be one so that the world may believe and I entirely accept that the divisions among your faithful people become an obstacle to belief for many. And when we focus on doing your work and share our faith in positive ways, instead of concentrating on the negatives, we get on very well.

But so often we end up having the involved conversations about all the details on which we profoundly disagree and widen our divisions instead of building bridges.

Is your invitation for us to become one in the sense of all worshipping in the same way? Surely not – we don't even manage that in one chapel, let alone across denominations!

Is it to become one united church, with an agreement about the meaning of Scripture and the creeds? Surely not – we don't even manage that in one fellowship group!

Does your invitation relate to the words we use when we seek to define what sort of union we are talking about? Does it fit with any of our institutional organizations at all?

And doesn't your invitation extend to all peoples? Are we not required to be seeking to be at one with the other faith communities in so far as that is possible? To be at one with the communities you have called us to serve? Where does the 'not belonging' fit in?

So every moment of paying attention seems to add to the confusion I confessed earlier. No wonder some people say 'Let's just concentrate on mission and stop worrying about ecumenism'.

Is the difficulty in fact from you? Like the way we see your Son at work, when he answers questions with another question – or with a story and then asks 'What do you think?' Are you yearning for us to learn more; to deepen our faith; to grow up in you?

Or is it of our own creation? Caused by our inability to let go of our security blankets; by our determination to hold fast to certainties which are often the barriers we build to defend ourselves and which become the walls behind which we hide from the wind of your Spirit?

Maybe, Living God, the answer lies in the challenging invitation to trust you – to trust not with unquestioning faith, but with a faith which is alive;

a faith which continually seeks the answers, but accepts that questions matter more;
a faith which longs to understand, but accepts that understanding may be slow in coming;
a faith which accepts the doubts and the confusions and even the darkness;
a faith which believes you are there, even when it is impossible to see or hear or feel your presence.

So perhaps you simply invite us to walk with you along the way and accept with loving trust the companions you supply, most especially the ones whom we dislike, or with whom we profoundly disagree. Perhaps we are required to accept that it is only through becoming one with you that we can become one with each other – and that only happens when we are prepared to offer each moment of our lives in trust.

If, then, we become one by walking with you, the focus of the journey is not even the destination, but you. The focus of the work is not even the task, but you. The focus of ecumenism is not to struggle to human agreements, but you. Even the focus of seeking justice and being peace-makers, is not only that, but you.

Help us, Holy God, to worship together as we are able, accepting each other's differences as your gift.
Help us to respect each other in every conversation, even when the other's opinion seems to us like painful prejudice.
Help us never to assume that there is only one way of being right, remembering that only One knows all truth.
Help us to hear each other's hurt, recognizing how much all of us need your healing.
Help us to listen for your voice as we work together, so that we may discover new insights about your love.
Then we may eventually, through prayer and conversation and hard work, discover your way of becoming one.
Guide us in each moment.
Strengthen us at each task.
Speak with and through us in every formal and informal conversation.
Inspire each attempt to create a closer unity.
Give us the patience we need with each other, and trust in the future that only you can give.
Then indeed may we be all that you call us to be, that your desires for your world may be fulfilled in and through us, and that the world may believe.

2 Does This Bring Us Closer to the Lord?

Vincent Nichols

Address to the Enabling Group of Churches Together in England, Manchester, September 2011

A London priest went to visit Pope Benedict. After three minutes, the priest did not know what to say next. He asked the Pope about his visit in 2010 to the United Kingdom, and what he remembered of it. 'I have never forgotten the profound periods of silence which were the hallmarks of the liturgies', the Pope replied, emphasizing the importance of a deep personal spirituality, and of knowing Christ in your heart.

Such an emphasis crosses the boundaries of the Churches. The spiritual life is the way we live wholly and thankfully in the presence of the transcendent. It is a quest and an adventure. The central calling of the Churches is to testify to the spiritual nature of the human person, to testify that it is necessary for us to sustain and nurture it. That spiritual quest to live in the presence of God is at the heart of our mission together.

It is vitally important in every field. The Catholic Church says the spiritual dimension of the human person has to be at the heart of every business and enterprise. It must shape economics. In education and Religious Education, the spiritual nature of the child is important and cannot be cast aside. It affects our attitude to the dying and the old, to patients and the bereaved. It affects how we support them. It is at the heart of our shared mission to affirm, witness to and nurture the spiritual dimension of each person.

Responding to the Pope's visit, the Chief Rabbi commented that at the heart of the inevitable decline of Western civilization was the neglect of the spiritual. A culture which ignores God becomes indifferent to truth. This is a real challenge for us. If we are committed to mutual wellbeing, then we must nurture the spiritual life of every human being. As Jesus said, what does it profit to gain the whole world and to forfeit one's soul (Mark 8:36)?

The Pope gave us three phrases to sum up the witness we must give: witness to the beauty of holiness, witness to the wholeness of truth, and witness to the joy and freedom which springs from relationship with Christ. In these, we can find a common attitude to mission.

In the ecumenical dimensions of the papal visit, there were two strands of challenge. The Archbishop of Canterbury asserted that whatever divides the Christian community cannot be of God. That is a profound challenge. And the Pope said that we need to gather in, and feed ourselves with, the spiritual lessons we have learned together over the last thirty years. Our relationships are not only theological, but spiritual.

The best attended London exhibitions have been related to faith; beauty can be more relevant than argument, it can feed the spirit.

My spirit and God's spirit bear united witness that we are children of God (cf. Romans 8:16). We are made for God. Let us approach each other in that way, asking of everything, 'Does it bring us closer to the Lord?'

3 *An Ecumenical Testimony*

Ernie Whalley

'Are you a Protestant or a Catholic?' a seven-year-old child was asked on his way home from school. I clearly remember this experience, as a young boy, who spent his primary school years in Northern Ireland. My response was, 'I don't know!' I still recall the look in my parents' eyes as I recounted this story over tea. Fortunately, I was brought up in a tolerant household but I still had a journey to make.

Almost twenty years later, I was training for Baptist ministry in Manchester and the College Principal arranged for us to meet up with a group of Roman Catholic ordinands at a seminary in Upholland. One particular day, the facilitator suggested we went on an Emmaus Walk where, in pairs – a Roman Catholic and a Baptist – we listened to each other telling our faith story. My partner called himself a Charismatic Roman Catholic. I, too, had been influenced in my own formation by Pentecostalism and Charismatic Renewal but I had not met anyone to that point from the Roman Catholic Church who had also been affected. That experience for me was not only 'in the head' but my heart was warmed to spend time with this brother-in-Christ, who loved the same Lord. I look back and see this now as one of the key ecumenical turning points for me.

Since then, other experiences have been gifts on the road. My ministerial training was with ordinands from the Methodist Church and United Reformed Church. As part of our theological journeys, this helped us to recognize what we held in common and to understand more deeply, and in an atmosphere of mutual respect, some of the areas where we saw things differently.

Ministry in inner-city, multi-cultural and multi-faith Bradford was a steep learning curve for me as a minister straight out of college. How do we share Christian faith through word and deed respectfully in a context with a Muslim majority? Mission was the driving force which brought together ministers from many different denominations to serve this community. We shared together in a local community project, engaged as governors in local schools and encouraged meetings for dialogue with the Muslim community. I recall one stimulating event when eight of us from different denominations, serving in similar contexts, were invited to Selly Oak Colleges for a week. We were privileged to spend quality time with eminent theologians such as Bishop Lesslie Newbigin.

Following ministry in Bradford, I was appointed a tutor at Northern Baptist College in Manchester and had the opportunity of working closely with ecumenical partners in Luther King House. Wider understandings were gained and deep friendships made. Learning to challenge one another respectfully, opening wider horizons to creative thinking and living with difference greatly enriched my life. This was the era when 'Faith in the City', the Report of the Archbishop of Canterbury's Commission on Urban Priority Areas (Church House Publishing, 1985) was published and which stimulated so much urban debate, profoundly in an ecumenical context. At the same time, I was able to work in a group of Baptist and United Reformed churches in South West Manchester. This kept my feet firmly rooted on the ground.

Thirteen years ago, I was appointed Regional Minister for Baptist Churches in the North East and then in Yorkshire. My ecumenical journey has not stood still! Through the West Yorkshire Ecumenical Council (WYEC) we have been able to focus attention on vital missional issues and to experience how we really can be 'stronger together'. Our Council meetings have broadened our understanding and enriched our thinking as we have listened to people sharing stories from the cutting-edge of mission. We have sought to discern the prophetic word in an ever-complex society. As church leaders, I have valued greatly the opportunity of meeting for conversation together – undergirded by the privilege of sharing in prayer. In an address to Westminster clergy in November 2002, Cardinal Gottfried Daneels warned about the contemporary 'deforestation of Christian memory' and our response to this requires us to pool together all our resources to ensure that the Gospel story is heard and understood within a diverse society.

I look back in gratitude to how the Holy Spirit has helped to nudge, open eyes, surprise and shock. And the journey is not finished yet: Christ beckons us forward, at times through risky territory, so that we can be one and serve him more effectively in these days of opportunity.

4 The United Reformed Church: A Story of Ecumenism

Val Morrison

The year 2012 is a significant year in the history of the United Reformed Church. It is 350 years since the Great Ejection when those ministers who, on theological grounds, could not accept the requirements of the Act of Uniformity were forced to leave the church, many suffering hardship as a result. I still visit churches which are set outside the boundaries of towns and villages as a result of the Five Mile Act which forbade the clergy from going within five miles of any city or town corporate or borough or any parish or place where they had preached or held a living.

What a long way we have travelled since that time. The United Reformed Church has, since 1972, been a 'work in progress' in the ecumenical world. It was in that year that the Presbyterians and Congregationalists united to form this new denomination – joined in 1981 by the Association of the Churches of Christ and in 2000 by the Congregational Union of Scotland.

But what have we learned over those years and what could be our contribution to the wider ecumenical scene?

Over those years we have learnt to live together, sometimes making compromizes and always recognizing the need to discuss the sometimes difficult and always challenging issues of theology, doctrine and ecclesiology. Within the denomination we hold together and practise different understandings of baptism, and have found ways to deal pragmatically, but with proper church order, with presidency at the sacraments. Our theology covers a wide spectrum and we hold the variety of understandings in tension, praying for God's guidance as we do that.

Our fundamental belief in the 'priesthood of all believers' leads us to value equally lay and ordained members, demonstrated in churches and throughout our structures not least by our appointment of two General Assembly Moderators – one lay and one ordained – but both with equal status.

Our founders had a vision that the 1972 union would be the first of many and their expectation was that this would be a denomination which would not live long enough to build its own traditions – it was born to die as others joined it. Forty years is long enough to build traditions and there are now many members who have no memory of the founding denominations. The failure to meet the vision is due in no small part to the changing ecumenical scene in these islands but that is not to say that what has happened has been a failure.

The experience of the United Reformed Church in learning to live together has given us opportunities to try new ways, with freedom to experiment and to reach new and exciting decisions about the way in which we can serve the kingdom. We believe that each denomination has treasures to offer to others and one of the treasures of this relatively new denomination is the possibility to question the status quo and to have confidence to move forward creatively. Many of our churches are now Local Ecumenical Partnerships with a variety of other denominations and many more are part of Churches Together Groups in their own geographical areas. It is in these places where ecumenism can be found to be alive and well and serving the world. As we listen to the stories which people share in these situations we hear where creativity is being allowed to flourish and the Kingdom with it. Experience which says 'we can do this' because we can point you to places where it has been successful encourages just such flourishing. I wouldn't wish to pretend that the United Reformed Church has the monopoly on any of this but I do believe that the lessons learned over the past 40 years have fed into the way in which ecumenism has developed, influencing in ways which are difficult to identify but which we would miss were they not there.

We might say that Christianity is at a crossroads in the year 2012 – criticized by many, valued by some, fearful of the future but at its best knowing that changes have to be made to meet the contemporary world. I like to think that the lessons and example of the best bits of the United Reformed Church over past 40 years will help the churches in these islands to have the confidence to take risks, to meet challenges, to respect and treasure difference and diversity all in the cause of serving a hurting and fragmented world.

5 Our Common Calling

Christopher Foster

This year of ecumenical anniversaries began in Westminster Abbey with the service of reconciliation and commitment on the fortieth anniversary of the establishing of the United Reformed Church. It both reinforced our approach and confirmed the pattern for our friendship and collaboration as we look forward.

The occasion was ecumenical not just bilaterally but much more broadly; increasingly our valued partnerships, which are often deep and lengthy, with individual churches are celebrated and developed with the involvement and support of other denominations. Together we reflected on the past with its sorrows and pains; for these cannot be forgotten or ignored as they have shaped our histories in separation as well as in unity. Powerfully the service gave expression to our commitment not simply to each other but to our faith in Jesus Christ and to the gospel, lived and shared.

Such an ecumenism is our common calling, recognizing one Lord within a plethora of church relationships, alive to what distinguishes us and committed to the developments of creative partnerships. We are engaged in these locally and nationally not because it makes organizational, administrative or financial sense, nor because it might be practically effective – and it might be some of these, or not – but because it is a Biblical and theological imperative. There is an indissoluble link in the scriptures and in our theology between Christian unity and the mission of God. As always our ministry is to keep up with God in his work and mission.

It is, therefore, encouraging for us in the Church of England that we are involved in a range of engagements that look to further and deepen the ministry of God's church for God's mission. Within Churches Together in England (CTE) we are thrilled to be involved with very many churches from across the nation, new friends and colleagues as well as those of longer standing. Membership is increasing, bringing challenges of communication and relationship which will, I judge, be an important issue in the coming period. The recent review of intermediate ecumenical life in England addressed some areas where perhaps our structures have been unable to keep pace with ecumenical developments both locally and nationally. We need to be nimble as we respond to the moving of the Spirit in the world as well as the Church.

As I become more deeply involved in CTE on behalf of the Church of England I am excited by the opportunity to be responsive and creative to ministry initiatives with our ecumenical partners, as we give expression to our common calling as disciples and apostles. We are called and sent. Fresh Expressions are increasingly ecumenical; shared ministry is high on the agenda with the Methodist Church as the Covenant develops; a new phase has begun in conversation with the Baptist Union.

Critically, I see and hear about local initiatives which are effective in service and witness. These inspire us and properly test our national and intermediate structures to be responsive and fit to serve the church, the gospel and the Lord.

II The Context of Unity

6 *An Overview of Ecumenism*

Clive Barrett

By all accounts, 1984 was an ecumenical winter. The General Synod of the Church of England was told that, 'For the first time since 1946 there are now no unity negotiations going on in England between any of the churches.'[1] There had previously been talk of the adventure of ecumenism, of local ecumenical scouts in advance of the main body of the churches, that 'this was to be the century of church union'. The adventure had come to an abrupt halt two years earlier with the Church of England's rejection of proposal for a Covenant with Baptist, Methodist, United Reformed and Moravian churches. 'The "scouts" felt betrayed, isolated and in many cases angry', and some felt that 'a generation's work has been wasted'.

The more indefatigable enthusiasts noted, however, that the extent of local ecumenism was such that the clock could not be turned back, that relationships between churches in many areas – including 'Areas of Ecumenical Experiment'[2] – had been built up to such an extent, and over such a period of time that mission would inevitably continue to go forward hand in hand with unity. Maybe that unity looked different from the model which the proponents of national Covenant schemes had anticipated. In rejecting the ordered and imposed structures of the Covenant, the churches had opened the way to a pragmatic approach which would allow for considerable diversity. After all, the very fact that there were no longer any national unity schemes being negotiated meant that it might more readily be possible to include the Roman Catholic Church, Pentecostals, Salvation Army, Quakers ..., all of whom, to a varying degree, took part in local ecumenical activities in different parts of the country. The potential for future partnership went beyond those churches which had traditionally engaged in bilateral or multilateral structural negotiations.

This analysis also transferred the emphasis of ecumenical progress to initiatives that were more local – or possibly 'intermediate', i.e., at Regional / County / Diocesan level (boundaries were always difficult, and remain so), with Sponsoring Bodies to oversee and encourage not only formal Local Ecumenical Partnerships (or 'Projects' as they were then) but local ecumenism generally. This was also the level of activity best suited for meetings of senior church leaders, and several areas had already developed such regional structures.

The launch of the Inter Church Process, 'Not Strangers but Pilgrims' in 1985, with a widely supported Lent Course the following year, complete with national radio coverage, was an ecumenical culture shift. It moved the centre of ecumenical attention away from councils and synods to grassroots prayer and practice, to local listening and to learning from each other.

The result was that, a mere three years after the trauma of 1984, the ecumenical scene in the British Isles was reinvigorated. Winter became spring as the phrase and concept of 'Churches Together' breathed new life into ecumenism at all levels. The year 1987 was the twenty-fifth anniversary of the first meeting of Vatican II, and in that spirit of renewal, Cardinal Basil Hume announced at a Swanwick Conference that the time had come for the churches, including the Catholic Church, to move from cooperation to commitment in ecumenical life. The Churches Together model, bringing partner churches together in presence and mission, respecting and listening to each other, acknowledging each other's integrity, enabled that fuller participation, alongside that of other churches which had never been part of the Covenant process. This would be fruit of the Swanwick Declaration of 1987.[3]

The 'four nations' would each have their own body (Churches Together in England, etc.) with a channel of communication through Churches Together in Britain and Ireland. Local Councils of Churches morphed, generally, into Churches Together groups. Instead of churches attempting to be a single entity and seeing difference as an obstacle, acknowledging difference at the outset produced a trustworthy basis for unity. As I suggest below, this could yet be an important British contribution to international inter church relations, given that the World Council of Churches and the Conference of European Churches have post-war structures which closely resemble those from which Britain moved on in 1987.

Thus, only three years after that ecumenical winter, the environment of Christian unity was transformed. The year 2012 is not only the fiftieth anniversary of that first meeting of Vatican II, it is the fortieth anniversary of the founding of the United Reformed Church,[4] the twenty-fifth anniversary of the Swanwick Declaration and the twenty-fifth anniversary of one of a number of Intermediate Bodies (intermediate between the local and the national), the West Yorkshire Ecumenical Council (WYEC). It is an opportunity to tell the stories, to review the ecumenical life of the churches, to discover the vast canvas of contemporary ecumenical activity, far greater than is generally acknowledged, and to consider the challenges and chances for this generation's indefatigable enthusiasts in the next 25 years. Such is the context of this volume.

Which stories to tell? The stories we choose, the stories we tell and the stories we hear, help to determine who we are, how we live, and what our priorities shall be. If we only tell stories of our local church, or even its environs, then our concerns will be parochial: rooted, but narrow and blinkered. If we only tell stories of our own denomination, then our concerns will still be narrow and blinkered, monochrome and fixated on organizational matters. The media we use for our Christian stories, however, is nearly all denominational, from the *Church Times* and *Methodist Recorder*, to diocesan, district and synod newsletters. It is little wonder that our interests are narrowed to the specific interests of our own denominations and that we are oblivious not only of the concerns of neighbouring Christians but also of the growing ecumenical reality around us. Our God is too small.

We are largely ignorant of ecumenical stories because we do not tell them, and, for the main part, we do not have the media through which to tell them. Little wonder that there is little awareness of ecumenism. Little wonder.

Yet there are countless ecumenical stories to be told, from local friendship cells to Churches Together groups to the affairs of those who take counsel for the international policies of the churches. There is far more ecumenical activity than we ever seem to admit. Let us tell those stories, and listen to them; let us open our eyes to see the Other in the other. As we appreciate neighbouring Christians more, seeing God in another's life, strange worship and witness, we grow closer to one another and to God. As our relationships become closer and our horizons become broader, we are strengthened by the awareness that we are not alone in being God's people in our place. There is solidarity and there is opportunity, each feeding each. We take each other seriously not only because of the greater mission potential that arises, but because in so doing we change and grow towards God. And we wonder.

If tradition can be seen as the story of the Holy Spirit, then it is a living, growing, changing entity. These are not threats to tradition, but part of it. The process of Receptive Ecumenism (see Paul and Andrea Murray's contribution) is rooted in the humility to recognize God's gifts in each other, with a willingness to respect and learn from each other, and to change in the light of awareness that our most unlikely neighbours may have gifts and practices from which we too may benefit. It is a readiness to ask about all things, from payroll administration to the way we read Scripture, 'Does anyone else do this better? What can we learn from them?' The only pre-requisites for this are an openness to the Spirit leading us to change and growth, together with sufficient ecumenical awareness, a mindset for unity, to make us look to each other in the first place. It is a way of looking at our faith and our churches which says of all things, 'Can we do this together?' The challenge for all the churches is to foster that mindset for unity at all levels, from the local to the international.

This volume aims to do just that, to foster a mindset for unity, beginning with Neil Richardson's excellent study of Unity in Scripture. It tells stories of ecumenical experience and activity from local grassroots Churches Together groups in one corner of England, through to international dialogues between Churches. The joys of ecumenism are real: contributors tell personal stories of building unlikely relationships, and of the way in which openness to others increased the depth of appreciation of one's own tradition.[5] The pains of ecumenism are also real: contributors have suffered ecclesial, racist or gender discrimination in the churches. The realities can be a joy – tell the stories – and a pain, an unfinished work of healing, as Barbara Glasson indicates. Pain is personal, and generally associated with a lack of respect or a disregard to an essential or important part of one's being. Such agencies as Interchurch Families, whose name speaks for itself, address such concerns head on.

Classic fields of pain include those concerned with racism (see Anthony G. Reddie's chapter) and issues of gender, where only a few churches have a record to be proud of. Theologies which emphasize gender distinction are often heard as – and at less reasoned street level are sometimes communicated as – blatant gender discrimination, with ecumenism taking the blame and the backlash. Even when thinking is clear, its expression might not be, with painful consequences. Good relationships depend on high quality, careful and respectful communication, both speaking and listening. Whatever the gender theology of one's own church, there may still be a need for men in particular to consider charitably, in a spirit of ecumenical hospitality, what an appropriate attitude might be towards, say, a woman minister from another church. If ecumenism is the process of building bridges, of making communication possible, then that includes addressing areas of pain, essential for growing relationships which go beyond superficial pleasantries and possess real depth.

In the building of relationships, and in the development of mutual understanding, there is no substitute for good communication. In a digital age, there are boundless opportunities. Churches Together in Britain and Ireland has an impressive interactive website. West Yorkshire Ecumenical Council recently 'tweeted' prayers by Church Leaders for young people. Nothing, however, can take the place of face-to-face meetings, of conversations and dialogue with Christians of other traditions and practices. Any forum which brings people together in this way is to be encouraged. Relationships and unity are intertwined; as Stephen Platten expresses it, the affective is the effective.

It remains a challenge, however, to make the transition from personal to institutional ecumenical relations. When I was a university chaplain, the team recognized that stability and permanence depended upon ecumenical relationships becoming embedded in structures which would be recognized by the constituent denominations. That applies at all levels of church life, through to Archbishops and national synods. The genuinely warm personal relationships which exist between national church leaders, and the joint public statements they make together, should inspire all of us to similar relationships and shared mission where we are. The non-trivial task then is to attempt to convert this personal warmth into structural changes which allow our successors to build on ever more secure foundations.

These issues are not new. Kirsteen Kim traces the relationship between mission and unity back to 1910. The Week of Prayer for Christian Unity can trace its origins to Anglo-American correspondence in 1908, with its revival in something approaching a recognisable form by the French priest, Paul Couturier in 1934. For many churches, a united liturgy during this week is the principal ecumenical event of the year. Church buildings close in order for congregations to come together, the people experience a preacher from a tradition quite unlike their own, and there is a sense of solidarity in the prayer of the wider community. How can this be built upon? (See the contribution by Kathryn Turner and Catherine McElhinney, for suggestions.)

I once wrote an article about so-called 'Messy Church' – informal children's worship with messy paints and craft materials – within a Local Ecumenical Partnership. I called it 'Yes to Messy Unity'. Ecumenism can be particularly annoying for systematic theologians; other people don't seem to fit the categories in which we want to place them. In my case, I was brought up to define the Church as the community of the baptized. Then I came across the Society of Friends and especially the Salvation Army, many of the adherents of which I realized to be far better and more committed Christians, baptized or not, than I could ever aspire to be. I long for the tidiness of my original understanding, but recognize that the reality is annoyingly messy. From my Anglo-Catholic heritage, I value the concept of the ontological state and order of priesthood, conveyed by the tactile laying on of hands by a Bishop similarly ordained and consecrated in an unbroken succession from the apostles themselves. It's just that, not only are there some decidedly iffy links in that Catholic chain of succession, but also I have seen, known and prayed alongside some Free Church ministers whom the Holy Spirit was clearly leading into a state of priestly being indiscernible from the best of those whose apostolicity I would happily acknowledge. My certainties have been challenged, and I warm to the Catholic bishop who rued that 'if only dogma had been written in poetry'. I have no alternative ready understanding of the ontology of priesthood to hand – that could be a scary denial of my own self-understanding and identity, and ecumenism is generally more about respect than denial – yet I am no longer in a position to deny the possibility of the Holy Spirit riding roughshod through the orders of my comprehension. Ecumenism is messy, because the Holy Spirit would not have it any other way, and it is getting messier.

In a post-modern world where the number of different churches is increasing all the time, the hopes of previous generations for unity through integration look increasingly unlikely in any foreseeable future. One Pentecostal congregation near me claimed to have spawned twenty new 'churches' in six months, mainly but not only gathering exiles, asylum seekers and immigrants from various African cultures and backgrounds into national and language-based independent churches. Some will be short-lived, while others will thrive in an increasingly crowded urban Christian scene. In the future, we may be thinking about partnerships of partnerships. West Yorkshire Ecumenical Council already has as a member the West Yorkshire African Caribbean Council of Churches; and recently in Leeds another network has grown up of black African churches (though it is open to broader evangelistic associates) under the moniker of TEAM (Together Everyone Achieves More).

The loose Churches Together structure gives us a freedom to explore this fluidity, this messiness. It is less concerned with the minutiae of legalistic punctuation, than with openness to how the Spirit has moved in the lives of others from different cultures and understandings. At its heart is an essential kernel of Trinitarian commonality, and beyond that a willingness to respect or at least tolerate the differences of members of other churches with whom one disagrees, much as one can reasonably expect respect from them towards that which one affirms as the interpretations, practice and Weltanschauung of one's own church. In a messy age, the Churches Together model, or least the best examples of it, gives a glimpse of an attainable form of unity. The churches should invest more heavily in it.

For its sheer breadth and diversity, the ecumenical endeavour in Britain is actually one of the best in the world, and deserves recognition for being so. This also means that the Churches Together model could be the gift that British churches can offer to international ecumenical structures. Our inward-looking society could receive much in return. Christian Aid, at least, makes us look ecumenically beyond our shores. There are commendable, if modest, examples of twinning, sometimes between ecumenical groups (in the context of twinned towns exchanges), but principally Anglican-Lutheran, across both national and denominational frontiers. Generally, though, UK churches have some way to go to see beyond Dover. Few would have heard of, much less engaged with, Charta Oecumenica, a significant vision and action statement which emerged in 2001 from collaboration between the Conference of European Churches (CEC) – a grouping of some 120 Orthodox, Anglican, Protestant and independent churches – and its Catholic partner, the Council of European Bishops' Conferences (CCEE). The Charta, a call to action for the local church, proclaims the churches' unity in faith and it upholds the visible fellowship of the churches. It speaks of shared responsibilities, not least towards the safeguarding of creation, and for building up relationships with Judaism, Islam and other religions, an agenda here discussed by Helen Reid and Celia Blackden. The Charta moves from Christ's revelation of the 'mystery of reconciliation' in the context of faith and unity,[6] to an explicit social context in which:

> reconciliation involves promoting social justice within and among all peoples; above all, this means closing the gap between rich and poor and overcoming unemployment. Together we will do our part towards giving migrants, refugees and asylum-seekers a humane reception in Europe.[7]

In an international context, the churches still have a significant role to play in pursuing peace and justice. Following the model of the influential 1985 Kairos Document in South Africa, Christians in Palestine issued a prophetic Palestinian Kairos Document in 2009; also, the World Council of Churches, whose activities are little noticed in Britain, has recently marked a Decade to Overcome Violence.

Conceivably, the Eurocentric emphasis of the Charta might narrow the horizons for some, but it would undoubtedly expand them for many others, without threatening one's own identity. In particular, the Charta states, 'We consider the diversity of our regional, national, cultural and religious traditions to be enriching for Europe.'[8] Note the movement back from the social to the ecclesial with the affirmation of diversity in religious traditions, which brings us back once more to the model of Churches Together.

What would it mean to finish? Where is ecumenism heading? Are all these relationships destined for an ultimate wedding – or should the metaphor be not marriage but community? We have our differing eschatologies, and that is part of the varied richness we bring each other, and one person's 'full visible unity' is another's 'reconciled diversity', while others still would distinguish between 'ecclesial communities' and 'the Church', a term which implies an eschatological timelessness very different from the ephemeral congregations mentioned above. If there is any single message permeating this volume it is that, as evidenced in the plethora of ecumenical stories that could and should be told, the fullness of unity is actually to be glimpsed in the journey, in the shared pilgrimage, in the messy process of unity.

I have always been drawn towards a sense of imminent, if not yet fully realized, eschatology, of the breaking in of the Kingdom and its values. That means, for example, that the moral counsels of the Sermon on the Mount are for living in the present, and not for delaying until the eschaton. Loving one's enemy, for example, is not an option to be deferred until the Kingdom comes in its fullness, but is a real individual and collective challenge for living today. Whatever our conception of an ultimate form of Christian unity, there is an imperative for us to live unity. There are those who say that peace is not so much a goal in itself, but the way in which one goes about trying to achieve that goal.[9] The peace one lives is the peace one achieves. Something similar may also be said for unity, that its eventual form will become clear by living it out. Of course, *pace* Murray and Murray, ' "Life and Works" ecumenism – doing things together – can never be enough.' However, the kind of unity we live will become the kind of unity we think of, which in turn will become the kind of unity we achieve. The goal is in the process because the process determines the goal. This is why local ecumenism is so important, because it is where, week in, week out, Christian people are engaging with each other across denominational divides. (See Mike Love's writing on local unity, and my own chapter on the priority of local ecumenism.) The nature of local unity is the root of ecumenical living for the vast majority of the Christian population. It is far from perfect, but it is what unity means for this age, in this place. We cannot defer ecumenical living until more pieces are in place in the interdenominational jigsaw. With all its current constraints, unity is for living out now, and in the process of ecumenical living and mission, outreach and service, in the process of unity, we will discover new depths of relationship and new understandings of the Body of Christ.

I have long found Barnabas (Acts 4:36) an inspiring and prophetic figure, a child of encouragement. As we recall the transformation of ecumenical hopes from the winter of 1984 to the spring of 1987, so we can be encouraged by the ecumenical journey we are on. We can be encouraged by how far we have travelled, we can rejoice at the huge ecumenical advances which have taken place, and we can, with confidence, bring before God our determination to engage with those things which appear as obstacles to us today. As Mary Tanner exhorts us, 'For God's sake, get on with it!'

The ecumenical story is an amazing and encouraging story, and the comforting and challenging Spirit will continue to encourage us to move further on together to a new chapter, towards a unity the full nature of which is beyond our current understanding. Unity is a process, and it is our privilege and responsibility to be part of that process today.

7 *Christian Unity in Scripture*

Neil Richardson

The New Testament is an ecumenical collection of documents. Redaction criticism taught us to listen for the distinctive voices of Scripture: not just Paul, but also John; not just Mark, but also Matthew and Luke. Earlier historical criticism enabled us to go further: we hear not just Paul, but interpreters of Paul, not just Peter, but an interpreter of Peter. In the writings which bear the name John we hear two, perhaps three voices, not one.[1]

Do its authors all 'sing from the same hymn sheet'? All of them – even James[2] – bear witness to what God has done in and through his Son, Jesus Christ. But there are differences: for example, Paul and James on faith and works (Gal. 2:16, Rom. 3:28, James 2:20–6),[3] and Luke and Paul on the solution to Jew–Gentile differences (Acts 15, Gal. 2).[4]

The New Testament testifies both to the unity and diversity which was there in Christian faith almost from the beginning.[5] This observation prompts two questions. First, in this inspired ecumenical chorus of witness to Jesus Christ, should we privilege one voice above all the others? Acts 2:42–7, perhaps, with its picture of the earliest Christian community? Or Matthew 16:16–18: 'On this rock I will build my Church ...'? The Petrine commission is clearly important, appearing also in Luke 22:31–2 and John 21:15,19 (cf. Mark 16:7). Yet 'Peter' needs to be in dialogue with 'Paul'; the two were partners in mission (Gal. 2:7–10), and, on at least one occasion, in sharp conflict (Gal. 2:11–12). There is also an ecumenical conversation to be had between Peter and the 'beloved disciple' of John's Gospel.[6]

The prayer of Jesus in John 17, however, merits special attention. John's Gospel 'gathers the sense'[7] of the other gospels, and, in a similar way, this prayer[8] gathers up Jesus' entire life's work. That life – and his death – became his eternal prayer, and so this prayer in John can be seen as an imaginative rendering of Christ's eternal intercession in heaven (e.g. Rom. 8:34). Three times Jesus prays that his followers 'may be one' (vv. 11, 21 and 23), 'as we are one' (v. 11), 'as you, Father, are in me, and I in you' (v. 21), 'I in them and you in me' (v. 23).

This is not a text to be fitted into a wider New Testament picture. Even when we have allowed for this evangelist's distinctive, sometimes uncomfortable voice,[9] this *is* the big picture. But we shall need the rest of the New Testament to discover what this prayer of Jesus means in practice.

As we eavesdrop on these ecumenical conversations in Scripture, questions of interpretation arise. What significance do they have for Christian pilgrims of the twenty-first century? In interpreting the Bible, a *consensus fidelium* is important, even though unanimity on everything is impossible.[10] For now, I simply note that the elevation of a writing to canonical status involved the recognition that its significance was now seen to transcend the original situation to which it was first addressed. So Galatians and its 'take' on the Judaizing controversy became Scripture not as valuable history, not even just because its author was the apostle Paul, but because this controversy has an abiding relevance for the Church.

So we return again and again to the New Testament trusting that our 'ecumenism' (as we, perhaps misleadingly, call it) may be refreshed, refined, and deepened by our encounter with these canonical texts. But first we turn to the revelation which is the foundation of all talk about unity.

I. God in Christ

We begin where the New Testament begins: with God's gracious initiative in Christ, and the resulting 'new creation' (Gal. 6:15, 2 Cor. 5:17). Church unity can only be properly understood against this background. (And I assume here, of course, all that preceded God sending his Son 'in the fullness of time' (Gal. 4:4): God's gracious dealings with Israel (Rom. 9:1–5). So we turn to other 'big picture' texts. One such text is 2 Corinthians 5:19:

> 'God was in Christ reconciling the world to himself, no longer holding people's misdeeds against them, and he has entrusted us with the message of reconciliation'.

Reconciliation language is surprisingly sparse in the New Testament. (The *theme* of reconciliation is another matter.) Found almost entirely in Paul's writings,[11] this language is one of his 'borrowings' from the wider world of Greece and Rome, pressed into the service of his mission to the Gentiles. It denotes the changing of enemies into friends.[12] It is not a word used of reconciliation between Christian communities.

Two later texts – whether Pauline or deutero-Pauline – provide a picture of a thoroughly Christ-centred universe which God is reconciling to himself:

> 'In him (that is, 'the Son') everything in heaven and on earth was created ... All things are held together in him ... In him God chose ... to reconcile all things to himself ...' (Col. 1:16a, 17b,19, 20a)

Ephesians 1:22 may be, in part, a re-write of this:

> 'He put all things in subjection beneath his feet, and gave him as head over all things to the church which is his body, the fullness of him who is filling the universe in all its parts'.

These texts – and many more could be added[13] – show that unity between Christians belongs to the wider context of God's grand project to reconcile everyone and everything to himself. So the New Testament challenges our church-centred perspectives, including our frequent distinction between those who are 'in' and those who are 'outsiders'. Karl Barth, commenting on Romans 5:15–19, and interpreting 'many' here in its semitic sense of 'all' (as in Mark 10:45) writes:

> 'In the light of this act of obedience (i.e. of Jesus) there is no man who is not in Christ. All are renewed and clothed with righteousness'.[14]

This 'universalist' perspective, expressed particularly clearly in the closing verses of Romans 11 (especially vv. 26 and 32), can be over-stated. Barth himself recognized that everyone being in Christ is a future hope, not a present reality (e.g. Rom. 5:17), and Paul draws a clear distinction between those who are in Christ and those who still live 'according to the flesh' (Rom. 7). Baptism into Christ (e.g. Rom. 6:1–11) is the all-important step. Nevertheless, some of the parables of Jesus, notably Matthew 25:31–46, suggest that we will be wise not to draw premature conclusions about who's 'in' and who's 'out'.

So the New Testament points us firmly in the direction of what Dietrich Bonhoeffer might have called 'worldly' ecumenism. The cross of Jesus is the central, seminal icon. God has 'moved the goalposts'. The place 'outside the gate' (Heb. 13:12–13) has become the centre of a new creation. The crucified Christ breaks open our religious worlds and invites us into God's new world.

All this is the work of grace (e.g. Titus 2:11, 3:4–8), and grace is, by definition, undeserved (e.g. Luke 15:11–32, Rom. 4:4 and 16, 11:5–6). Because it is undeserved, it is often destabilizing, subversive, even scandalous (Luke 19:1–10, Romans 5:19, etc.). Grace goes out to the radically 'other'; the more undeserving or hostile the 'other' is, the more grace 'abounds'. Karl Barth again:

> 'Grace is the distinctive mode of God's being insofar as it seeks and creates fellowship by its own free inclination and favour ...'.[15]

The Church began with the experience of grace. (Peter and Paul are prime examples.) So this same grace will be the hallmark of its life and mission. The Church of Christ will be recognizable by the way it extends friendship (reconciliation) to the radically other, and by crossing boundaries in its commitment to the cosmic unity which is God's grand design.

II. 'In Christ': One Holy, Catholic and Apostolic Church

The word 'Christian' occurs hardly at all in the New Testament.[16] It seems to have been a soubriquet attached to early followers of Jesus by others, probably Jewish and/or Roman authorities. The New Testament uses other – deeper – language to describe not only who these new people are, but also *where* they are. They are 'in Christ'. The first Christians had no religious buildings, no sacred space like the temple in Jerusalem. Instead, 'Christ himself functioned ... as the Christian sacred space'.[17] Wherever they were in physical or geographical terms, as the body of Christ they were 'holy'.

This kind of language is found mainly in Paul and John in the New Testament. But the reality is assumed or differently expressed in many other places. It is the reality behind the words of institution at the Last Supper (Mark 14:22–4, Matt. 26:26–8, Luke 22:19–20, 1 Cor.11:23–5). The life which is the response to divine grace is life 'in Christ', 'in the Spirit', 'in the Lord'.[18]

So the unity of the Church was, from the very beginning, a fact. How could it be otherwise, since all were 'baptized' into Christ (Matt. 28:16–20, 1 Cor. 12:13)? Though we have very little information about the early Christian practice of baptism, the evidence of Matthew's gospel, Luke-Acts (Acts 2:41 onwards), John 4:2, Romans 6:3–11, Heb. 6:2 (perhaps) and 1 Peter 3:21 suggests that baptism was the normal visible expression of entry into the Church. Baptism presupposes and expresses unity. No wonder it has been suggested that we are called not to create Christian unity, but to discover it.

This unity derives from and confirms the holiness of the Church. People in Christ are God's 'saints' (*hagioi*), his 'holy' ones. This is expressed time and again: Jesus prays for the holiness of his disciples (John 17:17 and 19), the gift of the Holy Spirit confers holiness even on 'unclean' Gentiles (Acts 10:44–5), so that they, too, are now God's 'holy ones' (1 Cor. 1:2, 2 Cor. 11, Eph.1:1, 1 Peter 1:15–6, 1 John 2:20, etc.).

They also belong to a community which may, from the beginning, be considered 'catholic' and 'apostolic'. Some may think this is to anticipate by at least a century or two. But even if the followers of Jesus are not yet obviously and visibly 'One, Holy, Catholic and Apostolic Church', these four notes of the Church are clearly there in the New Testament. Jesus commissioned twelve apostles (Luke 6:13), to whose company a number of others seem to have been added later (e.g. Andronicus and Junia, Rom. 16:7; cf. 1 Cor. 15:5, 7) and, belatedly, Paul (if that is what Paul's language in 1 Cor.15:8 implies). The apostles are described, along with the prophets, as the Church's 'foundation' in the probably deutero-Pauline Ephesians (2:20), and their teaching becomes a focus of the community's unity (Acts 2:42). As for the catholicity of the Church, the commissions of the risen Jesus (Matthew 28:16–20, Luke 24:47) place this, too, at the beginning, although it wasn't until a decade or two later, in the mission to the Gentiles, that the Church's catholicity came to fuller expression.

The New Testament indicates that the four notes of the Church belong together. Thus a Church which is not fully one cannot be fully catholic either. A Church which is not apostolic can hardly be catholic – and so on. But if the unity and apostolicity of the Church belong together, it follows that its mission and unity cannot be separated without both being impaired. Unity without mission is likely to degenerate into uniformity; mission without unity is likely to become Christian propaganda and proselytizing (as rival missions and evangelists engage in a numbers game).

Similarly, the unity and catholicity of the church cannot be divorced without damage to both. To revert to our earlier discussion of God's gracious purpose to draw all people to himself (John 12:32), the Church can only realize its vocation to unity and catholicity by constantly welcoming different people into its life. The Adam typology of the New Testament is important here (see especially Romans 5:12–19, but also 1 Cor. 15:45, Luke 3:38 (cf. v. 22) and, possibly, Mark 1:13; compare Heb. 2:5–9). It means that there has dawned in Christ a universal *humanum* – nothing less than a 'new creation'.

Since, according to Scripture, the four notes of the Church are indivisible, the unity and diversity of the church, like its unity and mission, are two sides of the same coin. Both are the gift of the same Spirit (Rom. 12:3–8, 1 Cor. 12:4, 12–27; compare Eph. 4:11–3, 1 Peter 4:10–1).

III Turning to 'the Other'

The mission to the Gentiles is a major theme in the New Testament, and we must take a moment to weigh its ecumenical significance. A good place to start is the need of the Church to receive the Gospel over and over again. *Ecclesia semper reformanda* is an abiding truth. The warnings of the apostle to the churches at Rome and at Corinth stand as a perpetual warning to the whole Church: '... by faith you hold your place. Put away your pride, and be on your guard ...' (Rom. 11:20); 'if you think you are standing firm, take care, or you may fall' (1 Cor. 10:12).

The Church's enduring need of conversion and repentance is a major reason why Christians must hear Scriptural words to or about Israel, whether from the prophets, the evangelists or an apostle, as a word to them. At least two evangelists seem well aware of this, as the language of Matthew 23:8–11 and Luke 18:9, occurring in apparently anti-Pharisaic material, might indicate.[19] Even if the writer of John's Gospel seems to write in an 'us' and 'them' vein, it will not do for followers of Christ to deflect the harsh word spoken of 'the Jews', as if it were inapplicable to them.[20] What Paul says of 'the Jew' in Romans 2:24 the Church has fulfilled over and over again: 'Because of you the name of God is profaned among the Gentiles'.

So the mission to the Gentiles and all its consequences are not simply early church history. (See, for example, Paul's words about the function of Scripture at 1 Cor. 10:11.) Passages about Jewish Christians and not-yet-Christian Gentiles may not seem to relate directly to issues of church unity today, but here two things need to be said. First, as I argued earlier, a major reason why New Testament writings were received as canonical was an ecclesial consensus that the significance of these writings transcended their original context and purpose. Second, mission and unity belong together; both, if separated, will be distorted, as the New Testament itself shows: subsequent controversies about the Church's unity and diversity arose directly out of the mission to the Gentiles.

We recall our discussion of the nature of the Church in the preceding section: the Church only realizes its true nature – catholic and apostolic – as it turns to the significantly different 'other'. In Simon Peter's 'second conversion', as it has been called (Acts 10 and 11), the leader of the apostles discovers a new dimension of the gospel and for the first time preaches that gospel to Gentiles. The Church breaks out of its old 'mould', as the Holy Spirit leads the way (Acts 10:44–9), and God's creation of a new unity-in-diversity begins.

But how much diversity should there be? Should Gentile converts conform to existing patterns of discipleship by becoming practising Jews – observing, for example, the Jewish Sabbath and Jewish food laws and, in the case of male converts, submitting to the physical rite of circumcision? The Church's answer – eventually – was 'No', largely thanks to Paul. Hitherto 'the Christians' had seemed to be just another Jewish sect; the Greek word *hairesis* is used of the Christians at Acts 24:5 and 14, and of the Sadducees and Pharisees respectively at Acts 5:17 and 15:5. Now they took a giant step towards becoming something else: a universal '*humanum*', in which unity and diversity would be two sides of the same coin.

But while the catholicity of the Church ensures its rich diversity, there is another, even more foundational source of both its unity and diversity. When a New Testament writer – in this case, Paul and his interpreters – discusses the Body of Christ and the gifts of the Spirit (e.g.1 Cor. 12:4,12–27), we have a picture of unity and diversity. (We return to this theme in section V below.).

Space does not permit an extended discussion of all the New Testament material relating to Jew and Gentile in the Church. The Judaizing controversy,[21] however, invites us to reflect on the danger of one group of Christians demanding of another the same 'type' of Christian faith as their own when the gospel itself does not require it. What the Church did require of the first generation of Gentile converts in the short- and medium-term is not easily stated. But whether we listen to Paul in Galatians 2, or to Luke in Acts 15,[22] the outcome of diversity was established.

It seems that by the time the epistle to the Ephesians was written, the dust had begun to settle. Addressing 'you Gentiles by birth, called "the uncircumcision" by those who are called "the circumcision" '... (2:11a), Paul – or 'Paul'- goes on to say:

> 'But now in Christ Jesus you who once were far off have been brought near by the blood of Christ. For he is our peace; in his flesh he has made both groups into one and has broken down the dividing wall, that is, the hostility between us' (Eph. 2:13–14)

The reconciliation language which follows is interesting. As always in the New Testament, the fundamental act of reconciliation is God's. Here both those who were 'far off' and 'those who were near' are reconciled and 'have access in one Spirit to the Father' (vv. 17–18).

Yet 'turning to the other' is only the beginning. Or, to put it another way, this is what the Church should always be doing. This is why 'living with "the other" ' is also a continuing task, and to that we now turn.

IV. Living with 'the Other'

The significance of Romans 14:1–15:7 for Christian unity has, I think, been largely overlooked. St Paul is addressing the tensions arising from the differences amongst the Christians at Rome. The differences were probably Jew–Gentile differences, though we cannot be certain about this.[23] The differences were not trivial. Both groups were in danger of unchurching the other by 'despising' or 'judging' – the two destructive attitudes which Paul several times condemns. The long discussion is 'framed' by the command 'accept one another' (14:1, 15:7).

It would be a mistake to label the differences discussed here as merely differences of lifestyle or of conscience. They were also *religious* differences; at least, they were so seen by one group, if not the other – hence the 'judging'. Paul urges on both groups the necessity of living with difference, however uncomfortable or even incomprehensible the differences of the other group might seem. All are to 'pursue what makes for peace' (14:19), and to refrain from all which damages or destroys the faith of another (14:15, 20–1). A corollary of this is that each must follow their own conscience: 'Let each be fully convinced in their own minds' (14:5).

Paul follows this a little later by one of the most remarkable definitions of faith in the entire New Testament:

> 'the faith that you have, have as your own conviction before God. Blessed are those who have no reason condemn themselves because of what they approve. But those who have doubts are condemned if they eat, because they do not act from faith; for whatever does not proceed from faith is sin (vv. 22–3)

This might appear to be a charter for rampant individualism in the Church. But Paul's argument in its entirety shows that this is not so. The unity of both groups in Christ is presupposed (14:8–9; compare the earlier v. 4, and the image of 'one body' in 12:4–5), as is the accountability of both at the final judgement: '... each of us will be accountable to God' (14:12).

What is more, the letter to the Romans, as, indeed, almost the entire New Testament, stresses that love (*agape*) is the defining characteristic of the Christian community (Rom. 12:9, 13:10, 14:15)

It is not possible to explore here all the contemporary implications of Paul's extended discussion in Romans 14:1–15:7. I am not alone in pointing out its relevance for the Church's anguished discussions about gay people in the Church.[24] But it is clearly an important example of early Christians' attempts to live with the significantly different 'other', as is Paul's earlier discussion about meat offered to idols (1 Cor. 8–10), where differences of religious conviction – and perhaps also of social status – were dividing the Church. These two extended discussions in Paul's writings point up the importance of relations between 'the strong' and 'the weak' in Christian unity.[25] In conclusion it is worth noting how Paul offers himself, in effect, as a role model: in faithfulness to the Gospel he sought to be 'all things to all people', practising what one scholar has called 'the adaptability of love' (1 Cor. 9:19–23).[26]

V. What kind of unity?

The frequency of the words 'every' and 'all' in the epistles underlines the unity of the Church. For example, churches are exhorted to greet and to love 'all the saints' (Heb. 13:24, Col. 1:4, Eph. 1:15). The many commands in which 'each other' occurs especially indicate the depth, warmth and practical nature of unity between Christians. For example, they are not only to accept and build each other up (Rom. 14:1, 15:7 and 14:19), they are to encourage (1 Thess. 5:11) and pray for each other (James 5:16), bear one another's burdens (Gal. 6:2), and humbly think each other better than themselves (Phil. 2:3; compare 1 Peter 5:5).[27] In short, they are to love each other as Christ has loved them (John 13:34–5, 15:12, 17; compare Gal. 5:13, Eph. 4:2, 1 Thess. 3:12, 2 Thess. 1:3, Heb. 10:24, 1 Peter 1:22, 5:14, 1 John 3:11, 4:7,11–2, and 2 John 5).

The remarkable frequency of the command to love brings us back to the prayer of Jesus in John 17: 'May they be one as we are one …' (e.g. v. 11).

The unity between the Father and the Son is, above all, a communion of love (John 3:35, 10:17, 14:31, 15:9, 10, 17:23, 26). It is also a unity of purpose to bring life and light to the world, and therefore a unity in mission.[28] Jesus prays that his followers may be one so that 'the world may believe that you have sent me' (v. 21; compare v. 23).

The divine unity is expressed in mutual reciprocity: the Father handed over all things to the Son (John 3:35) and the Son, in returning to the Father, offers all things back to him (e.g. John 17:13, 19).

Was God's own unity at risk, so to speak, in the Incarnation? That is a difficult idea. Yet a real incarnation suggests vulnerability and even risk, and those traits are certainly in evidence in Paul's cruciform self-portraits (e.g. 1 Cor. 4:9–13, 2 Cor. 4:7–12, and 6:3–10). In this context some words published in 1975 are worth quoting here:

> 'The challenge to ecumenical advance today is ... to be so engaged in bringing the world towards the purpose for which God created it that all the risks are taken of the Church's being torn apart. Christians ... will split down the middle about how to handle different issues. *The big ecumenical question is ... whether they have enough in Jesus Christ to hold them together against all the odds* [my italics]... It is a mistake to believe that Christians should be polite to one another. What they do owe to one another is courtesy'.[29]

And to 'courtesy', we might add, of course, the fruits of the Spirit (Gal. 5:22–3), as well as forgiveness (e.g. Matt. 18:15–18, 23–35), prayer, compassion, kindness (e.g. Col. 3:12–17), and thankfulness (i.e. for each other, as in Paul's opening thanksgivings).[30]

The New Testament writings fill out this picture of a community united in love in mission to God's world. According to Acts 2:42–7 it is a community united in and by the teaching of the apostles (v. 42), by grace, not law (v. 45),[31] united in hospitality of the table, in joy and simplicity of life, in the praise of God (vv. 46–7), not forgetting (Acts 4:33) its witness to the resurrection. In short, 'all who believed were *together*' (v. 42).

That last word begs a number of questions. Those first Christians were physically together in one place, meeting as they did in the portico of Solomon in the Temple (Acts 5:12). But 'together' also has a deeper meaning. House churches in Corinth, Rome and elsewhere imposed physical limitations on the size of the early Christian gatherings, as church buildings do today. Romans 16:23 might mean that the larger house of a wealthier Christian could accommodate several smaller house churches, but that may have been exceptional.

Acts adds a further dimension to the unity of Christians. Even if Luke's two pictures have been idealized, and even if the sharing of goods (Acts 2:44–5, 4:32–5) was an experiment later abandoned, the bridging and diminishing of the gap between rich and poor in the early churches remains a scriptural challenge. Paul's collection, discussed at length in 2 Corinthians 8 and 9 (mentioned more briefly in 1 Corinthians 16:1–2, Gal. 2:10 and Rom. 15:25–7), is the prime example of sharing in the early church. The

Romans passage makes clear its ecumenical – inter church and international – character: Gentiles, in grateful response for the gospel, sought to relieve the famine conditions amongst Jewish Christians in Judaea. Paul describes the collection by a word much used in recent ecumenical discussions: *koinonia* (Rom. 15:26, 2 Cor. 8:4 and 9:13). It is a *koinonia* rooted in the *koinonia* of the Holy Spirit (2 Corinthians 13:13).[32]

Christian unity in the New Testament has many facets. It is far from being purely 'spiritual' and theological. Life in Christ, in the power of the Spirit, challenges and transforms every relationship, not only between rich and poor (also James 2:1–7), but also between slave and master (Gal. 3:22, Col. 3:22–4:1, Eph. 6:5–9,[33] and between young and old (1 Tim. 5:1–2; 1 John 2:12–14 is more cryptic, but offers another glimpse of an all-age community). The Spirit also bridges, so Acts 2:1–11 implies, barriers of language.

The relationships between male and female in the Church should not be omitted from this catalogue of transformed relationships, even though the New Testament picture is more complex. Galatians 3:28 seems foundational, but its realization is not to be postponed to the *eschaton*, as Romans 16, for example, shows.[34] Even the so-called Household Codes of the epistles, cited above, although they reflect the patriarchal culture of the first century, point us towards the unity of a household 'in the Lord'. (1 Peter 3:1–7 is the most explicit reference to households in which the wife was a Christian and the husband was not).

Nor should we overlook what the later Church has called 'the communion of saints', foreshadowed in the (Old Testament) 'cloud of witnesses' of Hebrews (11:40, 12:1) and perhaps in the twenty-four elders of Revelation (e.g. 4:4). The sense of unity between the Church on earth and in heaven could only grow with the passage of time (1 Thess. 4:13–14).

In all of this, the authority, ministry and teaching of the apostles and their successors were important – even crucial. They are not portrayed as the guarantors of the tradition – i.e. the gospel – still less as its sole guarantors. But they were crucial witnesses to it (1 Cor. 15:3–11, etc.). Apostolic witness and authority implies, over time, apostolic tradition and succession, and we see the beginnings of this in the later writings (2 Tim. 1:13, 1 John 2:7, etc.). Our questions on these matters, however, are not answered directly by the New Testament – often, not even addressed. The authority of 'bishops' (*episkopoi*), and the question of who should preside at the Eucharist, for example, are issues addressed very soon after the New Testament period (e.g., 1 Clement 42, Ignatius, *Smyrn*. 8).

Obedience to leaders, whether apostles or not, is important (Heb. 13:17, though here the first verb may mean 'trust' your leader; 1 Thess. 5:12 reflects the same spirit). At the same time, leaders were to be 'icons' of Christ (1 Cor. 4:7–12, 2 Cor. 4:7–12; cf. 1 Peter 5:2–4), who are not to 'lord it' over their charges (1 Peter 5:3, cf. 2 Cor. 1:24), still less be a cause of division themselves (perhaps 3 John 9). The qualities required of *episcopoi* and deacons (1 Timothy 3:1–13) imply that such people are to be a focus of unity in the community.

Finally, in this section, what do the occurrences of the words 'one' and 'unity' add to this New Testament picture? The word 'unity' occurs only in Ephesians: unity is the gift of the Spirit (4:3), a unity 'inherent in' (so the REB) 'our faith and ... knowledge of the Son of God (4:13). As usual in Ephesians, prepositional clauses are piled one on top of another, but the Greek of 4:11–12 seems to mean that all the ministers named here ('apostles', etc.) equip 'the saints for the work of ministry' – which, in turn, builds up the body of Christ and leads towards the unity of the Spirit and the faith.

The occurrences of the word 'one' in ecclesial contexts are instructive. 'One God' and 'one Lord', one Spirit are the foundation (1 Cor. 8:6, 1 Tim. 2:5, Eph. 4:4), creating 'one body ... one faith, one baptism' (Eph. 4:4–5, cf. Heb. 2:11). 'One body' are two words found also at Romans 12:4, 1 Cor. 12:13, Eph. 2:16, Col. 3:15. What 'one body' and 'one faith' mean can only be answered in the light of the New Testament as a whole. But as we have seen, it does not preclude, but includes diversity – and also the gifts of the Spirit '*to each one*' (Eph. 4:7; cf. 1 Cor. 12:7, 1 Peter 4:10–11). It is a baptismal unity in(to) Christ (e.g. Gal. 3:16, 20, 26–8, where, again, 'one' is crucial to the argument). The 'one' language of Acts 4:32 and Phil. 1:27 and 2:2 denotes a unity of love, of friendship and of purpose. And to all of this there is a very definite doxological outcome: 'with one mouth' the praise of God (Rom. 15:7, cf. Acts 2:47, 2 Cor. 9:12–15).

The phrase 'one bread' occurs at 1 Cor. 10:17 – not surprisingly, given the divisiveness of the Lord's Supper at Corinth (1 Cor. 11:17–22). (Many scholars today attribute these divisions to the differences in social status amongst the Corinthian Christians). The 'one bread' derives directly from Jesus (Mark 14:22, etc., but also John 6:35 and 48). It is bread intended for the whole world; it is significant that the 'church' miracle of the feeding of the five thousand ('church' because of the role the disciples play), is the only miracle story recounted in all four gospels. It is ironic, to say the least, that the 'one bread' has become a prime cause of division amongst Christians.

VI. Ecumenism and '*he ecumene*': church and world

The word 'ecumenical' derives from the Greek word *oikoumene,* Luke's word for the 'inhabited world' (Luke 2:1). But the Church's mission to heal a fractured world has deeper roots: those New Testament texts offering a vision of a world united in Christ (section I above). Whether this vision lures us in the direction of a Christian triumphalism is a question to which I shall return But first we need to consider the relationship between the Church and that ill-defined entity to which Christian intercessions often refer: 'the world'.

Christian perception of the relationship between the Church and the world is easily distorted. This is due partly to the ambiguous meaning of 'the world' (*kosmos*) in John's Gospel. That relationship is often summarized as 'in the world, but not of it'. However, it would be more faithful to that gospel – and to Jesus himself – if we re-phrased it: Christians are not of this world (i.e., they are baptized into Christ; John's term is 'born again'), but they are *sent into the world* (John 17:18, 20:23).[35]

A proper understanding of the relationship between the Church and the world is essential to a proper understanding of Christian unity. Thomas Merton trenchantly sets out the spiritual and theological issues in chapter eight of *Contemplation in a World of Action,* 'Is the World a Problem?' A brief quotation must suffice:

> 'I am ... a man in the modern world. In fact, I am the world just as you are! Where am I going to look for the world first of all if not in myself? As long as I assume that the world is something I discover by turning on the radio or looking out of the window I am deceived from the start.'[36]

Merton, I believe, is profoundly biblical here. 'Church' and 'world' cannot be neatly identified with two discrete groups of people. That would be to misread John. Of course, John's Gospel almost certainly emerged from a situation where a Christian community felt beleaguered and threatened – whether from local Jewish communities or the Roman Empire or both. But even this community had not forgotten that 'God so loved the world' (John 3:16) and that disciples were called 'to be one, as we are one' so that the world might believe.

Ecumenism cannot be truly catholic if it leaves the world out. The way of unity embraces the world. The Bible's panorama – this is God's world – invites us to cross boundaries. For example, mysterious, surprising figures from beyond the boundaries of Israel testify to a ubiquitous God: Melchizedek (Gen. 14:18–20), Balaam (Num. 22:5), Rahab the Canaanite (Josh. 2:1–21, Heb. 11:31), Ruth the Moabitess, and, in Acts, Cornelius (Acts 10:1–2, 35). To this list we might add the 'strange exorcist' (Mark 9:38–41, Luke 9:49–50), and particularly the word of Jesus which this story includes: 'Whoever is not against us is for us' (Mark 9:40, Luke 9:50).[37]

And yet – it must be emphasized – the New Testament is unfailingly Christ-centred, and New Testament writers insist on seeing the Old Testament as Christ-centred too; Moses, for example, 'considered abuse suffered for the Christ to be greater wealth than the treasures of Egypt' (Heb. 11:26a; compare 1 Cor. 10:4, and Luke 24:27 and 44).

Nothing and no one is left out of the New Testament vision of a world brought to unity in Christ. The nature of grace (discussed in section I above) means that mission and unity are one whole.[38] This may sound like Christian triumphalism. Why it cannot be so is the subject of the next section.

VII. Costly ecumenism

The way of unity is the way of the cross. The equation can be reversed: the way of the cross is the way of unity. That is the meaning and purpose of God's self-giving in Christ: God's cosmic act of reconciliation (Col. 1:20–2, Eph. 2:14–16, 2 Cor. 5:17, John 6:51, 12, etc.).

What this means for contemporary ecumenism is well illustrated by the second half of Mark's Gospel. Each prediction of the Passion (Mark 8:31, 9:31, 10:33–4) is followed by a picture of the disciples denying by their words and conduct the cross and what it means; Peter wants to keep

Jesus from his cross (8:32–3), the disciples argue about who is the greatest (9:33–4), James and John request seats of honour beside Jesus in glory (10:35–7). The responses of Jesus indicate the only way in which disciples may be transformed from a quarrelling, self-seeking rabble into Spirit-filled apostles committed to the gospel and to the healing of the world: they are called to deny themselves and to take up their cross (Mark 8:34–8), to be 'last of all and servant of all', learning from a little child (Mark 9:35–7; so also 10:43–4).[39] Though Matthew and Luke soften a little Mark's portrait of the disciples, their message is essentially the same: the way of the cross is the only way to the kind of transformation which makes unity – the Church's and the world's – possible. The self-portraits which the apostle to the Gentiles gives in letters to a fractious church are, tellingly, cruciform (1 Cor. 4:9–13, 2 Cor. 4:7–12, 6:3–10).

The call to self-denial, like the Church's relationship with 'the world', can be misconstrued. It is not narrowly legalistic; but, rather, a grace-filled road to a deeper identity where we belong together in Christ (John 15:1–11). It points away from the sectarian flag-waving at Corinth ('I belong to Paul', 'I belong to Apollos', etc., 1 Cor. 1:12–13). Boasting of that kind exalts the individual, and destroys unity; the only legitimate 'boast'[40] for the Christian is the cross. Despite the terrible history of the Crusades, the cross is a 'No Entry' sign to the way of Christian triumphalism.

Conclusion

I once heard someone say 'The Gospel *is* unity'. An over-simplification, perhaps; after all, there are four written gospels, and harmonizing them, as Tatian did in the second century, means that we lose the distinctiveness of each.[41] Similarly, as we have seen, the New Testament illustrates and teaches a unity which includes diversity. But, with that important caveat, unity is the truth of Christian baptism. It is the measure of the Church's growth and renewal, and – despite the excesses at Corinth – a sign of the Spirit's presence in or absence from the Church. It is indissolubly linked to the other three 'notes' of the Church: one, holy, catholic and apostolic.

So mission and unity, unity and diversity are also inseparably linked. Mission, God's mission, *is* a movement for unity – the unity not just of the Church, but also of the world. Turning to 'the other' – exemplified in Scripture in the mission to the Gentiles – is an inalienable part of the

Church, and, therefore, of ecumenism. The divine grace that turns to the other in generosity, love and forgiveness is the lifeblood of the Church and its mission. Ecumenism without grace is empty and lifeless: a contradiction in terms. Similarly, a church-centred ecumenism is a contradiction in terms, or, at the very least, a malformed creature. Ecumenism grounded in the grace of God reaches out to the whole world, and therefore unity is 'not a project for completion, but a grace to be received', and therefore not a matter primarily of theological discussion and institutional negotiation. There *is* a place for theological negotiation, but it can only be a small part, and by no means the most important part of all that the word 'ecumenism' embraces.

Unity according to the New Testament is many-sided. All relationships, all differences and divisions, must come within the transforming orbit of the Spirit's power. Such unity cannot be measured only by what is seen; it is too deep and spiritual for that. But to describe Christian unity simply as a 'spiritual unity' is in danger of imposing a Gnostic-like distortion on Scripture. If we are to do justice to the concept of 'the Body', we need to recognize the down-to-earth dimension of unity. In this it is no different from *agape* (e.g. Luke 10:25–37, James 2:14–7, 1 John 3:16–7).

The writings of the New Testament may properly be called an 'ecumenical' collection of writings. They exemplify and so encourage conversations and dialogues. The conversations between Peter and Paul, between Peter and the beloved disciple, between Paul and later Pauline interpreters are especially important. Honesty, for the sake of the Gospel, rather than mere politeness, will be one of the hallmarks of such conversations, held within the *koinonia* of the Spirit and of love. This characteristic of the New Testament suggests that there is a proper place in the Church for legitimate diversity. The Judaizing controversy of the early period offers some scriptural warrant for Karl Rahner's suggestion that, outside an 'irreducible minimum' of doctrine, each Church should refrain from denying or rejecting dogmas held by another, and that no Church should be required to confess the dogma of another Church.

If today we are in something of an ecumenical malaise, it is important that we do not retreat into various kinds of denominational-based attempts at renewal and revival – as if this were the real business of the Church. The malaise must be faced. In North America and western Europe it is doubtless due in part to what has been called 'the churches' cultural captivity'.[42] But there are other, deeply-rooted causes of the malaise, including our grievous neglect of theology. 'A doctrine of the church is only as good as the doctrine of God which underlies it'.[43] Not least, our immersion in the New Testament will keep before us a searching, kaleidoscopic, theologically-rooted vision of unity.

III Unity and the Churches

8 *Mission, Unity and History: From Edinburgh 1910 to Edinburgh 2010*

Kirsteen Kim

The steep steps up to the doors of the General Assembly Hall of the Church of Scotland rise from the austere courtyard of New College, which resembles a tall Scottish castle, built of dark grey stone. Those who approach the steps pass under the forbidding statue of John Knox apparently in full flow against the evils of popery. The Hall has witnessed many historic occasions since it was built in 1846; more recently it was the temporary home of the new Scottish Parliament, and despite its associations with schism and nationalism, this same hall has been the venue for two significant events in the history of world mission and unity. These took place one century apart: the World Missionary Conference of 1910 and the closing service of the conference of the Edinburgh 2010 project. Although they were held in the same building, connected historically by the institutions which came out of Edinburgh 1910 and linked spiritually by the call to make disciples of all nations, Edinburgh 1910 and Edinburgh 2010 represent two very different visions of mission and unity. These cannot be separated from the constituencies on which they drew and the global contexts of their respective generations.

The World Missionary Conference which took place in Edinburgh in 1910 is probably the most important date in the history of the ecumenical movement and is sometimes even described as the beginning of it. (The definitive history of the conference is Brian Stanley, *The World Missionary Conference, Edinburgh 1910*, Grand Rapids MI, Eerdmans, 2009.) This is because that gathering of about 1200 Protestant missionaries led directly to unprecedented cooperation and good will between the churches. Protestant mission bodies came together in world evangelization through the International Missionary Council (IMC); strategic alliances were formed between churches in service of the wider society through the Life and Work movement; church leaders gave attention to issues of doctrine and polity which divided them through the Faith and Order movement; and theological educators collaborated through the World Council of Christian Education. All these bodies eventually became part of the World Council of Churches (WCC) at its formation in 1948 or later. In addition to its institutional legacy, Edinburgh 1910 has proved an inspiration for many other initiatives for cooperation and unity. For example, the Evangelical network of mission agencies known as the Lausanne Movement, which was formed in 1974, claimed to inherit the spiritual mantle of Edinburgh 1910 and its missionary aim of world evangelization. Edinburgh 1910 may even have influenced the open approach of Pope John XXIII when he called the second Vatican Council. Bishop Geremia Bonomelli of Cremona sent a message of greeting which was read out at the conference. The same bishop was a mentor of the future Pope John Paul XXIII and specifically discussed the need for a 'great ecumenical council' with him (Stanley, *The World Missionary Conference*, pp. 11–12). Edinburgh 2010 was also to be highly significant for Christian unity and mission for reasons that will be explained.

Edinburgh 1910: Cooperating to advance the kingdom of Christ

Photographs of the two gatherings in the Assembly Hall illustrate the contrasts between Edinburgh 1910 and Edinburgh 2010. The photograph of 1910 shows the 1200 delegates on the floor of the hall seated formally in serried ranks at right angles to each other. The photo is, of course, in black and white and the dominant impression is of grey-haired men in uniform suits. Indeed the conference was organized and dominated by the male elder statesmen of the Protestant missionary movement. But closer examination suggests colour from two quarters: First, the large decorated hats and brighter clothing of more than two hundred women missionaries who had been invited in their own right as delegates, and other women – the wives of missionaries, who were allowed seats in the gallery. The second source of colour was from the national costumes of several of the 'native' leaders who had been invited from churches in Asia. They included V. S. Azariah from India, Cheng Jingyi from China and Yun Chi Ho from Korea. Although they were only eighteen men, they made an impact out of all proportion to their numbers not merely by their appearance but by their informed and impassioned speeches and interventions during the conference.

The year 1910 was the high point of the British Empire and the imperialist mindset was not yet seriously challenged. The discussion of how to best 'advance of the kingdom of Christ' took place in an age in which most of the world's nation-states were kingdoms ruled by monarchs. The Conference received a message from newly ascended King George V, which was read out by the chairman, and was followed by a rendition of the national anthem, which it seems even the Americans joined in. The message sent by the conference in return confirmed the divine legitimacy of kingship and imperialism. (It began: 'That Almighty God, by whom kings reign, and who in His providence has called your Majesty to rule over so great an Empire ...', World Missionary Conference, 1910, *The History and Records of the Conference*, Vol. IX, Edinburgh and London, Oliphant, Anderson and Ferrier, 1910, p. 87.) The delegates in 1910 looked on the world as divided into 'Christian' and 'non-Christian', a division which paralleled that between colonizers and colonized, civilized and uncivilized or less civilized. Believing they represented the kingdom of Christ or 'Christendom', they regarded the rest of the world as both needing Christ and also as a possible threat to the lordship of Christ if not converted. Mission was understood as expansion of the territory of Christendom from its base in Europe 'to all nations' (Matt. 28:19) or 'into all the world' (Mark 16: 15). Although they left military conquest to their governments and they were reminded that 'Christ drew a sharp distinction between the kingdom of the Emperor and the Kingdom of God' (Professor Haussleiter, 'Thoughts on the Principles Underlying the Relations between the Religious and the Political Community', in World Missionary Conference, 1910, *Report of Commission VII*, Edinburgh and London, Oliphant, Anderson and Ferrier, 1910, pp. 142–3), the conference frequently adopted military metaphors to describe their activities. Hymns such as 'All hail the power of Jesus' name', 'Crown Him with many crowns', 'Thy kingdom come, O God' and 'Jesus shall reign where'er the sun' reinforced the analogy of Christ's kingship and earthly kingdoms which formed the theoretical basis of the model of Christian expansion as the aim of mission.

Although delegates understood that the lordship of Christ was exercized through service rather than by force, their close relationship with governments, and their dependence on colonial structures to support their activities, belied any firm distinction between the two kingdoms.

In 1910, mission was construed as a task of the church in obedience to the mandate of Christ (chiefly as recorded in Matt. 28 and Mark 16), and which they were obliged to fulfil by whatever means were available. It was described as 'carrying the gospel to the non-Christian world' or 'the evangelization of the world in this generation'. The post-Enlightenment focus on the agency of human beings and optimism about human progress resulted in great missionary activism, and discussions which focused on facts, numbers and strategizing. Mission was treated as a science in which 'method was everything' (Stanley, *The World Missionary Conference*, p. 5). The Edinburgh 1910 conference was also remembered for its spirituality and times of prayer but these were chiefly inspirational and motivational, for imparting the 'the superhuman factor' in the spiritual life of the missionaries and their home churches that was necessary to 'the success of the Kingdom of Christ' (World Missionary Conference, 1910, *Report of Commission I*, Edinburgh and London, Oliphant, Anderson and Ferrier, 1910, pp. 359–60). The prayer times were not an integral part of the discernment of the mission itself. The nature of mission was not a subject for discussion; that was confined to 'Missionary Problems in Relation to the Non-Christian World' (the subtitle of the conference). The reason for cooperation in mission was not chiefly biblical or theological but practical: to fulfil the task more effectively and efficiently, and in the shortest possible time.

In the imperial context of 1910, the churches of the world, of whatever continent, with the exception of the Oriental Orthodox, were led by Europeans. So the white missionaries at Edinburgh were making decisions for worldwide implementation. Were it not for the far-sightedness of John R. Mott, the conference instigator and chairperson, who realized that this would not always be the case, there would have been no 'native' leaders present at all. There were no indigenous black Africans at Edinburgh 1910 because of the racial stereotypes of the day by which Africans were thought to be much less developed and were therefore not expected to assume responsibility for their churches for several generations to come (Stanley, *The World Missionary Conference*, pp. 98–9).

A century of mission and unity in a changing world

During the next century the hints of colour in the photograph of Edinburgh 1910 would grow and transform the picture of world mission, from being carried out from the white West to the rest, into a vision of 'world Christianity' in which mission is understood to be a response to the initiative of God in the world, primarily through the witness of local churches of all kinds. This shift in paradigm, which transformed the understanding of mission and unity, emerged through the traumatic events of the twentieth century. (For post-1910 developments in mission thinking, the classic work is still: David Bosch, *Transforming Mission: Paradigm Shifts in Theology of Mission*, Maryknoll, NY, Orbis Books, 1991.)

The First World War was only four years in the future when the delegates met in Edinburgh and there was a sense even at the conference that the contemporary globalized situation which so facilitated world mission would not last for long. This sense of a world in crisis lent urgency to the deliberations. The War had two main effects from a mission point of view: political and moral. Among the political effects of the war was a new rapprochement of European Christians with the Orthodox churches due to the break-up of the Ottoman Empire to which many of them had been subject. In 1920 the first suggestion for a 'fellowship of churches' came from the Synod of Constantinople and the dialogue between Protestant and Orthodox churches in the WCC has proved very fruitful. For example, the Orthodox emphasis on unity as prior to and integral to witness challenged those Protestants who thought merely of cooperation. The First World War greatly increased the moral imperative for unity because the war of European nations, most of which had national churches, had also set their churches against one another. Furthermore, the War seriously damaged the credibility of the European Christians in the eyes of the churches of Asia, Africa and other parts of the world and quickened movements for independence of churches as well as nations from imperial control.

The IMC held its first meeting after the War in 1921 with a more sober assessment of the possibilities for world evangelization and a more humble approach to mission activity. By the second meeting at Jerusalem in 1928 profound questions were being asked about mission itself, particularly in relation to other faiths and social movements. The third conference was held in India, now clearly on the verge of independence and for the first time a majority of the delegates were from outside the West. It was 1938 and the shadow of fascism called into question totalitarian systems and visions, whether of church or mission, while also encouraging a focus on truth of Christ as against any human creed or ideology. When the IMC met for the first time after the Second World War in Whitby, Canada the world was radically changed. Western missionaries now recognized that the distinction between 'older' and 'younger' churches was a false one and that they could only work in partnership with fellow Christians in other lands in the urgent work of reconciliation, reconstruction and nation-building. With the human enterprise of building God's kingdom apparently in ruins, around the 1952 meeting of the IMC in Willingen, Germany a fundamental change took place in the understanding of mission and the new paradigm known as *missio Dei* (God's mission) emerged. Mission was no longer thought of in terms of the human enterprise of missions (plural), but as the activity of God the Father, in Christ and through the Holy Spirit, to redeem the world. Mission was now 'God's, not ours' and all were seen as partners with one another under Christ. Since all were now understood to be participating in the same mission, the barriers to unity now appeared more clearly as a direct affront to God.

In the paradigm of *missio Dei*, mission is not only practice but also theology and this encouraged a rethinking of the relationship of mission and church. The sending activity of God is revealed in Scripture in the sending of the disciples (John 20:21). That is, the church is sent into the world and, if so, the church is missionary in its very nature. The implications of this insight for both church and missions were profound because now it seemed church and mission belonged together. Mission was no longer an activity for enthusiasts carried out overseas but the calling of the whole church wherever it exists. This was the theology behind the decision of the IMC at Ghana in 1958 to integrate with the WCC, a decision that was agreed by the Council which, in 1961, created a division on world mission and linked it with its existing desk on evangelism. From then on WCC mission events were predominantly gatherings of church representatives rather than cross-cultural missionaries.

Not all mission bodies were happy about the merger, particularly the more Evangelical organizations, many of them in North America, which were now leading the Western overseas missionary movement and felt it was a betrayal of the missionary freedom exemplified by the Apostle Paul and of the enterprizing spirit of Edinburgh 1910 for world evangelization. In 1966 many of these came together for the World Congress on Evangelism in Berlin under the auspices of the Billy Graham Evangelistic Association, and again in 1974 to form the Lausanne Committee for World Evangelization. The Evangelical mission bodies became even more concerned about a loss of evangelistic zeal when the World Council of Churches was influenced by the secularizing movements of the 1960s and 1970s and seemed to drop its concern for eternal salvation in favour of humanistic or socio-political priorities. But ecumenical and evangelical mission movements began to come together again at Melbourne in 1980, which took the theme 'Your kingdom come', because both networks were committed to development activities internationally and to a holistic approach in mission. The 1982 WCC statement on mission (World Council of Churches, *Mission and Evangelism: An Ecumenical Affirmation*, 1982), in Jacques Matthey (ed.), *'You are the light of the world': Statements on Mission by the World Council of Churches 1980–2005*, Geneva, WCC, 2005, pp. 4–38, reflected a lot of common ground in terms of continuing concern to advance the kingdom, although not now thought of in terms of territory but rather in terms of fulfilment of the reign or will of God beginning on earth and continued in heaven. The Orthodox understanding of mission as witness (*martyria*) became more prevalent not only because it points to the priority of God's initiative in mission but also because it suggests a holistic activity by both word and deed and addressing body as well as soul.

The revolutionary decade of the 1960s produced many surprises including the new openness of the Roman Catholic Church to working with other Christians. WCC mission discussions now became much more representative of the world's Christians as they always included Catholic participants. Two movements which had their origins in the Catholic Church had a great impact on mission thinking in the next few decades: liberation theology and the charismatic movement. Liberation theology called attention to the purpose of the sending of Christ, and therefore the church, 'to bring good news to the poor' and 'liberty to the captives' (Luke 4:18–19). In its dialogue with Marxism, it drew attention to the need to challenge structures of oppression in order to bring about the transformation associated with the kingdom of God. The charismatic movement focused attention on the work of the Holy Spirit as the initiator, empowerer and guide of mission movements (see Acts especially) and redefined mission as the joyful fulfilment of the promise of Pentecost rather than obedience to a command (Luke 24:49; Acts 1:8).

Liberation theology, as a movement with its origins outside the West, and Pentecostal churches, which in Latin America at least were churches of the poor, were indications of what was described as the 'shift in the centre of gravity' of Christianity from the global North to the global South or the poor or majority world. The growing strength of Southern Christianity was reflected in the increasing centrality of justice in the mission, not only in economic but also in ecological matters. The twin concerns for the poor and the earth were linked together by indigenous peoples and other marginalized groups (cf. Rom 8:19–22). A growing maturity of relationships with other faiths, led particularly by Indian theologians, reached a large measure of consensus at the WCC conference on mission and evangelism at San Antonio in 1989. Post-colonial reflections challenged western missionaries to greater honesty about abuses of power in mission activities in the past and began a re-writing of the history of world evangelization which does not focus on missionary activity but rather on the reception of the gospel by local people, and recognizes that they are the chief evangelists and missionaries.

The 1990s brought an end to the Cold War and opened up fresh dialogues between West and East in which the emphasis tended to be on culture and religion rather than society and economics. Now more than ever in the highly globalized post-1989 world, we are living in an era of 'world Christianity' in the sense that Christianity is globally widespread, locally rooted and interconnected (Sebastian Kim and Kirsteen Kim, *Christianity as a World Religion*, London, Continuum 2008). As populations migrate around the world in large numbers, Christians of different regional origins increasingly find themselves living close together. The word 'ecumenical', which tended to be used in the twentieth century to describe activities across the boundaries of different Christian traditions, is now recovering the meaning it had in the early church of bringing together Christians from different parts of the world both locally and at a global level. As relationships between churches are now much more mutual and multi-directional, so movements of world evangelization are now emerging from many different centres around the world: Seoul, Lagos, Buenos Aires, Moscow, Sydney, as well as the older centres in Europe and North America.

Edinburgh 2010: witnessing to Christ together today

The representative photo of Edinburgh 2010 is in vivid contrast to that of one hundred years before, first, because in the intervening years the straight lines have been broken up somewhat and the seating arrangement in the Hall made more rounded, giving a less rigid appearance. Second, the colour which was suggested before is now overwhelming. Of course the photos were taken with a colour camera, but it is also more colourful because of the increased proportion of women and people of colour – especially in the African choir, which takes up much of the foreground. Third, the picture chosen is not of unsmiling faces as if engaged in serious debate but of a relaxed audience enjoying lively African rhythms.

The Edinburgh 2010 project was intended to gather the world's Christians together to renew the vision for mission and to celebrate the way in which the church has become truly global in the twentieth century. Whereas in 1910 it was estimated that nearly 70 per cent of the world's Christians lived in Europe, in 2010 more than 70 per cent live outside it. Africa and Latin America will soon be the continents with the largest Christian populations. (For statistics see Todd M. Johnson and Kenneth R. Ross (eds) *Atlas of Global Christianity, 1910–2010*, Edinburgh, Edinburgh University Press, 2009.) In 2010 the delegates were from all over the globe, and no distinction was made over whether their church was 'older' or 'younger', or who received the gospel first, and from whom. The descendents of the delegates of Edinburgh 1910 have learnt, as Peter did in the house of Cornelius, that 'God shows no partiality' (Acts 10:34) but blesses others in the same way. Edinburgh 2010 was also a celebration of the remarkable level of ecumenical cooperation that has been achieved over a century. Whereas the delegates in 1910 were all Protestants, Edinburgh 2010 was sponsored by bodies representing all the major strands of Christianity today. The Roman Catholic Church, the Orthodox churches, Pentecostal churches, and both the historic Protestant denominations and newer Evangelical movements and independent churches were all stakeholders in the project.

One of the reasons that Edinburgh 1910 made such a lasting impact was the research produced by eight commissions beforehand, which documented the state of mission activities at the time and examined what were considered to be the key issues of the day. (Reports of Commissions I–VIII and *The History and Records of the Conference*, all published by Oliphant, Anderson and Ferrier in Edinburgh and London, 1910.) Mindful of this legacy and hoping to stimulate new thinking and planning for mission today, a multi-national research project was set up in 2008 which brought together scholars from all continents and many different regions to work on what were identified as nine key issues in mission today. These included the questions of the foundations for mission, Christian mission among other faiths, the relationship of mission and power, the nature of mission spirituality, and of course mission in unity and unity in mission. Edinburgh centenary events were held in Aarhus, Accra, Aizawl (NE India), Bangalore, Belfast, Boston, Budapest, Buenos Aires, Cape Town, Geneva, Hamburg, Henderson (New Zealand), Hyderabad, Iloilo (Philippines), Liverpool, Minsk, Matanzas (Cuba), Melbourne, Nairobi, Oslo, Oxford, Rome, Santiago, Seoul, Seramban (Malaysia), Tokyo, Toronto, Utrecht, Wuppertal (Germany) and other cities.

As a member of the theology faculty at Leeds Trinity University College with a special interest in mission and world Christianity, I was delighted when the invitation came in late 2008 to serve the centenary project half of my time as Research Coordinator. In 1910 those who organized the conference, and those who convened the commissions which reported to it, were dependent on letters and surface mail for their communications with missionaries around the world, and journeyed by ship and rail. In 2010 email, the website (www.edinburgh2010.org), Skype and conference calls, Facebook and Twitter provided a variety of means to engage with mission thinkers globally from my base in Yorkshire. Air travel made it possible in 2010 for the study groups, which included people from many different countries, to meet face-to-face before the conference in Edinburgh in June 2010. I was able to participate personally in some of these and in other Edinburgh 2010-related conferences in Germany, Japan, South Africa and Switzerland, as well as many places in the UK. I produced the report of the study process which was the raw material discussed at the conference, and the conference report after it (Daryl Balia and Kirsteen Kim (eds), *Edinburgh 2010: Witnessing to Christ Today*,

Oxford, Regnum Books, 2010; Kirsteen Kim and Andrew Anderson, *Edinburgh 2010: Mission Today and Tomorrow*, Oxford, Regnum Books, 2011), and I continue to edit the series of nearly thirty Edinburgh 2010 volumes being published with Regnum Books in Oxford and distributed worldwide.

At the conference which preceded the final event I was busy coordinating the process by which the delegates representing the world's churches, and invited experts, interacted with and helped focus the work produced by the study groups on the different themes. The result was a short Common Call to mission, which can be downloaded from the website and is commended to the churches for further reflection and implementation in different contexts. Considering the theological and cultural diversity of the study process and conference, it was remarkable how much we were able to say together. The Common Call has this to say about Christian unity:

> Recalling Christ, the host at the banquet, and committed to that unity for which he lived and prayed, we are called to ongoing cooperation, to deal with controversial issues and to work towards a common vision. We are challenged to welcome one another in our diversity, affirm our membership through baptism in the One Body of Christ, and recognize our need for mutuality, partnership, collaboration and networking in mission, so that the world might believe.
>
> (Edinburgh 2010 Common Call, paragraph 9. Available to download from www.edinburgh2010.org)

9 *The Story of British Ecumenical Endeavour*

David Cornick

In his enthronement sermon at Canterbury in April 1942, William Temple (in)famously spoke of the ecumenical community as '... the great new fact of our era.'[1] He had seen the ecclesiastical world change in his lifetime. In 1909 he had chaired SCM's conference at Matlock on 'Christianity and social problems' in its heady days as the radical 'ecumenical think-tank' of Protestantism. The Movement also sent him to be a steward at Edinburgh 1910, and he never lost his sense of the church as an expanding, universal community.[2]

The world in which Temple came to maturity was dominated by the energy of ecumenism. It was at first not simply the gathering up of pre-war threads, but also a response to the horror of the trenches, an awareness of the need to fashion a new world order and build Christian bridges between nations. The list of developments between 1919–21 is impressive. What eventually became Faith and Order, and Life and Work, began their lives in preparatory conferences – the former in Geneva, the latter at Oud Wissemar in the Netherlands during these years. Temple was later to be a significant leader in both. He was a prominent player at the Lausanne Faith and Order Conference in 1927, which led him to suppose that '... all tendencies are towards unity'. He chaired its sequel at Edinburgh in 1937, and drafted the final statement of the remarkable Oxford Life and Work Conference the same year. The following year he became the chair of the provisional committee that designed the World Council of Churches, which was to come into being in 1948, delayed by the war.[3] It was no surprise that he considered ecumenism '... the great new fact'. It was.

If the thirties were, as Adrian Hastings argues, a 'remarkably dull' period in domestic church history, international ecumenism acted as a vivacious counterpoint as three outstanding British ecumenists – Temple, J. H. Oldham and Bill Paton – played critical roles in engineering the creation of these international institutional structures. As war loomed, those bodies had a resolve and resilience which their secular equivalent, the League of Nations, lacked. Elsewhere in Britain the Student Christian Movement was creating friendships amongst its staff which would shape the next generation of the ecumenical venture – amongst them Lesslie Newbigin, Eric Fenn, Alan Richardson, Ambrose Reeves, Oliver Tomkins, Ronald Preston, David Paton and Alan Booth.[4]

If the international scene was vibrant, the domestic front was hardly quiescent. The 1920 Lambeth Conference 'Appeal to all Christian People' has been convincingly shown to be part of that wider earlier activity, fed most notably by the meetings of 1916–19 between Anglican and Free Church theologians at Mansfield College, Oxford to prepare for the World Faith and Order Conference in Lausanne. That meant that the essential theological ground had been clearly defined by the time George Bell drafted the Appeal in 1920.[5]

The Appeal was a somewhat narrow fugue on the theme of the Lambeth Quadrilateral of 1888 – the Scriptures as '… the rule and ultimate standard of faith', the Nicene Creed, '… the divinely instituted sacraments of Baptism and the Holy Communion, as expressing for all the corporate life of the whole fellowship in and with Christ' and '… a ministry acknowledged by every part of the Church as possessing not only the inward call of the Spirit, but also the commission of Christ and the authority of the whole body.' But whereas the Quadrilateral presented the episcopate as a fact rather than a theory of ministry, the Appeal spoke of '… the episcopate [as] the one means of providing such a ministry' (albeit in a rhetorical question). Nonetheless, the spirit was eirenic and hopeful, positing an agenda of '… mutual deference to one another's consciences …' so that Anglican bishops and clergy would seek '… a form of commission or recognition which would commend our ministry to their congregations, as having its place in the one family life', and non-episcopally ordained clergy would accept '… a commission through episcopal ordination, as obtaining for them a ministry throughout the whole fellowship.'[6]

The rootedness of the Appeal in wider ecumenical discussions explains the rapid progress which was made between 1920 and 1925 between the Church of England and the Free Churches. There was broad agreement that the two constituencies were united in one faith, and that the Appeal offered a reasonable practical roadmap towards unity. But the talks ended because the participants could not find a route across the contours of episcopal ordination. Was conditional ordination a way of disowning ministries of Word and Sacrament non-episcopally received?

However, the Appeal quickly revealed the theological fault-line which was to dominate the English ecumenical agenda for the next century. Episcopal and non-episcopal churches could cooperate effectively within councils and consultative bodies, and were to do so as the World and British Councils of Churches came into being. Organic unity or full communion dictated different demands, and in England at least the nature of episcopacy and attempts to reconcile episcopally and non-episcopally ordained ministries became the dominant ecumenical contour of the ecumenical landscape while the main ecumenical players were the Free Churches and the Church of England (that is until Vatican II and its aftermath) – indeed, it is still a major question in the Anglican–Methodist covenant.

However, Scottish union in 1929 and Methodist Union in 1932 showed that unity was perfectly possible. Granted both were familial unions, but the differences between the family members shouldn't therefore be minimized. Similarly, throughout the interwar period, work towards the creation of the Church of South India (1919–47) continued, as much an English debate about the nature of the early church as it was about India.

Temple remained frustrated by the responses to the Lambeth Appeal, but he consistently backed the South India negotiations, and inevitably became the first President of the British Council of Churches in 1942. That in itself was a unique achievement. It brought together for the first time the leaders of all the non-catholic churches in Britain.

It was that remarkably successful, potent, cohesive and essentially Protestant ecumenism which shaped the nature of post-war ecumenism. On 23 November 1946, in the midst of the needs of post-war reconstruction, Temple's very different successor, Geoffrey Fisher issued another appeal, this time from the pulpit of Great St Mary's Church in Cambridge. Fisher appealed to the English Free Churches to take episcopacy into their system. Unlike the Lambeth fathers of 1920, Fisher dreamt not of organic unity, but 'full communion'. 'What I desire is that I should be freely able to enter their churches and they mine, in the sacraments of the Lord and in full fellowship of worship.'[7]

A generous interpretation would suggest that Fisher had seen enough of the difficulties to realize that there was no other way around the difficulties of reconciling episcopal and non-episcopal ministries, but it is more likely that the innately conservative Fisher saw no reason why the Church of England should change, but every reason why the Free Churches should alter their polities. The Methodist Church responded most positively, ironically setting in train a process of negotiation to achieve what Fisher didn't want, a united church.

The war and its immediate aftermath witnessed the emergence of a significantly new ecumenical atmosphere. It is hard to overstate the importance of the British Council of Churches as a meeting place for non-Catholic church leaders.[8] There was also a proleptic significance in the slow involvement of Cardinal Hinsley in public statements by church leaders during the war, and in the astonishingly ecumenical platform provided by the radical and short-lived Sword of the Spirit movement which Hinsley nurtured so carefully.[9] It barely survived his death in 1943, yet it was a pointer towards the new relationship between English Catholics and their fellow Christians which would eventually take new institutional shapes in the 1960s and 1970s.

A generation was dying – Bill Paton in 1943, Temple in 1944. Only George Bell of the first rank of pre-war ecumenists lived on to play a significant role in international ecumenism as chair of Central Committee of the World Council 1948–54 and as President until his death in 1958. But the mood had changed. Ecumenism remained the '... great new fact.'

The Church of South India finally came into being in 1947, a union of Anglicans, Methodists, Presbyterians and Congregationalists. It seemed to square the circle of episcopal and non-episcopal ministries, albeit with mixed success, at least as far as the Anglican Communion was concerned. The scheme stated that all ministerial ordinations after union would be episcopal, but that existing ministers did not have to be episcopally re-ordained. The Lambeth Conference of 1948 decided that it could not remain in full union with the new church, a situation which continued until 1988.[10]

That the union of small churches in a predominantly Hindu culture thousands of miles away should produce such a pamphleteering storm in England during the 1940s gives pause for thought. Although there was sympathy for the Indian church, many English Anglo-Catholic commentators interpreted the union as an incipient threat to the very being of the Church of England. T. S. Eliot was amongst the most prominent, ungenerously describing the process as '... twenty years to construct a pantomime horse' and dismissing the new church as '... a pre-fabricated church.' The heart of his concern was, of course, the nature of episcopacy and the validity of the sacraments, and his fear was of a church being designed according to the lowest common theological denominator.[11]

The shape of the Church of England was changing. Although never a part of the 'establishment', and although internally divided, Anglo-Catholicism had come of age in the interwar period. Eliot's shrillness owed something to his repudiation of his New England Unitarian background, and something to the confidence of a convert into the third generation of Anglo-Catholicism. Fifty thousand laity and clergy had gathered at White City Stadium in 1933 for Pontifical High Mass to commemorate the centenary of the Oxford Movement.[12] As a movement it was at this stage at best ambiguous about the Roman Catholic Church in England, convinced that the Church of England was the true *ecclesia Anglicana*, although for some (such as Eliot) the Malines conversations of the 1920s were a flicker of hope. The Church of England, whether it liked it or not, was becoming more demonstrably aware of its catholic, as well as its protestant, heritage.

However, the impetus of ecumenism seemed unstoppable, for hot on the heels of the creation of the Church of South India came the first meeting of the World Council of Churches at Amsterdam in 1948. In England these were years of hope and idealism – the 1944 Education Act, Atlee's post-war administration and the creation of the Welfare State. Post-war church life, caught up in the realities of re-building and creating new structures for mission, reflected that. These were the years of Christian Action, of the consolidation of the British Council of Churches and the emergence of its overseas development arm, Christian Aid, of Leslie Hunter's creation of Industrial Mission in Sheffield, of the Parish and People movement which sought to make the eucharist the central act of Anglican worship, and of the growth of Evangelicalism – Billy Graham's first mission in England was in 1954.

The Methodist response to Fisher's 1946 Appeal needs to be understood within that context of optimism. Progress was steady, but painfully slow, and the final scheme was not presented to both churches until 1968, by which time England was a very different country. But, during the 1950s and early 1960s, the very existence of such discussions which might end a schism of two centuries seemed profoundly hopeful.

In 1957 it seemed as if Fisher's call might bear fruit in relationships between the Church of Scotland, the Presbyterian Church of England and the Church of England in *The Bishops' Report*, which proposed episcopally ordained permanent Moderators of Presbytery both north and south of the border. The Scottish press flailed it with clubs of nationalism and imperialism, and it died the death of the floor of the Church of Scotland Assembly.[13] If the creation of the Church of South India had indicated that one brake on ecumenism might be the complex chemistry of the Church of England's own pathology, the perceptive might have noticed that the increasing complexity of the British Isles was another. Stakeholders other than Christian theologians were to be reckoned with as the ecumenical pilgrimage continued.

Two years later, in Rome, a remarkable event occurred. An elderly, supposedly caretaker Pope, John XXIII, announced on 25 January 1959, the last day of the octave of prayer for Christian unity, his intention to call a General Council of the Church. Observers from other Christian communions would be welcomed. It was not a move for which the English hierarchy were prepared. He spoke of *aggiornamento*, intuitively sensing the unrest in continental Catholicism. Yet, with the possible exception of B. C. Butler, the Abbot of Downside, the English Catholic leadership did not swim in those intellectual waters.[14] Indeed, the English Catholic Church was prospering. While the Protestant churches were embroiled in decline, Catholicism enjoyed its highest percentage of English baptisms between 1959–64, and 12.6 per cent of all marriages in 1961 (its highest ever). The annual figure for converts over the same period ran at about 12,000 per year.[15] The need for a council eluded Cardinal Godfrey.

A few months after summoning the Council, Pope John instituted the Secretariat for Unity in the Curia. Its first head was the distinguished German Jesuit, Cardinal Bea. Later that year (1960) Archbishop Geoffrey

Fisher became the first Archbishop of Canterbury since the reformation to visit the Pope. Despite the efforts of the Secretariat of State, there could be no disguising its significance. As the two elderly leaders sat in the Pope's study, the Pope expressed the hope that the day would come when our 'separated brethren return to Mother Church'. 'Your Holiness, not return', said Fisher. 'Why not?' asked John. 'None of us can go backwards', replied Fisher, 'we are each now running on parallel courses; we are looking forward, until, in God's good time, our two courses approximate and meet.' The Pope thought a moment. 'You are right', he said.[16]

Ecumenism had taken a decisive, momentous turn. The Council opened on 2 October 1962, ending in 1965. English observers were there, including the Congregationalist Biblical scholar George Caird, and the Bishop of Ripon, John Moorman, who attended every session. Once again, the air was pregnant with ecumenical hope. If that was the mood in Rome, it was echoed in the deliberations of the World Council of Churches. The 'young' churches of the global South and East were coming of age, and corporate unions were burgeoning across the world, in North India, Zambia, Canada and Nigeria. The Church of England's ecumenical guru was Oliver Tomkins, the Bishop of Bristol and a former WCC staff secretary. He returned from the Council's Faith and Order Conference at Montreal in July 1963 with a sense of all-enveloping ecumenical speed and '... a sense of panting along in the rear of events.'[17]

That sense remained with him as he chaired the British Council of Churches Faith and Order Conference at the University of Nottingham in September 1964, which for the first time included ten Roman Catholic observers. Five hundred and fifty representatives gathered from virtually every church in England, together with the General Secretary of the World Council of Churches, Visser t'Hooft, and representatives from the Russian and Greek Orthodox, the Lutheran Church, the Pentecostal churches, the Church of South India and the Taizé Community.[18] Tomkins hoped that 'It would raise the temperature in the churches and make it easier for unity to go forward at every level'. The intent was to create a forum from which new initiatives could arise.

Archbishop Michael Ramsey preached the opening sermon at Southwell Minster, gently warning the conference that younger churches came to the ecumenical table with less historical and institutional baggage than the ancient churches of the west, and that the task before them was therefore intellectual and doctrinal.

In his opening address Oliver Tomkins stressed the urgency of union, arguing that the question was no longer why Christians should unite, but 'why do Christians not unite?' To a '... bomb-threatened, half-starving, rioting, population-exploding world' the church appeared too often to be talking to itself about itself. Unless Christians could convincingly show that '... they were concerned with unity because a divided church was disastrously the wrong-shaped tool for doing the work that God wanted his church to do in the modern world', they would forsake the support of many.[19]

The Conference had two notable outcomes. The first was a challenge to the churches to covenant together for unity – '... in appropriate groupings, such as nations'. And, they added, '... we dare to hope that this date should not be later than Easter Day 1980. Although the motion was passed by an overwhelming majority (53 against out of 550), it had been vigorously debated. John Moorman, fresh from Rome with a draft of the Council's proposed decree on ecumenism in his briefcase told the Conference that it was 'one of the most remarkable and hopeful documents which have been issued in the whole history of the ecumenical movement'. He confided his dislike of the proceedings to his diary, particularly '... a determination on the part of the young (especially nonconformist young)' to force through the 1980 date. Although never a friend of the Free Churches, Moorman was uniquely placed to see that the pivot of ecumenism was about to be changed forever by the Council's Decree on Ecumenism. However, even the Catholic observers sided with Tomkins.[20] Had Moorman been heeded, English ecumenism might have taken a very different route.

Having issued the challenge, the Conference then authorized a practical way ahead, what it called 'Areas of Ecumenical Experiment' (AEEs), which would permit local experiment. It was an attempt to allow the Lund Principle of 'acting together in all matters except those in which deep differences of conviction compel them to act separately' (which had been essentially Tomkins' draft at Lund in 1952). Local unity was far from new. Mervyn Stockwood looked back fondly on his wartime ministry at St Matthew's Moorfield, Bristol and the community of Anglican, Methodist, Baptist and Congregational colleagues as the deepest ecumenical experience he ever had.[21] However, Nottingham 1964 lent a new depth to local ecumenism. These AEEs were the harbingers of the national unity which would arrive in 1980. Five years later the Sharing of Church Buildings Act passed through Parliament, providing a legal framework for the Areas. They took off on a wave of excitement.

The 1960s was a decade of cultural and largely failed political revolution. For the churches the early 1960s were shot through with optimism and possibility. There were new cathedrals – Guildford in 1961, Coventry risen like a phoenix from the ashes in 1962 along with the extraordinary Metropolitan Cathedral of Christ the King, in Liverpool. Theology was on fire, pregnant with revolution. The *New English Bible* was the bestseller of 1961, the Cambridge Divinity Faculty produced *Soundings* in 1962, and John Robinson's *Honest to God* followed hot on its heels in 1963. The radical journal *New Christian* began in 1965. A new beginning seemed possible. Ferment and creativity were all around. Vatican II and Nottingham were also part of that ecclesiastical culture, which in its turn reflected a world of economic growth, political liberalization, and the whiff of cultural revolution. Keith Clements, the Baptist ecumenist and historian, who was a student at the time, captures the mood exactly.

> '... I was in a circle who believed we were entering into the era of an unstoppable ecumenical advance. Undefined, maybe naive, but it was a feeling that we were all somehow 'on the way to unity'. We were being welcomed at each other's communion tables and altars. Extraordinary reports were reaching us from Rome as the Second Vatican Council got under way. The Abbot of Downside made history by coming to preach in Great St Mary's, Cambridge. Bliss was it in that dawn to be alive, as over our bread and cheese lunches we argued and speculated. In such an atmosphere it did not really seem to matter which denomination you presently belonged to. It made little sense to transfer from one to another because one's real loyalty lay to the coming Great Church'.[22]

But below the surface dangerous currents were swirling. The gentle decline in Protestant churchgoing continued unabated, apart from a slight increase in Anglican Easter communicants in the mid-1950s. Even that failed to regain its pre-war level. Allegiance to concept of a Christian culture was weakening – post-war Sunday School observance had been in serious decline since the mid-1950s, and the number of Anglican baptisms per 1,000 live births dropped from 67 in 1950 to 52.6 in 1964. Children were no longer being socialized into the church.[23] Christianity was beginning to lose its privileged position in English society, and religious choice was increasing, as was individualism and the concept of spiritual 'seeking'.[24] The far-sighted realized that. In 1962 Christopher Driver, a Congregational layman, better known as the editor of the *Good Food Guide*, published a withering analysis of the present state of the Free Churches in *A Future for the Free Churches?*

If Nottingham was a high-water mark of hope, by 1969 it was clear that the deep-seated tensions of 'the long 1960s' (1958–74) were seriously distorting the ecumenical dream. In 1960 Kenneth Slack, the Presbyterian Secretary of the British Council of Churches wrote a book called *The British Churches To-day*. It was republished in 1969, and Slack noted how 'passage after passage' seemed strangely optimistic and had to be excised.

Ironically, as the churches drew ever closer together, the divisions within each church deepened, and that polarization made the possibility of inter-denominational union the more unlikely. The Anglican-Methodist scheme suffered from precisely that when a minority combination of Anglo-Catholics and Evangelicals ensured that General Synod in 1969 failed to obtain the necessary 75% in favour (it achieved 69%).

When a revised version was presented in 1972, the vote was 65.8 per cent in the house of clergy (tantalisingly close to the required new two-thirds majority), and less than 63 per cent in the house of laity.[25]

Vatican II had changed the ecumenical scene completely. Michael Ramsey's meeting with Paul VI in 1966 was a marked contrast to that between Fisher and John XXIII six years earlier. Pope Paul spoke of the Church of England as a sister church and presented Ramsey with the Episcopal ring he had been given when he became archbishop of Milan. It was symptomatic of a new relationship, which was enshrined in the founding of the Anglican Centre at Rome and the ARCIC process.[26] It was John Moorman who led the opposition to Methodist union in General Synod because as a member of ARCIC he believed that giving Methodist ministers the same authority as Anglican priests would greatly weaken the Anglican argument with Rome about the validity of their orders.[27]

Although the Congregationalists and Presbyterians did achieve a union in 1972, the failure of the Anglican-Methodist talks was a devastating blow. The world was changing. The seventies were not the sixties. Edward Heath's government came to power in 1970, and English society was dogged by the politics of division and dispute. Dreams of Protestant unity were fading.

The Churches Unity Commission was created in 1974, in part at least as a response to the creation of the United Reformed Church. Eight denominations were represented, from the Catholics to the Baptists. Its remit was daunting – to see if the kind of union which had prevailed in the Church of South India and the Church of North India could be replicated on English soil. So, it was faced with the reconciliation of episcopal and non-episcopal ministries, women in ministry (General Synod did not finally accept the ordination of women to the priesthood until 1992), believer's and paedo-baptism, establishment and disestablishment. It issued Ten Propositions about unity, and recommended the formation of the Churches Council for Covenanting, under the chairmanship of Bishop Kenneth Woolcombe. The participants were the Churches of Christ, the Church of England, the Methodist Church, the Moravians and the URC. The Catholic Church and the Baptist Union sent observers. It was, as John Huxtable later wrote, doomed to failure, not least because it attempted too much too quickly. However, that was part of the funding conditions. In 1982 it came to naught on the floor of the House of Clergy.

Looking back, Huxtable commented that he (and by implication his ecumenical generation) '... had been working on a set of assumptions which I could now see were too much of a pipe-dream.'[28] He realized that he had misunderstood the Church of England, or perhaps more accurately, he had not realized that it had changed. The ecumenism of Temple and Tomkins was being eclipsed, but it is important to realize just how close it had come to success. It was derailed by a mere handful in the House of Clergy in 1972. Had six clergy voted the other way, the twentieth century history of ecumenism would be told in a different key.

The tensions within the Church of England, accentuated by the growth of Anglo-Catholicism in the interwar years and evangelicalism from the 1950s onwards, meant that it was a divergent coalition of ecclesiologies held together by episcopacy. More hopefully, as relations with Rome improved after Vatican II, it could have become the arena for a serious dialogue between Protestantism and Catholicism. As it is, movement towards the ordination of women bishops has rendered that less likely than it seemed to John Moorman and his colleagues in 1972. However, the demise of the Covenant spelt the end of the phase of English ecumenism which dated from Lambeth 1920. For the first time since 1958, there were no discussions about unity in progress.

Yet 1982 was an oddly ambiguous year ecumenically. ARCIC I reported, arguing for the establishment 'of a new relationship' between the Anglican Communion and the Roman Catholic Church as the next stage of ecumenical commitment, and that coincided with the World Council of Churches Lima text, *Baptism, Eucharist and Ministry* which revealed remarkable convergence, and invited all churches to prepare a theological response. And, most significantly for English ecumenism's future shaping, Pope John Paul II's visit lent a new and wider perspective to the English ecumenical enterprise. It was not unprepared. Both the BCC and the Catholic Bishops Conference of England and Wales had been involved in discussions since the announcement of the visit in 1980, and Cardinal Hume and Bishop Murphy-O'Connor were clear that they wished it to have an ecumenical dimension.

At Bellahouston Park in Glasgow the Pope addressed the 'larger community of believers in Christ' with the words: 'We are only pilgrims on this earth, making our way towards that heavenly Kingdom promised to us as God's children. For the future, can we not make that pilgrimage together hand-in-hand?'[29] During the visit he spoke of how heavily the sin of disunity weighed on the shoulders of the church, and emphasized that the restoration of unity, beginning with that '... interior conversion which is the essential condition for ecumenism' was the responsibility of all Christians. Unity was the work of the Spirit.[30]

That precipitated a search for new ways of seeking unity. Thus encouraged, the English Catholic Church's commitment to English ecumenism was deepened, and that led to the creation in 1984 of the Inter-Church Meeting which brought together not just the Anglican, Catholic and Free Churches, but also the Orthodox and Lutheran communities, and some African and Caribbean Independent, Pentecostal and Holiness churches. The leaders of some 32 churches in England, Scotland and Wales agreed to launch a three year process, the Inter-Church Process, *Not Strangers but Pilgrims*, which included the 1986 Lent course *What On*

Earth is the Church For?, as well as English, Welsh and Scottish national conferences. The intent was for the churches to pray and reflect about the nature of the church in the light of its mission.

The British Council of Churches was in a difficult position. Its General Secretary, Dr Philip Morgan, immediately saw that the events of 1982 needed something different. The Roman Catholic Church had been considering the possibility of joining the BCC since 1970, but by 1982 it was clear that it would not, whether for financial reasons or anxieties about the locus of authority or both – that was never made clear. It also suffered from the structural weakness of all umbrella organizations – namely, that its members could (and did) ignore its decisions, and from the beginning all member churches had (quite properly) reserved decisions on unity to themselves. Similarly, its propensity to concentrate on English issues in the absence of an English instrument had exacerbated the growing irritation of the Welsh, Scots and Irish.

Nonetheless, it was a noble and costly decision that it took when it resolved to dissolve itself by the end of August because the end of the Inter-Church Process was not yet visible, and the implications for the staff were considerable.

The process culminated at Swanwick in September 1987. It was clearly a remarkable occasion, all the more so because the lead up to it had revealed many tensions between the varying communions, not least around the subject of Eucharistic celebration. Indeed, the organizers knew that Cardinal Hume's briefing of Catholic delegates had been fairly negative. So, when the Cardinal and Archbishop Runcie arrived, Canon Martin Reardon made sure that he was there to meet them. Runcie threw his arm around Hume's shoulders and said, 'Now we all know that we've come here to get you to join the British Council of Churches!' Runcie always knew how to take humour to the edge, and this time it worked.

Hume presided at the first Catholic Eucharistic, inviting non-Catholics to come forward for a blessing, and he found himself blessing Archbishop Runcie, and the leaders of most of the British churches. There was an unusually long pause after communion, and the congregation slowly realized that the Cardinal was so moved that he was finding it hard to finish the mass. The following day's Eucharistic proved equally moving as Catholics, led by the Cardinal, in their turn came forward to receive blessings from Anglican and Presbyterian ministers.

By the Wednesday, however, the conference seemed to be going nowhere, so John Habgood, who was chairing it, and Derek Warlock decided to visit the Cardinal Hume to persuade him that he now needed to say something about Catholic intent. The following afternoon Hume addressed the conference, 'I hope that our Roman Catholic delegates ...will recommend to members of our Church that we move now quite deliberately from a situation of cooperation to one of commitment to each other.'

He added: 'Christian unity is a gift from God and in these last few days I have felt He has been giving us this gift in abundance. It is also a process of growth ... One step at a time, and Swanwick has been a very decisive one.' The Archbishop of Canterbury and other leaders welcomed this shift from what Runcie called '... ecumenism as an extra which absorbs energy' to 'ecumenism as a dimension of all that we do which releases energy, through the sharing of resources'.[31] And so, on September 1987 the church leaders and others gathered at Swanwick, judging themselves 'the broadest assembly of British and Irish churches ever to meet in these islands', declared their '... readiness to commit ourselves to each other under God', to become in God's good time '... the one Church of Christ, united in faith, communion, pastoral care and mission.'[32]

The headiness of Swanwick turned in the following year into necessary detailed planning, and the so-called 'Marigold Booklet', *The Next Steps for Churches Together in Pilgrimage* became the bible for negotiation between the churches and then the implementation of the new bodies. The Council of Churches for Britain and Ireland replaced the BCC, a new English instrument was created, Churches Together in England, in Wales Cytun succeeded the Council of Churches for Wales, and in Scotland ACTS (Action of Churches Together in Scotland) replaced the Scottish Council of Churches. The report also envisaged what it called an 'intermediate level' of ecumenical activity. This again was of particular significance to the Catholic church because this was the level at which a good deal of decision making happened, and in Cardinal Hume's words '... there can be no authentic evolution which does not take place at a local level.'[33]

The new structures were illustrative of a profound philosophical change. The switch was simple. Ecumenism was no longer to be, as the Marigold Booklet put it, '... an extra, which absorbs energy, to ecumenism as a dimension of all that we do, which releases energy through the sharing of resources.' This deep change of mind-set was precisely what the churches had committed themselves to in the heady atmosphere of Swanwick. The weakness of this Churches Together model was clear from the beginning. It depended on the churches' commitment to Christ's call, and on their commitment to each other. In other words, it placed the responsibility for Christian unity into the hands of church leadership, and by extension (for no church leader is omnicompetent or omnipresent) to a not necessarily theologically literate bureaucracy, which could be unsympathetic, or even hostile, to its goals.

Colin Davey was a member of staff who bridged the two eras. He found the new way of working a positive liberation. He felt himself now working for an enabling body which was encouraging the churches to come together and work together, whether that in creating a joint report like *Unemployment and the Future of Work* (1997) or sending delegations to visit places like Malawi, Ethiopia or Albania, where it truly mattered that Anglicans, Catholics and Orthodox were making these visits together. The ecumenical tent was larger under the new dispensation, and the voice more authoritative, because it was the voice of the churches themselves.[34] The new mind-set could work. This was truly a way of ecumenism that exuded rather than absorbed energy because the churches were actually doing their work together. When that happened at any level, the new model worked.

However, that was far from the whole story. The transition from the first phase of English ecumenism to the second was rocky and difficult, and the early history of CCBI is a sorry tale of incompetent planning and inadequate costing. The hoped for level of funding from the Roman Catholic church failed to materialize, the original budgeting hadn't included any provision for Steering Committee expenses (including travel), and some churches under financial pressure (the early 1990s were years of high inflation) refused to send delegates to the Church Representatives' Meeting, which had been envisaged as the principal forum for deepening ecumenical relations. Those problems were exacerbated by the cost of creating an entirely new English instrument, and of accommodating it within a British structure.[35]

The transition from the culture of a British council to national and local ecumenism has not been either simple or easy. 'Britain' has never been a straightforward concept politically or ecclesiastically, and as the pressure for devolved political power in Wales and Scotland gathered pace in the 1990s, the need for a four nations instrument became less obvious. The new instruments worked hard to establish new modes of working, each with its distinctive national dimension. In England CTE concentrated on inter-church cooperation and fostering local ecumenism while relying on CCBI for public affairs and international work.[36] However, the structural and financial issues would not go away. After a review in 1997 CCBI re-branded itself yet again in 1999, becoming Churches Together in Britain and Ireland. Further downsizing was to follow in 2008–9 as some major funders cut their ecumenical funding dramatically.

Ecumenical bodies do not exist in a vacuum. Their fortunes are intimately entwined with the churches they seek to serve. Late twentieth century church history has been dominated by institutional decline. The population of England increased by 4 million between 1979 and 1998, but the number attending church declined over the same period from 5.4 to 3.7 million. Anglican attendance declined by 41%, Catholic by 38%. Only Baptist, black-led and independent churches appeared to be holding their own.[37] By the end of the century some historians were talking about the death of Christian Britain. That was to mistake church attendance for emotional commitment to Christianity. The 2001 Census suggested that 71 per cent of the population still considered themselves Christian, although quite what that means is subject to interpretation.

Yet, if decline is one salient reality, diversity is another. Successive waves of immigration have brought the world church to the high streets of English cities. From 1995 to 2005 black led churches grew by 50 per cent, and now constitute 10 per cent of the churchgoing population, despite being 2 per cent of the population.[38] That is highly significant as Pentecostalism as a world movement becomes increasingly engaged in ecumenical discussion and partnership. The main black-led churches have a long history of commitment to the ecumenical instruments, as indeed do the Orthodox churches. They are increasingly being joined by some of the 'new' or community churches which have previously sat at some distance from formal ecumenism.[39] Christianity in England is becoming increasingly pluriform, albeit still within a pattern of overall, if slowing, decline.

Ecumenically there is a sense of being at a crossroads. Current trends are never easy to analyse, but three aspects are significant. The first is that increasing pluriformity. Some mission focused initiatives, like Hope and

More Than Gold (the churches' response to the 2012 Olympics), have a brand quality which has enabled them to gather to themselves a mixed constituency of partners who in previous decades would have shunned each other. Indeed, More Than Gold probably represents the widest ecumenical coalition yet achieved in England, founded though it was by the Archbishop's Council, the Catholic Bishops' Conference of England and Wales and Churches Together in England amongst others. That bears theological reflection – ecumenism is changing, unity is being discovered in mission, but it is a unity which is essentially relational rather than structural or institutional. In a sense what is happening is reminiscent of the early days of modern ecumenism, in the discovery of friendship and common purpose which (for example) marked SCM in the 1920s and 1930s. If ecumenism is turning into an iterative cycle, that is an essential component of spiritual growth.

The second aspect is revealed by reflection on international dialogues. When Cardinal Kasper's stewardship of the Pontifical Council for Christian Unity was drawing to close, he initiated a review of the main Western dialogues in which the Catholic Church had been involved. Looking back on the forty years of dialogue and the remarkable degree of doctrinal convergence that it had revealed, he commented, 'There is no reason to be discouraged or frustrated, or to speak of an 'ecumenical winter'. We have achieved more than we could have imagined or dreamed forty years ago. Yet we must also admit, realistically, that we have not yet reached the goal of our ecumenical pilgrimage but are still at an intermediate stage.'[40]

The divisive matters that remain – authority, the nature of the human person and theological anthropology, the sacramental nature of the church, and the eucharist – will not bear a quick solution, so the question then becomes, 'What shall we do in the interim?' That in turn provides a basis for the essentially Catholic development of receptive ecumenism. Vatican II recognized the ecumenical impulse amongst the Catholic Church's 'separated brethren' as a work of the Holy Spirit, and spoke of unity as of the essence of the church.

Catholics and Protestants perceived unity differently, but that is unsurprising because there is one Catholic church, but many Protestant churches. As the Protestant churches gathered in council did their theology, they perceived the unity of the church to have been given once for all in Christ, and concluded that it had been masked by the divisions of history, so the ecumenical task was to make that given unity visible (New Delhi 1961). The Catholic view, on the other hand, was that the unity of the church 'subsists in' the Catholic church, which is in historic continuity with the church of the early centuries. So, there is a tension between the Protestant ecumenical method which is about making visible the unity which Christ embodies, and the Catholic method which is about 'restoring' the shattered unity of the church.

However, the logic is compelling and hopeful. As Paul Murray has recently written, 'The logic is that if we believe the Holy Spirit is really at work in other Christian traditions sustaining real elements of the Church of Christ there ...why need we wait for full ecclesial unity before being enriched by them?'[41]

Formal dialogues will continue during the interim. In England the Anglican-Methodist Covenant of 2002 was devised as 'stepping stone' on a journey whose eventual goal is still the full, visible unity of Christ's church.[42] Similarly, a new phase of ARCIC was announced in 2010, with receptive ecumenism as its avowed methodology.

The third aspect is the sense amongst some serious and lifelong ecumenists that new patterns are needed. The Methodist theologian Frances Young has recently written, 'I speak as a life-long ecumenist ...but I now find myself asking, "What kind of unity?"... We need, not a unified top down totalitarian ecclesiastical institution, but public demonstrations that, though diverse, we Christians love one another. I seriously wonder now whether ecumenism needs a different model of unity.'[43]

The opposite of unity is, of course, not diversity but division. And the opposite of diversity is uniformity, not unity. But her point is well made. In a sense, the reassessment of the route to the ultimate goal of unity being mapped out by receptive ecumenism, the broadening of the tent which is characteristic of both national and intermediate ecumenism in England as well as task-centered movements like Hope and More Than Gold, and the struggles to move to a truly 'Churches Together' model, are part of the organic evolution of a new and appropriate ecumenical shape.

Traditional ecumenism, which was largely by default Protestant (and Orthodox at world level) has many remarkable achievements to its name. Reviewing the history of Christianity in England in the twentieth century, Adrian Hastings concluded 'A sense of one Christian community with a common mission and a common faith had become central to the experience of all the main churches in England in a way that it had never been previously. And that was a very great achievement.'[44]

That Protestant voice is still the default accent of English ecumenism. It badly needs supplementing. The Catholic theological accent is still not properly understood or appreciated, still less those of Pentecostalism and the new churches. The uncertainty and flux of present ecumenical activity is symptomatic of the beginnings of that wider conversation as structures mutate and evolve to accommodate the changing nature of the body of Christ.

Local engagement will increase in importance in that flux precisely because it is mission-focused and relational. That, in a sense, is the turning of a circle because local ecumenical engagement pre-dates national structures. From 1917 onwards Councils of Christian congregations had been formed in cities and towns like Bolton, Manchester, Bristol and St Alban's.[45]

We need to discern anew the movement of the Spirit in the flux that surrounds us, and recover our confidence that the church is God's, and that the gifts we enjoy in all their diversity are God's gifts. Interim there undoubtedly is, but no one doubts the eventual goal. It was the last Pope, John Paul II, who in *Ut Unum Sint* re-stated the classic theological case for unity, 'This unity, which the Lord has bestowed on his Church and in which he wishes to embrace all people, is not something added on, but stands at the very heart of Christ's mission. Nor is it some secondary attribute of the community of his disciples. Rather, it belongs to the very essence of this community. God wills the Church, because he wills unity, and unity is an expression of the whole depth of his *agape*.'[46]

The ecumenical question that we need to answer is not the ultimate one, but the penultimate. What of the interim, as we seek together to find ways of living out the mission of Christ in the complex and ambiguous context of an England that, in Richard Chartres' prophetic words will become increasingly 'secular, religious and Christian all at the same time.'[47]

10 *The Roots, Range and Reach of Receptive Ecumenism*

Paul D. Murray and Andrea L. Murray

Introduction: what is Receptive Ecumenism?

As is independently mentioned in some of the other essays in this volume, Receptive Ecumenism represents a fresh approach to the contemporary ecumenical task. It seeks to serve the traditional Faith and Order concern to work for the structural and sacramental unity of the churches while also seeking to move beyond the impasse and energy-drain that much Faith and Order style ecumenism has suffered over the past decade or so when compared with the remarkable achievements of the latter part of the twentieth century. Although having only come to named articulation and full development in recent years through a series of initiatives running out of Durham University's Centre for Catholic Studies,[1] Receptive Ecumenism can be viewed as bringing to the fore certain background values and assumed dispositions that have always been quietly recognized as being essential to good ecumenical work.[2] It operates by bringing these background values and dispositions to the fore and giving them explicit shaping influence and strategic priority as no longer just ancillary to the ecumenical agenda but as actually constituting its core contemporary task and challenge.

At the heart of Receptive Ecumenism is the conviction that further substantial progress is indeed possible on the way towards full structural and sacramental unity but only if a fundamental, counter-instinctual move is made away from denominational traditions wishing that others could be more like themselves to instead each asking what they can and must learn, with dynamic integrity, from their respective others. Moreover, this required receptive ecclesial learning is envisaged as operating not only in relation to such things as hymnody, spirituality and devotional practices but as extending to doctrinal self-understanding and, even more so, respective structural and organizational-cultural realities.

There have thus far been four key strands to the Durham Receptive Ecumenism projects. Where the first two focused in international research conferences concerned to articulate and scrutinize the basic idea and to test it out (first in relation to Roman Catholicism[3] and then in relation to as many other traditions as possible,[4]) the third has taken a directly practical turn, concerned to test the relevance and viability of Receptive Ecumenism on the ground in the local church. This has been done in collaboration with nine of the major denominational groupings in the North East of England.[5] The fourth strand, to be hosted by Fairfield University in Connecticut, USA, will gather together the various individuals, groups and organizations throughout the world that have been putting Receptive Ecumenism to work in their own respective contexts and spheres of responsibility.[6]

The specific invitation in relation to the present essay was less to do with rehearsing the theological rationale for Receptive Ecumenism (for this, see the various essays identified in n. 1 earlier) and more to do with our being asked to reflect more personally on the roots and reach of Receptive Ecumenism and the various influences that have shaped it. It is, of course, very difficult to trace such things adequately. Autobiographical reflection is notoriously partial as reconstructed from hindsight. With these caveats in mind, the reflections that follow fall into three sections: 1) *the roots of Receptive Ecumenism*; 2) *the guiding principles and theological range of Receptive Ecumenism*; and 3) *the reach and potential of Receptive Ecumenism*.

1. The roots of Receptive Ecumenism

In different ways we each grew up deeply marked by Catholic faith and practice, alive to it as a privileged place and means of encounter with grace, holiness, and the forgiving, strengthening presence of God in Christ and the Spirit in a way that has sustained an adult lifetime of committed participation. Equally, we each arrived at adult Catholic faith well aware of various ways in which Catholic life can seem thwarted and even resistant in some respects to engaging vital questions about its own growth and renewal. This, of course, is a dissonance, that runs through each of us personally every bit as and considerably more sharply than it runs through Catholic life and organization in their more institutional forms. Accepting that and genuinely so, for each of us at different points the more institutional, organizational and cultural forms of this ecclesial dissonance – between calling and deep integrity on the one hand and lived response and integrity on the other – has led at times to periods of ecclesial frustration and even of longing desire for what variously appears differently attractive and of God-given grace in other Christian traditions. The live option has ultimately, however, never been to leave Catholicism for ecclesial residency elsewhere in the household of faith but rather to desire Catholicism's own further deepening, enriching, freeing and fulfilling and to lament its falling short, as also our own.

At its core here is a continuing sense of being called to be Catholic; of being indelibly shaped by Catholic sensibilities and understanding; of 'at-homeness' and a continuing appreciation for Catholicism's distinctive gifts. Andrea once summed this up with the pithy comment: 'Leaving Catholicism would be like divorcing your parents.' The most important things in life are generally given happenings rather than chosen actions – or at least given happenings before they become chosen actions – starting with life itself, about which we are all singularly unconsulted. As what we have written here suggests, Catholicism for each of us is basically one of these fundamental givens. It is through Catholicism that we each came to Christian life and it is within the context of Catholicism, duly supported through much ecumenical learning, that we have grown in Christian life. Further, this long habitation and familial love goes beyond mere cultural habituation and accidental givenness and manifests in an appreciation for some of Catholicism's distinctive gifts as being essential for the good of the whole church. Equally, this long habituation and familial love supports also the recognition that these very gifts are at once sites of difficulty as well as grace; gifts that need liberating and re-performing if their God-given quality is to be released and realized in a manner attractive to the other Christian traditions – as Pope John Paul II recognized most remarkably in relation to the Papacy itself in his 1995 encyclical *Ut Unum Sint*.

In many respects this is already to have identified the core principle at the heart of Receptive Ecumenism and to have situated it within our own faith stories. This is not yet, however, to have identified the various factors and influences that served to bring it to explicit voice. Some of these are now traced briefly here.

For Paul a profoundly shaping experience over an extended period was that of receiving his initial introduction to, and much of his subsequent formal training in theology, at the hands of great Protestant, particularly Anglican, teachers: most notably Stephen Sykes, Ann Loades, Dan Hardy (all at Durham) and later David Ford (at Cambridge). In addition to opening up an appreciation both for the sheer richness of the Christian tradition in all its depth and breadth and for the vital role that critical-constructive theological conversation has to play in serving the health of the churches, they each had the tremendous generosity of spirit to encourage their students to go more deeply into their own respective traditions and to take ownership of same rather than to promote an assumed commonality. To put it in the later terms of Receptive Ecumenism, their shared commitment was that ecumenical theological learning should be about the enrichment rather than diminishment of identity. This is a great gift to bestow: to help another become him/herself in all his/her difference from you.

This basic value received more explicit formal stimulus during the years spent pursuing doctoral studies with David Ford at Cambridge and the opportunity this presented to engage closely the kind of approach to theology that he and others were pursuing. This version of 'post-liberalism' characteristically combined a concern to take the particularity of Christian practice and understanding seriously with due recognition of the need always to hold such particularity open to appropriate expansive scrutiny and potential revision.[7] In David's own work the clearest practical expression of this is in the practice of Scriptural Reasoning that he was developing during this period in the context of inter faith encounter and inter faith theological reasoning, in collaboration with Dan Hardy, Peter Ochs and Aref Nayad. In this regard, Dan Hardy notably describes Scriptural Reasoning as 'one way of going deeper simultaneously into one's own faith and into the faith of others through study and mutual mentoring'.[8] In many respects Receptive Ecumenism can be viewed as seeking to do something directly analogous in the intra-Christian context.

At a more affective level, another key influence for both of us was the experience of sharing in a series of Ignatian-inspired Lenten retreats in daily life organized for interested staff and students of Newman College, Birmingham (where we were each then Senior Lecturers) by Barbara Stafford and Avril O'Regan of the Sisters of La Retraite. At the heart of all such Ignatian-style prayer, reflection and direction is a call to personal conversion but understood explicitly as the call to greater life, interior freedom and flourishing. With this, the offered path to such increased interior freedom is through bringing the movements of one's imagination and the desires of one's heart into clearer view (through imaginative prayer in relation to given texts of Scripture and subsequent heart-to-heart conversation with one's prayer guide) and the discerning of these movements in terms of what binds and what frees relative to the movements of the Holy Spirit who is understood as leading from frustration and confusion ('desolation') into life and peace ('consolation'). There is a direct link between the emphasis placed in Receptive Ecumenism on continuing conversion – both personal and institutional – as a principle of life rather than diminishment, and our involvement in these guided prayers experiences and the tangible benefits they brought, as there is also in relation to the place accorded within Receptive Ecumenism to the imaginative, the creative, the 'dreaming of dreams' and their critical testing and scrutinizing.[9]

Somewhat later, following a decisive relocation from Birmingham to Ushaw College, the then Catholic seminary for the North of England and the Diocese of Shrewsbury, other factors that would subsequently play a role in shaping the Receptive Ecumenism projects, particularly the regional comparative project, included an eighteen month period that Andrea spent conducting research for the Bishops' Conference project on Evangelization in England and Wales.[10] This served to connect Andrea's expertise in contextual social-scientific analysis with the empirical life of the church in a more formal capacity than hitherto and to confirm for her the pastoral and ecclesial value of such studies. Throughout this period also Andrea was serving as a Pastoral Tutor at St John's College, Durham, an independent Anglican College within the University, wherein she both enjoyed the warm fellowship and lively worship of an evangelical community and lived the pain each week of not being able to share fully in the community Eucharist.

For Paul's part, of immense significance during these years was the experience as the new boy on the staff of being given the responsibility to act as the Ushaw staff member on a compulsory double module on Church and Ministry in an Ecumenical Context that was co-taught and co-studied in collaboration with staff and students of Cranmer Hall and the Wesley Study Centre, the Anglican and Methodist training institutions situated within St John's College. Few if any of the students were particularly positively disposed to the module. Quite apart from its being compulsory, which tends to bring out the adolescent in students, the prevalent attitude – amongst some staff also – was that the formal ecumenical project had basically arrived at an irresolvable dead-end: consequently, beyond praying together, being nice to each other and generally trying to do what we can together, the common assumption was that formal ecumenism simply does not justify the required expenditure of time and energy. Amongst the Catholics the tendency was to view the 'others' as just not being prepared to get sufficiently serious about the importance of ecclesial unity and what it entails. In contrast, for the Anglicans and Methodists the tendency was to regard Catholics as simply *being* the problem on account of Catholic refusal to embrace other Christians into full communion in the face of continuing structural and institutional differences.

For all this, however, and for all the real challenges that teaching on the module entailed, not least not having taught either ecclesiology or ecumenism before, Paul found that the regular experience of having to prepare materials relating to difficult issues in one's own tradition for use in an ecumenical context served to release something in him. As with Andrea's experience more broadly in St John's, this involvement, surpassing all expectations, became a privileged opportunity to ask how the experience, practice and understanding of other traditions can speak into Catholicism's own experience and so help address the specific problems and difficulties that can be found there. With that, the basic core principle of Receptive Ecumenism was born if not yet either precisely articulated or named. Beyond this, the continuing preparation for the module provided ample further opportunity to come to appreciate just how well this basic principle coheres both with the teaching of Vatican II on ecumenism (most notably in the Declaration on Ecumenism, *Unitatis Redintegratio*) and with Pope John Paul II's remarkable encyclical, already referred to earlier, *Ut*

Unum Sint. For each of us, then, our respective involvements with the communities of St John's College had something of the feel of a graced happening that was expanding us affectively, intellectually and ecclesially in ways pregnant with possibilities and implications that were as yet unclear.

Reinforcing this sense was another related happening about this time in the shape of Paul being invited by the late Bishop Ambrose Griffiths to share in the work of the Methodist–Roman Catholic Committee of Great Britain. Again somewhat contrary to expectations, there was a similar experience of the work of the Committee going considerably beyond each party simply explaining itself to the other and allowing rather for each to be genuinely challenged and enriched by the other.[11] The idea of a research project in transformative Catholic ecclesiology in ecumenical perspective was beginning now to emerge clearly into view.

The final decisive event, following after Paul had moved to a post within Durham's Department of Theology and Religion, was the good fortune to be able to participate in a remarkable day conference in the nave of St Alban's Cathedral in early summer 2003 at which Archbishop Rowan Williams and His Eminence Cardinal Kasper each expounded upon their shared vision of Spiritual Ecumenism.[12] Spiritual Ecumenism articulated precisely the vision of receptive ecumenical hospitality and fruitfulness that we had each been experiencing and towards which Paul had been moving in his thinking. The one caveat was that Spiritual Ecumenism could potentially be heard as speaking of the need for receptive learning purely at the level of one's personal spirituality or, if extended to the collective level at all, to the need for such learning merely in relation to respective spiritual and liturgical traditions. If so, this would be to leave out of account the crucial need also for deep structural, institutional learning from each other in relation to such things as respective processes and structures of decision-making.

The point is that without such institutional learning it is unlikely to be possible either to find a means of fruitfully addressing the various respective difficulties within each tradition or for any real further ecumenical progress to be possible. Spiritual Ecumenism, while absolutely right in its basic orientation, appeared to be in need of being taken forward in a more obviously institutional direction. In order to emphasize this, in the process of preparing for the first international research colloquium (Ushaw, January 2006) that was to explore this strategy and concern, the decision was taken to refer to Receptive Ecumenism rather than to Spiritual Ecumenism.

For all the undoubted success of the first event and for all the genuine attempts made there to move away from the theoretical alone and to engage in analysis of the lived, practical, organizational dimensions of ecclesial existence, the fact remained that the analysis operated at a relatively theorized, academic level. Speaking into this from her newfound vantage point of now working as the Ecumenical Officer for the Diocese of Hexham and Newcastle, together with her long experience of contextual social-scientific analysis, Andrea helpfully suggested that 'Getting real about Receptive Ecumenism supposedly being a means of shaping the lives of the churches would require close engagement with such people as local ecumenical officers and the formulation of an initiative directed at the level of the local church.' It is this that led directly to the five-year comparative regional project in Receptive Ecumenism and the Local Church that is reviewed in the final part of this essay. For now we turn attention to summarizing the key guiding principles at work in Receptive Ecumenism. The resonance that variously exists with the principles less formally presented in the current section will be clear.

2. The guiding principles and theological range of Receptive Ecumenism

The various essays cited in n.1 here, as also those in n. 2, each provide systematic articulations of and reflections upon the various theological and strategic principles at work in Receptive Ecumenism. In the light of the freshly articulated autobiographical and contextual reflections on the roots of Receptive Ecumenism that have been offered here, no attempt is made in this present section either to repeat or substantively to supplement these various extended systematic accounts of its guiding principles. Rather, we settle for simply summarizing in point form and in ordered sequence the most important of these principles. By doing so their relationship with the various guiding influences on the articulation and development of Receptive Ecumenism formulated in the previous section should be all the clearer to view. These are:

- as called forth and held within the Trinitarian communion of God, the churches are called to grow ever more deeply and more visibly together in this communion and to come to express the union-in-relation it implies in appropriate structural and sacramental unity;

- 'Life and Works' ecumenism – doing things together – while absolutely vital, can never be enough;
- while always in need of testing by the 'head' – by critical theological scrutiny – all effective receptive ecumenical learning consists most deeply in an affair of the 'heart', as a matter of being attracted by, even falling in love with, the grace-filled beauty in another tradition and being impelled to move towards this even at cost;
- the authentic Spirit-led vitality of Christian life and tradition consists not in steadfast identical repetition but in the preparedness to return to our core calling and to ask what fresh performances of this, with dynamic integrity, are appropriate to the specific challenges and opportunities of our times and contexts;
- the integrity of traditions consists not merely in doing the same things in different ways and different locations but in doing, as required, genuinely fresh things in familiar or recognisably coherent ways;
- we need to resist exclusively past-oriented views of tradition and exclusively problem-solving understandings of the ecumenical task relative to such past articulations and to engage also future-oriented understandings of the tradition as all it is and might be relative to the saving purposes of God in Christ and the Spirit;
- traditions are better conceived as dynamic webs than as inflexible structures;
- our traditions are limited as well as life-giving, wounded as well as grace-bearing: we need to show rather than to hide our wounds and to ask our others to minister to us;
- the openness to growth, change, examination of conscience and continual grace-filled conversion that lies at the heart of Christian life pertains as much to the ecclesial as to the personal: to allowing, that is, one's own tradition to be challenged to expand and to re-think how it understands and does things in relation to specific issues;

- this due emphasis on the ecclesial dimension of conversion needs to extend beyond the doctrinal-theoretical alone to include also the organizational, the structural, the cultural, and the broadly practical;
- truth is ultimately something lived and not simply something thought;
- whether personal or ecclesial, the call to conversion requires to be lived through attentive hospitality to the truth of the other in specific circumstances;
- in this regard it must be remembered that Christian living and ecclesial existence is not a zero-sum game in the sense that the call to graced conversion is always the call to greater life and flourishing, never, fundamentally, to diminishment;
- consequently, rather than worrying unduly about what learning others may need to do, each should take responsibility for their own learning, mindful of the adage that 'We cannot change others, we can only change ourselves but changing ourselves will enable change in others';
- with this, receptive ecumenical learning requires a move away from the presupposition of mutuality – 'we'll move if you move' – to the embrace of a certain unilateral willingness to walk the path of ecclesial conversion for the sake of the greater flourishing one's own tradition's and regardless, to some extent, of whether others are also currently prepared so to do;
- the primary aim is not the promotion of increased mutual understanding and appreciation *between* traditions but of continuing ecclesial conversion, deepening and expansive growth *within* traditions;
- throughout, it must always be remembered that progress towards our ecumenical goal is fundamentally God's work and calling into which we are being drawn rather than any merely human project of our own creation, possession and control;
- living this requires *both* active trust that we *are* being resourced for this and led into it in the ways that we require *and* patient recognition that any real receptive ecclesial learning necessarily takes time to be realized;

- as such, the ecumenical scene is best viewed not simply as a problem-strewn field but as one of open possibilities, across which the only path is one of long, slow learning into greater life and maturity – this is not a second-best accommodation compared with a supposedly alternative faster route but the only route possible, the golden highway;
- the time we have is a time of grace and time for the eventual unfolding and present anticipating of God's success, not a time of irredeemable failure;
- the fact that some problems and differences can now appear insuperable does not mean that they will always so appear;
- we must neither give up on the God-given calling to be one, nor allow it to mutate into merely getting along with each other but rather seek to live courageously and imaginatively in hope;
- we need to 'lean-into' the promise of God's purpose and the presence of God's Spirit and to ask what it means in practice for us to enter into this more fully in the here and now;
- we are changed by love not by anger and if we are in turn to effect creative ecclesial change then it must be through the sustained passion of love rather than frustration: 'By love alone' the way of ecclesial transformation.

3. The reach and potential of Receptive Ecumenism

Having traced something of the back-story to Receptive Ecumenism's emergence into clear voice and some of the experiences and influences that promoted this (sec. 1 here) and having also surveyed its core guiding principles (sec. 2), both theological and strategic, it is now fitting to take a brief look at what Receptive Ecumenism can look like in practice. Without this it would be in danger of sounding like a fine vision that does not in any way connect with the nit and grit reality of ecumenical work and encounter.

One way in which we could do this would be to review and reflect upon a selection of the creative theological analyses that were pursued during the course of the first and second international Receptive Ecumenism conferences, engaging respectively what Catholicism might have to learn with integrity from other traditions and what the full range of

Christian traditions might each have to learn from one or more of their own other traditions. There is certainly a great deal of very high quality work here that requires considerable further engagement. As noted earlier, however, there is also a sense in which for all their strengths, the analyses in each of these first two phases of Receptive Ecumenism tended to operate at a relatively theorized level. As such, for present purposes it will probably be most helpful to attend awhile to the regional project in Receptive Ecumenism and the Local Church that has been underway in recent years in the North East of England in partnership with nine of the major denominational groupings in the region.[13]

The core purpose of the project has been to examine how respective specific difficulties in the organizational cultures of each of the participant groupings – and the doctrinal theological commitments associated with these – might fruitfully be addressed by appropriately learning from and receiving of examples of 'best practice' in the other traditions. As such, the idea has been to use practical and organizational matters – and the social-scientific means of analysing these – as portals into the ecclesial and the ecclesiological. This comparative analysis of respective organizational cultures has been pursued at the three levels of: *regional processes and structures* (e.g. Diocese, District, Synod, Association, etc.), *local processes and structures* (parishes/congregations) and, where they exist, *intermediate processes and structures* (e.g. deaneries, circuits, mission groupings, etc.).

In order to do this an interdisciplinary and diversely skilled and situated overall project group was brought together, comprizing philosophical and systematic theologians (Department of Theology and Religion, Durham), sociologists and anthropologists of religion (Department of Theology and Religion), practical theologians (St John's College, Durham), organizational and human resource experts (Durham Business School), adult Christian educational experts (North of England Institute for Christian Education), and local ecumenical offers and local church practitioners. This overall group was in turn sub-divided into three research teams: one focused on matters pertaining to *Governance and Finance*, another focused on matters pertaining to *Leadership and Ministry*, and a third focused on *Learning and Formation*.

The work itself has ended up being divided into six interrelated phases. First for each research team was a detailed mapping, on the basis of extant documentation and some initial interviews, of what is in principle happening on the ground within each denominational grouping relative to the interests of the particular research team in question and at the three relevant levels of region, intermediary, and congregation.

Second was a more detailed empirical testing of how this relates to actual practice (again at all three levels of region, intermediary and congregation) and the strengths and issues this raises: in the case of the *Governance and Finance* team this was largely done through structured interviews; in the case of *Leadership and Ministry* by questionnaire; and in the case of *Learning and Formation* by focus groups and participant-observation.

In turn, taking the respective strengths and open questions cum areas for possible development that had been identified in Phase Two, the third phase consisted in a series of cross-trajectory participant-observer congregational studies focused on examining how the various denominational groupings are responding to the challenges raised by the declining numbers of ordained, or authorized, ministers. This generic change serves to bring into focus issues relating to all three trajectories of *Governance and Finance* (e.g., in the shape of the need for fresh structures or ways of organizing), *Leadership and Ministry* (e.g., in relation to the need for fresh models and patterns of ministry and ways of relating between clergy/ministers and lay), and *Learning and Formation* (e.g., as regards the formational work required to enable a congregation to make a smooth transition through this period).

For each denominational grouping the various materials and interim reports deriving from the three respective research teams in relation to the first three phases of work are, at time of writing, currently being used as the empirical basis for the production of one integrated, multi-perspectival report for each participant grouping. Each of these Phase Four preliminary integrated reports will culminate in identifying respective strengths and weaknesses for each denominational grouping and specific areas worthy of further consideration for potential receptive learning at one or more of the levels under investigation and from one or more of the other participant groupings.

These will be working documents for purposes of: a) consultation with the respective stakeholder groupings to test initial reactions both to the integrated account in the round of how their groupings are being presented in the project and to the specific examples of potential receptive learning that are being identified in their regard; and b) the subsequent rigorous testing and, where possible, sharpened re-articulation (Phase Five) of these aforementioned examples of potential receptive learning relative to considerations of ecclesiological integrity and real possibility, pastoral appropriateness, and sheer practicality. The respective possibilities for real receptive learning that survive this robust process of ecclesiological, pastoral and practical testing and associated refinement and re-articulation will then be finalized and accordingly offered, along with their worked-out justifications, to each denominational grouping for potential reception, or otherwise.

The sixth and final phase will then consist in a process of widespread dissemination of the findings and proposals arising from the project both throughout the participant groupings themselves and for widespread consideration by others much further afield.

Interesting while all of this is, and not just for the substantive findings and constructive proposals that will emerge from the project but also in relation to the fresh methodological light it casts on the systematic task of ecclesiology,[14] there is nevertheless a major limitation with the project when viewed as a potential model of Receptive Ecumenism in action. That is, while it certainly engages closely with the lived reality of the local church, the extensive use made of expert social-scientific analysis in the Receptive Ecumenism and the Local Church Project means that it does not represent a practice of Receptive Ecumenism that, in this particular form, can easily translate into the ordinary practice of the local church or be easily continued and further applied by those without specialist social-scientific training. For this to happen then, rather than the kind of expert consultancy model prevailing – which in no small part is what is being played out in Receptive Ecumenism and the Local Church – what is required is for groups in diverse local contexts themselves to take on the responsibility of identifying what is difficult and in need of repair in their respective contexts and with that in view to turn to pursue the Receptive Ecumenical question as to how their particular difficulties can, with integrity, be creatively addressed and tended to through appropriately receiving from the gifts of other traditions. In this regard it is heartening and humbling to see that this local reception of Receptive Ecumenism is indeed well in progress with groups, to our knowledge, in Australia, New Zealand, Canada, the United

States, Germany, Scotland and England exploring what it means in their own respective contexts.[15] Also significant here is the fact the staff of Churches Together in England have been tasked by one of the Presidents with devising resources to help promote and support the practice of Receptive Ecumenism at the level of the local church.

If, then, the fruitful reception of Receptive Ecumenism requires it to be capable of being adopted, in appropriately adapted form, into the ordinary practice of the local church, it equally depends on it being taken into the formal ecumenical practice of the churches in their institutional relating to each other. On this front, highly significant has been the interest shown by the Faith and Order Directorate in thinking and practice of Receptive Ecumenism.[16] Of greater significance still, however, is the explicit adoption of Receptive Ecumenism by ARCIC III as providing an appropriate way of proceeding and theological orientation as it sets out on this crucial next phase of the Commission's work focused jointly on the relationship between the local and universal levels of the church and on the dynamics and substance of ethical discernment.[17]

In terms of how this will shape and change the practice of ARCIC III when compared with previous rounds of the Commission's work, it first and foremost implies that the key question will no longer be, as it once would have been, 'How can Catholics and Anglicans seek to come to a common mind on issues such as decision making at local and universal levels?' but 'What respective difficulties are there in each of our traditions around decision making and how can these potentially be helped by learning from what is strong in the other tradition?' With that it also means that ARCIC III will both seek to model this process in its own work and seek to stimulate similar processes at all levels of the lives of the churches through creating appropriate consultation documents and resources. Here the process of receptive ecumenical learning and showing forth its transformative potential in clear, useful, attractive and convincing ways is actually more important than seeking to arrive at a theorized conclusion in a convergence statement.

As such, the final statements arising from ARCIC III will very likely include clear acknowledgment of continuing areas of substantial and substantive disagreement between the traditions. It is hoped, however, that what they will also do is to articulate, witness to and serve a process of real receptive, life-giving learning on behalf of each tradition precisely in the context and in face of such continuing substantive disagreement. If so, each tradition will be called to grow in specific ways in its respective practices and structures of decision-making through effective receptive ecumenical learning.

In terms of what it means for the theology and practice of Receptive Ecumenism that ARCIC III is explicitly taking it up in this way, one friend, on reading the official communiqué, commented: 'Receptive Ecumenism has now moved from being a good idea discussed by some academics and ecumenists with some church support to being embraced by the most significant international bilateral process in the English-speaking world that has in turn tended to influence the methodology of all the other dialogues.'

This, of course, all needs to be kept in perspective. As indicated earlier, while the specific language and systematic articulation of Receptive Ecumenism as an explicit strategy fit for our times might be of relatively recent articulation, it is a way of thinking and acting that has long been incubated in the ecumenical movement and which has, in part at least, been assumed in all good ecumenical work throughout. If Receptive Ecumenism is indeed fruitful for our times, it represents the coming of age and to full voice of a gift born within and given by all *that* has and all *who* have gone before in the ecumenical movement. As such, the appropriate attitudes are those of gratitude, rejoicing, humility and confidence that in as much as Receptive Ecumenism is indeed right and fitting for our times, it will be shown to be so by its fruits and, in as much as it is not, it will in due course be similarly discerned not to be and so be suitably adapted and developed by the community of the church.

11 *Focusing a Vision: Affect and Effect in Ecumenical Dialogue*

Stephen Platten

In 1989, Robert Runcie, then Archbishop of Canterbury visited Pope John Paul II in Rome. It was an iconic moment. Alongside the famous picture of the two church leaders praying together at the place of Thomas Becket's martyrdom in Canterbury in 1982, the visit completed the circle which marked out their joint contribution towards closer Anglican–Roman Catholic relations. Over lunch in the Vatican, the Pope coined a memorable aphorism which might be the motto or text for all who would work for the unity of God's Church on earth. Reflecting on their common meal together, the Holy Father said simply: 'Affective communion leads to effective communion.' It was a phrase that he would frequently return to when talking of the nature of the Church. The sentiment which it expresses underpins the complexity and the multi-layered nature of ecumenical dialogue. Dialogue refers not only to formal theological conversations and the statements which are their fruits. It also refers to a much richer tapestry which begins with individual personal relationships, broadens out into the engagement of otherwise separated church communities and issues in common discipleship with its commitment to the religious and moral life of our world.

The seed of the harvest of Anglican–Roman Catholic dialogue is just one interesting example.[1] In 1955, Wilfrid Browning, a young Anglican priest was at that time the secretary/editor of the *Bulletin Anglican Ecuménique*. The *Bulletin* had been launched in Cambridge by Professor Owen Chadwick and others. Father Louis Bouyer, a noted Patristic scholar in France was also supportive of this group. Bouyer was a priest of the Oratory. He encouraged the setting up of a visit of four Church of England clergymen to Milan. Browning was asked to write to Monsignor Giovanni Battista Montini, then Cardinal Archbishop of Milan, later Pope Paul VI and a friend of Father Bouyer. Browning wrote a diplomatic note (in Latin) and received a charming reply (in Italian). The reply included an invitation for four Church of England clergymen to visit Milan.[2] The group was to include the then Bishop of Ripon, John Moorman, the Franciscan scholar (who ultimately could not go because of ill health), who would later be one of the Anglican observers at the Second Vatican Council over which Pope Paul would preside for most of its work. Bernard Pawley (later Archdeacon of Canterbury, and another Anglican observer at Vatican II) did take part in the Milan visit. The visit brought forth much fruit. Montini had already visited Britain and knew something of the Church of England. This augured well for Archbishop Michael Ramsey's 1966 visit to Pope Paul. During that visit the Pope removed his episcopal ring and gave it to the Archbishop; some have likened this to an 'engagement' between the two communions. The ring is still worn by Archbishops of Canterbury on all visits to the Pope. The fourteenth century fresco which was also given by the Pope to Archbishop Ramsey still hangs on the north side of the sanctuary of the crypt chapel at Lambeth Palace.

The 1966 visit, which benefited so much from Montini's earlier links with Anglicanism was very fruitful. Out of it grew the Malta Commission which produced a preparatory report establishing the parameters of the future Anglican–Roman Catholic International Commission.[3] Founded, at the same time, with the encouragement of both Pope and Archbishop, was the Anglican Centre in Rome which acts as the base for the Archbishop of Canterbury's Representative to the Holy See.[4] That same person, as Director of the Centre, administers a library of ecumenism and ecclesiology, directs courses on a variety of ecumenical themes and acts as a focus for Anglicans and other visitors to the *eternal city*. This brief set of vignettes illustrates the interconnectedness of *affective* and *effective* ecumenism. Affective simply refers to the need to build up personal relationships, whereas effective fairly clearly describes positive progress more generally in ecumenical dialogue. Good human relationships are the foundation of more formal dialogue. They are also an essential part of what is now known as 'receptive ecumenism.'[5]

The ARCIC dialogue is considered by many to be seminal amongst the many bilateral theological conversations between two world communions. Starting its work in 1970, ARCIC I engaged with three doctrinal areas: the eucharist, ministry and authority. There were included elucidations within this work and the 1982 *Final Report*,[6] as it was known, declared full agreement on the eucharist and ministry with more work to be completed in the area of authority. The 1988 Lambeth Conference received this report and endorsed the agreement noted by the Commission. There was another three year wait before the publication of a document in response to ARCIC I from the Vatican.[7] This document allegedly took into account the earlier fairly positive responses from certain Roman Catholic Episcopal conferences, including those of France and of England and Wales. The Vatican document, however, did not reflect the tone of these positive responses and required from ARCIC II further clarifications on certain issues.

It was during the present author's time as Anglican Co-Secretary of ARCIC II (1990–5) that the report of ARCIC II was published.[8] The document's publication rested again on personal relationships nurtured over the years within and beyond the Commission. Soundings were taken with the then President of the Pontifical Council for Promoting Christian Unity, Cardinal Edward Idris Cassidy. He agreed to consult with the Congregation for the Doctrine of the Faith who confirmed that a formal response from ARCIC II could be a positive step forward. The document was published in 1994 and eventually a further response came from Cardinal Cassidy, as President of the Pontifical Council for promoting Christian Unity saying that no further work needed to be pursued in the two areas of eucharist and ministry where there was now said to be substantial agreement. There were negative reactions to *Clarifications*, however, from within Anglicanism, notably from Evangelicals who were unhappy with some of the conclusions of the document.[9] Furthermore there was widespread concern that there was a tendency for the document to forsake the ARCIC method, which was to go behind the controversies of the sixteenth century and seek those areas of theological consonance which exist between our two communions. In 1981 at Castel Gandolfo Pope John Paul II received the members of ARCIC, after welcoming them, he continued, 'your method has been to go behind the habit of thought and expression born and nourished in enmity and controversy, to scrutinize together the great common treasure, to clothe it in a language at once traditional and expressive of the insights of an age which no longer glories in strife but seeks to come together in listening to the quiet voice of the Spirit'.[10]

This period of the early 1990s was a fruitful time for ARCIC II. In 1991, the agreed statement *Church as Communion* was published.[11] Little notice was taken of its publication than otherwise might have been the case for three reasons: first it was launched on the first day of the first Gulf War; second, the controversial Canberra Assembly of the World Council of Churches followed immediately and overshadowed it; third, it is a consolidating document rather than an agreed statement breaking entirely new ground. Nevertheless, the rigour of its ecclesiological work and the gathering together of this material in one ordered argument offers one of the most succinct statements of the key elements of the doctrine of the Church found in recent ecumenical dialogue. It presents a clear matrix on which further theological work can be hung in other areas. Indeed the first substantive paragraph of the 1999 agreed statement, *The Gift of Authority*, takes *Church as Communion* as its starting point: 'In Jesus Christ's work of redemption God renews his promise to his creation, for 'God's purpose is to bring all people into communion with himself within a transformed creation' (ARCIC, *Church as Communion*, 16)'[12] In the paragraph that begins the final section of *Church as Communion* we read:

> 'Progress in mutual understanding has been achieved. There exists a significant area of doctrinal agreement between our two communions even upon subjects which previously divided us. In spite of past estrangements, Anglicans and Roman Catholics now enjoy a better understanding of their long-standing shared inheritance. This new understanding enables them to recognize in each other's church a true affinity.'[13]

This again presages the recent emergence of the term 'receptive ecumenism.' Some might argue, however, that such mutual understanding is far from complete. They would cite the establishment of the Anglican Ordinariate as an obvious example of a misunderstanding of the nature of Anglicanism and its so-called *patrimony*.[14]

Perhaps the most significant innovative publication of ARCIC II in this period was the document on morals. Here new ground was broken with the Commission moving outside the strict realms of ecclesiology and sacramentality. The reasoning behind this move outwards is explained in the Preface of the report:

> 'We have prepared this statement in response to requests from authorities of both our Communions. These requests have given voice to a widespread belief that Anglicans and Roman Catholics are as much, if not more, divided on questions of morals as on questions of doctrine. This belief in turn reflects the profound and true conviction that authentic Christian unity is as much a matter of life as of faith.' [15]

This extract raises two key issues essential to the pursuit of Christian unity. The first is that already focused upon in the title of this essay. Affective relationships are an essential part of different churches understanding each other and moving closer together: we have already seen the significance of personal relationships in the vignettes with which we began. But this takes on a still greater significance when placed in a wider historical context. The longer churches live apart from each other, the more likely it is that understandings of theology and morals will develop differently and sometimes in contrast or even conflict with each other. This is clear in the divergence of the eastern church from the church of the west after the schism of 1054. The schism was itself a product of divergent cultures; that divergence had been unfolding for centuries. So, after examining the shared vision and common heritage of Anglicans and Roman Catholics, the morals document openly acknowledges the significance of separate development in a chapter headed *Paths Diverge*. So the chapter begins:

> 'For some fifteen centuries the church in the west struggled to maintain a single, living tradition of communion in worship, faith and practice. In the sixteenth century, however, this web of shared experience was violently broken ... It is in this context of broken communion and diverging histories that the existing differences

> between Anglicans and Roman Catholics on matters of morality must be located if they are to be rightly understood.'[16]

The document examines four areas of assumed or explicit disagreement. These include human sexuality and marriage, marriage after divorce and contraception. There is then a short section adverting to other subject areas. The discussions on marriage and human sexuality exposed an interesting facet of the life of the Commission which had existed throughout, but became more obvious in discussion of these topics. The fact which was highlighted was simply that in these discussions disagreements were as sharp within the two separate ecclesial groups – Anglican and Roman Catholic – as they were across the divide between the Communions. Indeed at certain points internal disagreements were more profound than between Anglicans and Roman Catholics. The ability to expose and live with this difference within each group illustrated a growing trust between members of the Commission as the work continued over a period of years. A real *affection* emerged. Admittedly this had both positive and negative by-products. Positively it led to the important progress made within the ARCIC dialogue: it demonstrated on the 'micro level' the importance of investment in human relationships between the churches. Negatively, it meant throughout the dialogue that both our Communions have often found it difficult to receive the work of bilateral commissions. As others have not been part of that growing relationship, that living together, that foretaste of a deeper communion, so those outside have found the substance of some agreed statements difficult to receive.

Nevertheless, *Life in Christ* is clear that we may move closer to a deeper mutual understanding and communion by working and speaking together on morals. The final section of the document is titled *Towards Shared Witness*. So, the ante-penultimate paragraph of the statement notes:

> 'We propose that steps should be taken to establish further instruments of cooperation between our two Communions at all levels of church life (especially national and regional), to engage with the serious moral issues confronting humanity today. In view of our common approach to moral reflection, and in the light of the agreements we have already discovered to exist between us, we

believe that bilateral discussions between Anglicans and Roman Catholics would be especially valuable.'[17]

The unfolding landscape in the past fifteen years suggests that we have ignored this call at our peril. Anglican disagreements on human sexuality might have at the very least have been informed by mutual dialogue with Roman Catholics. Then, too, the crises both Communions have faced on the abuse of children argues for closer cooperation and mutual reflection, not only on the avoidance of such tragedies, but also on understanding more clearly the moral and pastoral issues which may underlie the emergence of such abuse. These questions are also seminal in our better understanding of how the Church of God discovers, and more effectively prosecutes its part in effecting the *missio Dei*. It was this realization that assisted ARCIC II in prompting the inauguration of the International Anglican–Roman Catholic Commission on Unity and Mission (IARCCUM).[18] In the consultation at Missisauga in Canada in 2000 which set up the commission, once again, personal relationships, that is *affective* communion played a key part. Cardinal Walter Kasper freely admitted that until that moment he had had little experience of Anglicanism. He acknowledged the strong resonances within the Anglican and Roman Catholic Churches and was impelled therefore to encourage the establishment of the new commission.

Here once again, however the report is already becoming something of a text book for peoples' library shelves, another volume in the gathering deposit of ecumenical documents rather than a stimulant to further work together. Without proper responses to its challenges, dialogue remains at the formal level of intellectual reflection. In West Yorkshire, in England, this prompted a determination to respond to IARCCUM. In the past three years, the Roman Catholic dioceses of Hallam and Leeds and the Anglican diocese of Wakefield have held a joint assembly, a joint Lent course, and the four bishops in these dioceses have committed themselves to regular meetings including a common meal, prayer and study. The faithful of both churches have been encouraged by this 'extension' of our partial communion and have asked for further engagement.

Thus far, these reflections have been entirely rooted in one bilateral dialogue. We have kept this focus simply to illustrate through example and practice the essential need for keeping affective and effective communion together. During the early 1990s there were, however, very positive and conclusive initiatives within the churches of northern Europe and the Nordic countries whose roots lie in the Reformation period. Similarly in the United States of America, Anglicans and Lutherans have been able to move into full organic unity. The present author was involved in three of these conversations and many of the insights provided by the examination of Anglican-Roman Catholic relationships have been paralleled within Lutheran and Reformed/Anglican dialogues.

The Porvoo Common Statement of October 1992[19] formed the conclusion of a dialogue which sought to bring together existing agreements on communion between the Church of England and the Church of Sweden and Finland (these had extended back into the first forty years of the twentieth century) with a wider communion of churches in northern Europe. Ultimately this dialogue included representatives of the Lutheran Churches of Denmark, Estonia, Finland, Iceland, Latvia, Lithuania, Norway and Sweden, together with the four Anglican churches of Britain and Ireland. In the case of Finland and Sweden there had been an unbroken line of episcopal ordination since the Reformation. In Norway, Denmark and Iceland there had been a break in episcopal ordination through an ordination by a German pastor, Johannes Bugenhagen in 1536, thus during the Reformation period itself. The succession in the Baltic republics was complicated by their absorption into the Soviet Union during and after the Second World War.

The successful dialogue, resulting in the Porvoo Common Statement of 1992, was built initially on the basis of agreement in faith. Together with this went the fact that in most of these countries the Lutheran Churches had retained the ancient sees and so there was, alongside the agreement in faith, a continuity of apostolicity in these churches which paralleled that in the Church of England and in Ireland and Wales. Once again *affective* issues were prominent. In both Sweden and Finland strong friendships had been built up over almost 100 years. The friendship between the doyen of Swedish ecumenists, Archbishop Nathan Söderblöm and Bishop George Bell is perhaps the most famous example, but there are many others. The links with Denmark can be traced back even to the nineteenth century with the theologian and hymn writer, N. F. S. Grundtvig's interest in the Oxford Movement.

As with ARCIC, the building up of trust through good human relationships and a common theological understanding within the group was essential. Between Anglicans and Lutherans there remain significant differences, since the two traditions grew independently in different cultural milieu. Lutheranism is an explicitly confessional ecclesial expression of the gospel: the key document is the *Confessio Augustana*, also known as the *Confession of Augsburg*, which with Luther's *Small Catechism*, has acted as the sign of mutual recognition for 450 years. In contrast to this, Anglicanism rests upon an implicit *lex orandi, lex credendi* approach to its doctrinal title deeds. So the Book of Common Prayer acts as a foundation in relation to the Church of England's place in the wider stream of western catholicism, albeit a reformed catholicism. The agreement in faith in the Porvoo dialogue allowed a bridge to be secured between these two contrasting starting points. The bridge also secured agreement on ministry. Where Anglicanism preserved the threefold pattern of bishop, priest and deacon, Lutheranism has spoken of one ministry but with bishops and pastors (priests/presbyters). The Porvoo Common Statement has encouraged the Lutheran churches to examine and develop the diaconate; it has also encouraged Anglicans further to examine and understand *diakonia* as the Church's service to the world.

The Porvoo Statement built upon earlier agreed statements between Anglicans and Lutherans.[20] The meetings of the commission comprised common worship and a common daily pattern of life which included a broader engagement with the cultures which have nurtured both traditions. So, for example, in the meeting at Smidstrup Strand in Zeeland in Denmark, time was spent visiting local churches and the world renowned museum of visual art, *Louisiana*. The final document was unanimously agreed at Järvenpäa, the Finnish city in whose cathedral the eucharist had been celebrated on the previous Sunday: Porvoo is the Swedish name for that same city. The conclusion of the agreement was celebrated by the signing of the Common Statement followed by a eucharist in three centres. These were Nidaros Cathedral in Trondheim in Norway, Tallin Cathedral in Estonia and Westminster Abbey in 1995. In his sermon at Westminster Archbishop John Vikström from the Church of Finland commented:

> 'Our churches live and have their being in a part of a world that longs for reconciliation and hope. Once it was the war – both 'hot'

> and 'cold' – that gave rise to rifts and differences. Now it is nationalism that sunders peoples, and economic ideologies and policies that divide our peoples into winners and losers. At the same time as the process of outward integration advances, our part of the world is threatened with collapse from within. Marginalization and alienation of more and larger sections of the population is a catastrophic trend in our countries today. In this very serious situation we are in crying need of visions that will bring us together, and concrete expressions of a fundamental fellowship.
>
> The Porvoo Declaration aims at a deeper realization of the unity that has already been bestowed upon us both as people and as Christians. It is also a promise of the perfect unity that we will one day celebrate before the throne of God.'

Part of the commitment required by the agreement was to establish a continuing contact group and also regular meetings of bishops, alongside bishops participating in episcopal ordinations in both our traditions. There have been occasional consultations on specific issues including a continuing seminar on the diaconate, and in November 2011, a consultation on marriage at Turku in Finland, following the Church of Sweden's move to align itself with the Swedish state's legalization of same sex marriage.

In the Lutheran–Episcopal Dialogue (LED) in the USA, the Church of England was invited regularly to send a participating observer. I attended one residential meeting in New Orleans, towards the conclusion of the dialogue. The dialogue eventually resulted in the unity scheme which brought together the two churches in organic but not structural unity.[21] Once again the effectiveness of the dialogue was rooted in human relationships which have developed over a long period of time. Despite this history of friendships, the New Orleans meeting was complicated by three factors. First, there is a strong 'pietist' tradition in the Evangelical Lutheran Church of America (ELCA) which viewed unity with Episcopalians with suspicion. Second, the observers from the Lutheran Church – Missouri Synod (not in communion with the ELCA) further fuelled the fire of this suspicion. Third, the agreement required the Episcopal Church to suspend certain of its canons to allow unity and interchangeability of ministries with a church which had not until then inherited the ordination of bishops within the historic episcopate. These difficulties were overcome but not without some loss of ministers from within the ELCA.

There is insufficient space in this brief essay to do justice to the Meissen process with which the present author was also involved. This process brought the Evangelische Kirche von Deutschland (EKD) (the main Protestant Church in Germany) into partial communion within the Church of England. The origins of this dialogue issue from the Archbishop of Canterbury, Dr Robert Runcie's visit to the EKD in 1983 on the occasion of the five hundredth anniversary of the birth of Martin Luther. The Archbishop challenged the churches to consider setting out on the path of unity. The agreement reached allows so-called 'table fellowship', that is communion *in sacris* but not interchangeability of ministries. The reason for this movement to a halfway stage derives from the fact that the EKD is effectively a federation of *Landeskirchen* (regional churches within the separate German Länder or states). These churches vary in theology and polity. Some are purely Lutheran, some purely Reformed and still others *United* Churches (Lutheran and Reformed).[22] This presents the Church of England with a dilemma in moving forward toward greater unity and notably again over the issue of the historic episcopate. Nonetheless the Meissen Declaration[23] has led to growing relationships on both the individual and wider church level and good links between different landeskirche and dioceses of the Church of England. In this case, theological dialogue is further stimulating *affective* communion.

Where, then, do these reflections leave us? Perhaps four comments might offer promptings towards further discussion. First, the number, variety and complexity of these dialogues requires the Anglican Communion, and indeed other churches, to be clear that each of the dialogues with its own theological basis is consonant with other dialogues: are we all saying the same thing to our different ecumenical partners? Second, there are a number of fundamental theological building blocks which remain crucial. Some of these are set out in the Chicago–Lambeth Quadrilateral; key issues are the historic episcopate, unity in faith, the patterning of the ordained ministry and scripture as the basis for Christian theology and life.[24] Third, we have seen that theological rigour is crucial but that it must be rooted in the life of the Christian community. Theology, moral reflection, pastoral issues, the relationship with the state, and other practical concerns should inform each other. This is a lesson still to be learned by the World Council of Churches where *Faith and Order* and the engagement with moral issues remain isolated from each other. Neither dialogue alone, nor experience and moral reflection alone are sufficient. This takes us to our final point which is effectively to return to the place from which we began. *Affective* communion leads to *effective* communion and vice versa. This is why the continued existence of agencies like the Anglican Centre in Rome, the Centro Pro Unione in Rome and the Irish School of Ecumenics remain so important in their work.

Much also, of course, depends on personalities. The search for heroes can take us down dangerous paths, but it may not be unwise to seek out beacons along the path to unity. Looking back over these reflections, one individual stands apart from the rest in the past half century. Pope Paul VI is frequently vilified for his loss of nerve over *Humanae Vitae*. Focus on this one issue, however, obscures his extraordinary contribution to the life of God's Church and to the cause of greater Christian unity. Forgotten are the opening up of his *Ostpolitik* with the Soviet Union and its satellites; the permissive attitude to the explorations of the 'liberation theologians' who struggled to interpret the gospel amidst the poverty and injustice in Latin America;[25] the revision of the liturgy; and the presidency of the Second Vatican Council which transformed the face of the Roman Catholic Church. Finally, of course, we should mention the promulgation of the Decree on Ecumenism, *Unitatis Redintegratio* in 1966. It happened in the same year as Archbishop Ramsey's visit to Rome, which itself was informed and made effective by that visit of four Anglican clergymen in 1955. It was a profound friendship and understanding of other churches that enriched and stimulated Giovanni Battista Montini's outstanding contribution. That short Latin missive from Wilfrid Browning, in 1955, made possible more than any of those involved could possibly have imagined.

12 Ecumenism and Covenant

A Reflection on Personal Experience of the Anglican–Methodist Covenant, and pointers for effective ecumenical relationships

Liz Smith

In this chapter I reflect upon a particular experience of ecumenical working and some of the lessons it offers us if we are to take seriously our covenanted ecumenical relationships.

I begin with my memory of a pivotal conversation:

'And what will I be called?' I asked the Bishop.
'The curate, of course!' he replied.

The context for this exchange was a conversation in which the diocesan bishop had just confirmed that arrangements were set to go ahead, by which I would serve as a probationer Methodist presbyter in a Church of England parish in his diocese. This was in the mid-1990s, when unofficial consultations were taking place exploring the possibility of more formal conversation being re-opened between the Church of England and the Methodist Church in Britain. The personal context was that I had just completed three years of ecumenical ministry training as a candidate accepted for ministry in the Methodist Church, and I had previously been employed as a Church-based community worker in this same diocese, in a neighbouring parish. Faced with personal circumstances that made a geographical move difficult at the time for my family, I became the focus of a creative mix of pragmatism, ecumenical experimentation and ecclesiastical risk-taking. The bishop agreed that in such circumstances, 'they should be able to help out ...'; the incumbent who was asked to consider inviting me to work in his parish met with me, decided that I might 'fit in', and was willing to take the risk that all practicalities would be worked out along the way; the Methodist Conference was persuaded that this would be a suitable station for a probationer minister, under the direction of the Chair of District. Having previously worked in a community role, I assumed I might be called something like 'community minister'. I was completely unprepared for title of 'curate' that was rather casually flung in my direction, but decided that since it seemed to be the only course of action open to me, I had better catch it and make something of it! With the benefit of hindsight I would suggest that the title may not have been thought through at all by any of those involved, and that it was the first of many instances when we all simply fell into default Anglican mode. While I am able to smile at this now, at the time the 'what will I be called?' question felt pivotal, as such titles and forms of address are deeply connected with our sense of denominational identity and sense of belonging.

While my own roots are in Cornish Methodism, my journey has woven its way in and out of the Church of England in every place where I have lived. This began at a young age, when I was conscious of attending 'chapel' for Sunday School, but the C of E Infant & Junior Schools from the age of four. Later, in teenage years, I shared in the activities of both Methodist Youth Club (on Saturday night) and the Anglican Youth Fellowship (on Sunday night), with many of the same people. As a student in London I became President of Methsoc, but formed significant ecumenical friendships. A little later, I found myself employed on two separate occasions, and in different dioceses, on community projects in Church of England parishes. Nevertheless, my primary Christian commitments have been made within the Methodist Church, from membership through to office holding and becoming an accredited Local Preacher. In responding to the call to explore ordained ministry, I was very clear that this was to be in the context of the Methodist Church and its disciplines, despite my close working relationship within an Anglican parish, funded by the Church Urban Fund. When I found myself, therefore, about to be made 'a curate', I needed everyone to be very clear that I was still completely and genuinely a Methodist. In effect, this became the basis of the experiment: was it possible for an ordinand in one of our two churches to embark upon this final 'training' stage of pre-ordination ministry in the other's context? What would be the particular challenges for all involved?

I am very aware that I can only tell this story in the first person, and that others – those exercising oversight, colleagues and parishioners – might tell it very differently. The pragmatism and risk-taking referred to earlier, created for me a fresh context for ministry, while enabling me to continue living in the same community as the previous ten years. It was a very focused ministry in an inner urban parish with an attractive and busy church building, which incorporated a sports hall and youth facilities. I joined a pre-existing team of vicar, youth worker and others – some paid, some voluntary – working in a challenging community where the everyday needs and experiences of parishioners rightly took precedence over ecclesiastical or ecumenical niceties. I immersed myself in the life and work of the parish, and was only required to relate to the Methodist structures that were concerned with my being a Probationer minister and member of District Synod. The arrangement worked well for three years.

During this period of time, once relationships were established, I suspect I was simply regarded as 'the next curate' by many of those in the parish, and indeed in the wider deanery. On one occasion I willingly took on an organizational role for the deanery in relation to creating a banner and other representation at a splendid diocesan celebration in the Cathedral. In doing so, it was intimated to me that I would 'become one of them, eventually'! However, the entire appointment had the effect of confirming in me a much stronger sense of my own Methodist identity, not in any antagonistic way, but simply a stronger recognition within me as to who I was – and continue to be – while relating to others in this context, for whom I had every respect.

The particular appointment and circumstances in which I found myself occurred before we had entered into the commitments and affirmations of the Anglican–Methodist Covenant, signed by the Archbishop of Canterbury and the President of the Methodist Conference in 2003. It serves as a reminder that where there is a will to work together, and differently, often a way can be found, even without Covenant commitments. Those in authority in both denominations were determined that my appointment in the parish would not 'break any rules' or be seen as exceptional. Both parties simply used the means of operating that were open to them, a little more creatively and collaboratively. The appointment received a brief mention in *Releasing Energy: How Methodists and Anglicans Can Grow*

Together (The Archbishop's Council, 2000), a booklet anticipating the later Covenant commitment of both Churches.

The Anglican–Methodist Covenant drew both Churches into interdependent Affirmations and Commitments 'in a spirit of penitence for all that human sinfulness and narrowness of vision have contributed to our past divisions, believing that we have been impoverished through our separation and that our witness to the gospel has been weakened accordingly, and in a spirit of thanksgiving and joy for the convergence in faith and collaboration in mission that we have experienced in recent years.' (Preamble to an Anglican–Methodist Covenant, 2001, formally signed in 2003.)

Having sketched the situation in which I found myself, I want to proceed in this chapter by asking a number of reflective questions. They arise out of my experience, but are questions that continue to be very real ones in the context of the Covenant, and possibly in other ecumenical contexts. Some may prompt us to feel penitent, others to be thankful. We first note two of the foundational affirmations of the Anglican–Methodist Covenant:

> We affirm that one another's ordained and lay ministries are given by God as instruments of God's grace, to build up the people of God in faith, hope and love, for the ministry of word, sacrament and pastoral care and to share in God's mission in the world. [Covenant Affirmation Number 4]

> We affirm that one another's ordained ministries possess both the inward call of the Holy Spirit and Christ's commission given through the Church. [Covenant Affirmation Number 5]

1. A partnership of equals?

A Covenant relationship is a formal agreement between two or more partners. The most commonly cited parallel is that of marriage, although in conversation that is frequently adjusted in the context of the Anglican–Methodist Covenant to engagement or betrothal, as these terms acknowledge the unfulfilled nature of the Covenant relationship at present. On numerous occasions I have felt a degree of discomfort when I have listened to (usually male) church leaders using this analogy in talking about the Covenant, perhaps because I was left wondering about their understanding of equality within a marriage relationship. This serves as a warning to all of us that if we take imperfect human institutions as our models we must guard against replicating their imperfections. In practice, it is difficult in many contexts to speak of the Covenant relationship as a relationship between equals. The Church of England, as the 'established' and numerically bigger (in terms of places of worship, ordained ministers, active church participants) and more wealthy partner, has implicit claims to be regarded as the stronger/ dominant / 'more significant' partner. If we are to pursue the 'betrothal / marriage' analogy we have to be careful at this point not to cast the Methodist Church in the role of weaker / oppressed partner / victim. Within any relationship there will be strengths and weaknesses on both sides. Any healthy relationship requires the ability of both partners to stand in their own shoes, to take initiatives, and not to be overshadowed by the other. Put bluntly, the Covenant affirmations should enable both of our Churches to stand firmly within their own history and self-understanding and act in adult ways in expressing affirmation, appreciation and a willingness to engage, through working in partnership with one another.

In my appointment as curate there were a number of imbalances of power to be acknowledged, but an essential feature of the appointment was that I was not requested to change my identity. When I prefaced my comments at a church meeting or in a staff conversation with the words, 'as a Methodist woman ...', I did so not to be awkward, but to be clear of the basis for what I was sharing. The challenge as to how far, as a guest, one is able to exercise leadership was not explicitly examined at the time. In spite of much emphasis on team working and shared ministry, there were constant reminders that authority (and therefore real leadership) was located elsewhere – certainly not embodied in the curate! I found this occasionally bewildering, but I was mostly able to work collegially as I would have expected to in any Methodist circuit.

While working as the curate I once chose the story of the slave, Onesimus, in the New Testament book of Philemon, as the basis for theological reflection upon my position. With hindsight it was an interesting choice. It enabled me to focus a little on the lack of power implicit in my situation there, as one waiting to be handed back to the Methodist Church in order to exercise my future ministry. At the same time it enabled me to acknowledge that I was in the receipt of considerable care and thoughtfulness in many aspects of that appointment. It provided a window for me on questions of exile and abiding identity, and of being in a provisional place, yet still held within God's grace and God's call.

When we seek to work in ecumenical partnership, we need to be sensitive to imbalances of power, and capacity. Each partner should feel able to bring their distinctive contribution and be willing to receive the gifts of the other, while not feeling threatened or overwhelmed. A partnership that acknowledges some of the tensions and challenges of difference, promises to be a healthier relationship than one where one or both of the parties feel under pressure to conform to a single ideal, in order to create a false sense of uniformity. Partnership language invites us to explore what it means to celebrate difference, which is itself a challenge right across the spectrum of church traditions in our generation, as we wrestle with notions of inclusion and diversity.

2. Whose ground?

A particular gift – and potential tension – of the appointment, was that of being a guest in space that belonged to others. For three years I consciously ministered within, and from, a setting that was not my own. When I took up this appointment I had been an accredited Local Preacher for sixteen years, and had served in that capacity in four very different circuits in different parts of the connection. One of the distinguishing – and sometimes confusing – features of being a Methodist Local Preacher is that in making oneself available to be planned across a circuit, one is constantly leading worship 'on someone else's patch', relating to congregations about which one may know very little, other than what becomes familiar over time. On reflection, this experience proved to be an important asset in my new context. More challenging was the practice of leading worship alongside others, ordained and lay, and listening to other's sermons but not as a member of the congregation. I would also, however, cite this as an enriching feature of the appointment.

For three years I lived with the ambivalence of working in a very focused way – one building, with much daily activity, and a strong emphasis on lay ministry – yet with an ever-present awareness of being the 'resident alien'. The experience has continued to serve as a reminder to me that we can all too easily become unhelpfully possessive about our buildings, and especially our pulpits and communion tables or altars. It is no bad thing to be reminded that we break bread at 'the Lord's Table', and that we stand to preach and to preside on holy ground: neither pulpit, nor table, nor ground are ours to possess. Ironically, in my ministry since this time I have served in a rural circuit where ministry was spread across many chapels, and now as a Chair of District find myself the perpetual guest in others' space.

While reminding ourselves that we stand on holy ground, we also need to remind ourselves that no ecclesial space is 'neutral'. When engaging in ecumenical activity a helpful question to ask is 'whose space are we in, as we do this?' In holding this question we can be alerted to matters of respect, custom, expectation and hospitality that can be attended to with some degree of intentionality, rather than tripping us up along the way.

3. Expediency or integrity?

As I have already suggested, an integral aspect of the novel situation in which I found myself, was the need to retain a clear sense of my own identity, while being open to further learning and formation in my journey of faith and ministry. This is, of course true for all of us whatever our context. However, in the context of ecumenical relationships it requires us to pay good attention to our own story, as well as the ability to listen to the stories of others, and to be open to signs of God's grace in the other, as well as in our own experience. For much of my ministry in that urban parish I had to be content with being identified with the mission and ministry of the Church of England. It was expedient to do so, not least when my credentials were questioned in relation to the conduct of a funeral service. I was asked, when I visited one family whether I really was an Anglican. Fortunately, before I could reply they went on to voice their anxiety about Jehovah's Witnesses, after which a simple reassurance that I was 'from the parish church' was sufficient.

Each of us has many facets to our sense of personhood. In ecumenical relationships we can sometimes focus almost exclusively upon our denominational sense of identity, while ignoring other signifiers such as gender, race, sexuality and ability. We all feel uncomfortable when assumptions are made about us that are not true, or when others have expectations of us that we are not able to fulfil. In highlighting the need for honesty and mutual respect in our ecumenical relating we run the risk of stating the obvious, but there is a need to be intentional in pursuing our own journey with integrity and openness.

The most helpful model I came across at the time of my appointment, was that of an Anglican priest intentionally spending a period of time – 12 months I think – working and praying wholly within the Jain community in Leicester, in order to explore inter faith relationships. When we find ourselves intentionally working and praying in an alien context, we can discover a surprising strength of spirit in our own sense of identity and integrity, that enables a warmth and generosity towards colleagues of difference alongside us. Paradoxically, in such contexts it can feel a deep honour to be associated with a tradition that is not our own, but which can offer us a different kind of space in which to be ourselves.

4. To what extent is working ecumenically formational?

Every first appointment in public ministry is formational. In both the Church of England and the Methodist Church this period of time is acknowledged as a continuation of initial training in preparation for ordination. It will be clear from the reflections already shared that my experience in this experimental appointment has proved formative for my continuing ministry. If working ecumenically and building good ecumenical relationships are to become second nature for us, implicit in the outworking of our journeys of discipleship, ministry and ecclesiology, we cannot ignore such formative experiences or leave them to 'chance'. While the nature of my own first appointment was exceptional, there has been a growing trend, over the past forty or more years, for initial and continuing ministry training to be undertaken within various shapes of ecumenical partnership. We have begun to reap the benefits of our ecumenical training programmes, not only in terms of personal enrichment, but in the willingness of many in ministry to engage in ecumenical ways of working in their developing ministries. My own experience of training on an ecumenical ministry course was that Methodism was offered back to me afresh, with the valuable insights of those from other traditions.

At the time of writing the initial training agendas of the Methodist Church and of the Church of England are under intense scrutiny, due to changes in the Higher Education sector, pressure on the budgets of institutions and dioceses, and challenging questions about styles of learning and dispersed ways of working. This is not the place to tackle this complex agenda. However, if we take seriously the formative nature of all initial and continuing training, we need to be alert to the potential detriment to future ecumenical relationships if we each retreat into the familiarity of our own traditions. There can be much enrichment in being open to the practices and traditions of others at this formative stage of ministry, and I believe that only through such personal experience of each others' riches will each of our denominations be equipped to offer effective leadership in this generation and the Church of tomorrow.

In terms of my own story, if the metaphor of 'ecumenical guinea pig' were to be taken literally and the question asked, 'if we do this to someone at an early stage of their ministry, what do we get further down the line?', the answer would be 'a Chair of District like this one!' That is to say, a Methodist Chair of District who regards working ecumenically as a significant plank in our shared ability to engage in God's mission; who wishes to take seriously the Anglican–Methodist Covenant, and use its affirmations and commitments as the starting point for intentional partnership working; who remains convinced of a distinctive Methodist identity, but wishes to be open to receive the giftedness of other traditions; who considers it an honour to be associated with other Christian traditions, while not experiencing them as a threat to my own sense of identity or integrity; who is delighted to be Chair of West Yorkshire Ecumenical Council as it celebrates its Silver Jubilee!

5. The gender question

As I have written this reflection I have been conscious throughout of the significance of gender weaving through my own story and implicitly in the thoughts I have shared. I wish to state openly that this is inevitably the case, and that being a woman in all of the contexts that I have shared has brought to them a particular dimension, which has sometimes been challenging for others as well as for myself!

In the parish in which I served as the Methodist curate, there were women colleagues in lay ministry, but I was the first woman to serve there in stipendiary ministry. When I moved from that appointment to rural

Lincolnshire, I was the first woman presbyter to serve in that circuit. I am at present one of a relatively small number of female Chairs of District in the Methodist Church.

Each of our Christian traditions and denominations has been challenged in recent decades over the question of the role of women in ordained and leadership roles. It is my belief that we must all continue to rise to those challenges if we are to be faithful to the gospel of Christ and if we are to be credible witnesses in the age in which we live. There have inevitably been some painful experiences in my own journey, but there have also been moments of sheer grace in unexpected places on that ecumenical odyssey, for which I am deeply grateful.

6. For whose benefit?

The context for the experiment conducted at the outset of my ministry was an inner urban parish, with all the implicit challenges for ministry and discipleship. I will always be grateful that the pressing needs of being an effective Christian presence in that community far outweighed any engagement with ecumenical theories and programmes. The ministry team, lay and ordained, were very clear in their commitment to the people of that community in the name of Christ. While members of the worshipping congregation(s) very quickly accepted my presence as the next curate, and were gracious towards my Methodist identity, to those in the wider parish I became identified with that church's ministry – rather than the Methodist Church building twenty yards away.

In that context and in many others since, I have found myself challenged by the reminder that when we work in ecumenical partnerships in mission contexts, we engage together in God's mission which always has bigger parameters and more exciting possibilities than our own limited vision. The affirmations and commitments of the Anglican–Methodist Covenant are currently the impetus for joint working between the Leeds Methodist District and the Ripon and Leeds Diocese, in a number of areas such as the challenge of issues of racial justice and inclusion, and inter faith work.

Since the signing of the 2003 Covenant, a number of interim publications have encouraged both Churches to explore the Spirit of the Covenant, to Live God's Covenant, to Embrace the Covenant, and most recently to Move Forward in Covenant. Prompted by this latest publication, we are currently exploring together the possibility of a Covenant relationship over an Extended Area of the same diocese and district as above. In doing so we are mindful that the real test of such a commitment will be twofold: its effectiveness in enabling real partnership in ministry and mission on the ground, especially in the most challenging and deprived communities that we seek to serve, and its ability to welcome additional working partners across the ecumenical spectrum.

In more recent years the Fresh Expressions and Pioneer Ministry initiatives have presented new possibilities for ecumenical working, especially within the affirmations and commitments of the Anglican–Methodist Covenant, but also with other partners. We should take great encouragement from the insights gained in these new ways of working, but need to be attentive to the fresh questions that they pose for our often denominationally bound thinking.

Covenant working, whether within the Anglican–Methodist Covenant or the Covenant commitment made by Church Leaders in West Yorkshire, offers a shared foundation and framework. The signing of a formal Covenant does not itself bring any guarantee of different ways of working. Our Covenant commitments, however, should help us to hold our nerve as we continue to engage in creative pragmatism, ecumenical experimentation and ecclesiastical risk-taking, as co-participants in God's mission to all people in every place.

Postscript

I began this chapter with an exchange between myself and a bishop: I close it with another one.

The very recent invitation to become an ecumenical canon of Wakefield Cathedral was a delightful surprise. Having been installed as such for no more than a few weeks, I cannot yet comment upon how this new relationship in which I find myself will enhance ecumenical and Covenantal relationships. However, a number of themes already explored above were very present in the liturgy of the installation.

The importance of identity and formation were acknowledged explicitly by the Bishop in his informal remarks and woven into his sermon for the occasion. In this act the Bishop explicitly shares with the one to be made canon, 'the cure of souls', and declares the canon to have 'place' and 'voice' in the cathedral. I found myself once more acutely aware of being a guest, and of standing on ground that is not my own, yet being generously offered a real and physical place within it. My own sense of Methodist identity was acknowledged and celebrated – including the singing of a great Charles Wesley hymn. When invited to kneel before the Bishop, I was very clear in my own mind that this was a gesture of humility and dignity, not of submission. Kneeling for a second time, to receive a blessing, I sensed that the words of blessing were articulated by the bishop, but the gift of blessing also came, silently, from the company of believers, Anglicans, Methodists and others, gathered in the nave behind me.

While the gesture could be interpreted as a personal 'honour', my own understanding is that this is primarily a representative act. For me and for others, the test of its true value will not be about my own finding of place and voice, but the degree to which it enables and enhances the mission of both of our Churches alongside those for whom ecclesiastical and ecumenical niceties of any flavour are an utter irrelevance.

References

Releasing energy: How Methodists and Anglicans Can Grow Together (London, Church House Publishing, 2000)

An Anglican-Methodist Covenant (London, Church House Publishing, 2001)

In the Spirit of the Covenant (2005) (available to download from http://www.anglican-methodist.org.uk/)

Living God's Covenant (2007) (available to download from http://www.anglican-methodist.org.uk/)

Embracing the Covenant (2008) (available to download from http://www.anglican-methodist.org.uk/)

Moving Forward in Covenant (2011) (available at http://www.methodistconference.org.uk/media/48508/moving%20forward%20in%20covenant%202011.pdf)

Appendices

The Affirmations and Commitments of the Anglican-Methodist Covenant

The Covenant signed by Church Leaders in West Yorkshire

IV Unity and Mission

13 *The Priority of Local Ecumenism*

Clive Barrett

Ecumenism is local

There is a philosophy for doing ecumenism. Essential to this process of unity are relationship and trust, from which come reconciliation and unity. As Stephen Platten expresses it in this volume, the affective becomes the effective. It is a process that occurs at all levels of relationship and interaction – including the local. Indeed, without the local there would be no basis, no foundation for ecumenical endeavour by theologians and senior church representatives.

There is a dialectic relationship between local and global ecumenism, which means that each feeds the other, each can inspire the other, and neither can make complete progress without the other.

So often the temptation is to regard the outcomes of Councils, Congresses and Synods as the most significant actions, the goals of Christian activity. The worst aspects of this can be reinforced by inevitable media focus on tension and division – issues of sexuality, gender, negative attitudes towards the Ordinariate ... Below the media threshold, however, is the slow, steady business of developing theological understanding – the cognoscenti rattle off the buzzwords: 'ARCIC', 'Leuenberg', 'Meissen', 'Porvoo'. Though lacking the peaks of expectation of the first half of the twentieth century, this conciliar ecumenism continues its steady and inexorable progress in building the ecumenical understanding of those who take counsel for the affairs of the churches.

Even further below the media threshold, but much more dynamic by far, can be the substantial ecumenical progress that is being lived daily in many local communities. Often this is unacknowledged, little known, disregarded, not least because the principal channels for promotion and affirmation of local Christian activity tend to be denominational. (Notable exceptions include *The Way*, the new thrice yearly newspaper of the churches in Cumbria, and *Unity Post,* an annual paper of West Yorkshire Ecumenical Council – 'WYEC' – produced since 1999.) This, in turn, can lead to low self-esteem among those most closely engaged in ecumenical endeavours, as their achievements, however impressive, are not always recognized.

The ecumenical mindset, which prioritizes working together, needs to be nurtured and encouraged at every level of the churches, including those involved in communications and especially within local churches. The shared wonder, worship and witness of any two or three local churches are not token gestures but, as if sacramental, they effect that which they signify. In a small, flawed, yet real way, local ecumenical life is real unity, and a fundamental part of the total process of unity.

Unity is not only something restricted to the professionals in their councils, important though those are. Such gatherings gain their significance precisely because of the firm foundation of ecumenism permeating all levels of the Churches, especially the local. Let us value, affirm and relate that wealth of hidden stories which contribute to such a foundation. In the end, the councils of the churches matter precisely because the realizations that come from them, and the relationships across boundaries that are built up by them, affect the life and relationships of ordinary churches in ordinary communities. Here, is where unity happens. The local matters precisely because, in microcosm yet in reality, the Body of Christ is in that place, in all its fractured wholeness.

Churches Together groups

The core text for reflecting on the image of Church as Body of Christ is 1 Corinthians 12:12–27, with the context set by verse 4, 'varieties of gifts, but the same Spirit'. There is the call to humility (v.14), 'the body does not consist of one member but of many'. There is the call to recognize the gifts of others (v. 17), 'The eye cannot say to the hand, "I have no need of you," nor again the head to the feet, "I have no need of you." ' And in between we see that it is simply not possible to opt out of being part of the body (vv.

15, 16), of being in that state of mutual dependence with others from whom one may differ enormously in outlook and practice. For all the diversity of the members of the body, 'If one member suffers, all suffer together with it; if one member is honoured, all rejoice together with it,' (v. 26).

This basis for ecclesiological relations fits well with a Churches Together approach to local ecumenism. However difficult or diverse local understandings of theology and practice may be, there can often be an awareness of mutual need and support. Admittedly, despite 1 Cor. 12:15–16, there are some churches and congregations, large or small, unwilling, perhaps through overwork or spiritual pride, to recognize their need for ecumenical relationships, and in those cases they and all neighbouring churches are diminished.[1]

Preventing that, in many places, are those who faithfully engage in the local ecumenical process but who feel on the margins of their own churches, doing work which is perceived as an expendable luxury, not central but additional to the maintenance of their own church. In a sometimes indifferent climate, a Churches Together committee of the tired and overworked are not remnants but saints! They are doing holy work, however imperfectly.

As we shall see, below, however, many other places are much less myopic and are more outward in their orientation. In such places, Churches Together becomes the primary vehicle for transformation not only of the churches but of the entire suburb, town or village. Such examples are to be proclaimed.

Regional 'intermediate' bodies like WYEC are charged both to foster an ecumenical mindset among people whose focus is constrained by single-church concerns, and also to champion, encourage, and celebrate local ecumenical activity. How often have I been to small, ageing, committees of local Churches Together groups to be told, 'we don't do very much here'? When pressed, they continue with a subset of, 'We only run a Unity Service in January, a pulpit exchange, Lent courses, Holy Week services, an outdoor procession of witness and Passion Play on Good Friday, a sunrise vigil on Easter Day, Christian Aid week, Pentecost Praise in the Park, Harvest Supper, One World Week, alternative Halloween, a memorial service for the recently departed …' and the list continues through peace trails and prayer walks between the churches, passing round an 'ecumenical cross', shared overnight residentials, prayerful retreats and quiet days to Christmas carols outside the supermarket, and a Watch Night service – and those are only the events involving shared worship and prayer. All this prayerful activity, however, can be underappreciated because the principal communities of affirmation, and their media channels, are within denominational structures. Unless the intermediate body celebrates ecumenical life, nobody will hear of it or value it. Unity can be the churches' best kept secret.

That list, however, is not half of it: a lot of ecumenical endeavour does not even pass through local Churches Together groups. Three examples come immediately to mind.

The Women's World Day of Prayer is one of the largest single ecumenical actions in the country and is marked in thousands of communities. It is usually quietly run by ecumenical groups of lay women meeting quite independently of ministers, church councils or even Churches Together groups. Often unheralded, it is one of the oldest ecumenical endeavours, with an outward, international perspective and the ability to bring women together – Catholic, Anglican, Free Church – across the ecumenical spectrum.

Also, many local ministers belong to informal ecumenical clergy cell groups (previously called 'fraternals'), meeting regularly for Bible study, conversation or a prayer breakfast. In such groups there can be mutual support and the opportunity to consider the local landscape together, with a number of significant ecumenical initiatives being germinated in resulting discussions. These groups may only contain representatives of a subset of local churches but they are among the most important ways of building up relationships and mutual trust, the pillars upon which so much local ecumenism is built. A recent telephone study of the deaneries of the Diocese of Wakefield, conducted by the Diocesan Ecumenical Affairs Group, discovered that Anglican clergy in around two thirds of all parishes were involved in some kind of ministers' prayer fellowships or other ministers' informal support gatherings.

Thirdly, a consultation of people involved in Churches Together groups and other ecumenical activities in North Yorkshire – one of a number WYEC has held to support regional Churches Together groups – revealed the extent to which ecumenism can be almost taken for granted in rural areas where church buildings are few and denominational affiliation has a reduced significance. It's more than simply Churches Together stalls at country shows (Bentham and the Northern Dales, and also Mirfield, West Yorkshire). As one lay preacher remarked, 'You meet the same people at the Gala Committee and the Village Fair as you do in the churches'. In other words, as church members are more likely than others to be involved in community activities, a lot of relationship-building among church people in rural communities takes place in contexts that are not overtly church-related. Such ecumenism may not be named as such, but it may be part of the fabric of many rural societies and country church life.

The principal vehicle, however, for local ecumenical activity remains the Churches Together group. Elsewhere in this volume, Neil Richardson writes on the relationship between mission and unity:

> Ecumenism without grace is empty and lifeless: a contradiction in terms. Similarly, a church-centred ecumenism is a contradiction in terms, or, at the very least, a malformed creature. Ecumenism grounded in the grace of God reaches out to the whole world, and therefore unity is 'not a project for completion, but a grace to be received'.

Ecumenism, by definition and etymology, is concerned above all with the whole inhabited earth, or, to put it simply, 'God so loved *the world*...' Ironically, this can be appreciated most in a local context. Apart from formal Local Ecumenical Partnerships, ecclesial structures are usually seen locally as part of what is 'given' and unchangeable. The emphasis instead is on what life may be shared in full acknowledgement of the inherited constraints of one's own tradition and others'. In the best Churches Together groups, mission comes to the fore and the focus of attention is not on church structures but on 'the world', or at least that part of it for which the Churches Together group has responsibility and opportunity. The best Churches Together groups not only engage in the full cycle of prayer and study, above, but are characterized by their mission, outreach, and contribution to the transformation of their locality. They respond to the specific needs of local communities and help to build up community in the neighbourhoods which they serve. They take tentative steps towards the Lund principle of striving 'to act together in all matters, except those in which deep differences of conviction impel them to act separately.'[2]

In the WYEC area alone – and we are far from unique – Churches Together groups have run: diverse youth projects, many employing paid staff, whether detached youth workers on street corners of challenging estates at night (Middleton, Leeds) or youth clubs in church halls; schools projects, some of which also have paid staff (Calderdale and Keighley), perhaps using the Scripture Union REWIND programme (Gomersal and Birkenshaw) or addressing behavioural and lifestyle skills (Horbury, Wakefield); young people's summer camps and caravans (Todmorden) and holiday projects; mobile drugs information units; local 'Christian Resource Exhibitions' (Calderdale); shared visiting projects, and prayers, in residential homes; preaching and healing 'on the streets'; charity shops (Meltham); cafés (Skipton); countless lunch clubs; drop in support for homeless people and people suffering from addictions (in Dewsbury this not only includes lunches but also computer provision and access to benefits); drop in support, advice and ESOL provision for asylum seekers and refugees; providing food parcels for homeless and asylum-seeking people (Halifax); community building dialogue, sharing scriptures and food with neighbours of other faiths (East Bradford; see also the chapter in this volume by Helen Reid and Celia Blackden); Bible exhibitions; exchange projects with ecumenical groups in other countries (Wakefield, and Moor Allerton and Shadwell, Leeds); negotiations with local councils to tell the Christmas story at the switching-on of Christmas lights (Ilkley and Huddersfield); cultural engagement projects through exhibitions and drama; rock concerts (Ilkley); fundraising for external charities, through Shoe Boxes and similar initiatives (Dewsbury); public statements and campaigning against the rise of the far-right (Middleton); open air café church worship in a town centre with free hamburgers for all (Keighley); Hope 08 / Hope Together evangelistic events; More Than Gold sporting events based around the Olympic Games; Street Pastors (Chapeltown, Leeds and Ripon) and Street Angels (Halifax, Bradford, Huddersfield, Harrogate, Wakefield, Leeds, Headingley, Skipton …)

Street Angels was pioneered by Churches Together in Halifax, with a town centre base in their Fair Trade Café. The presence on the streets of Christians in their luminous vests, late night at weekends, escorting the vulnerable to bus stops, providing safety and shelter for those who were worse for wear, soon led to the local police recognizing a fall in town centre crime and the Street Angels initiative spreading rapidly to many other cities, towns and suburbs.[3]

One of the best examples of a project which could only be undertaken by a Churches Together group is the community festival. Pioneered in Rastrick, and successfully copied in Newsome (Huddersfield), this involves a weekend when the churches take over a high school, inviting stalls from a range of community businesses, charities and service providers, as well as from numerous church-related organizations, with music and art events including children's art competitions, and a closing 'event' (i.e. 'service') with schools' choirs, quizzes, local speakers and community singing. It's a marvellous expression of 'God loves you', and a way of the churches conveying a message to hundreds of local people that this is a good place to live, and that the churches, united, are at the heart of it. Significantly, the festival idea expanded from Rastrick to Newsome because of an article in WYEC's *Unity Post*; sharing good practice makes a practical difference.

One of the most innovative Churches Together group is in Settle and District, in North Yorkshire. They have even purchased a traditional red telephone box as a notice board for gospel messages and church activities!

Some of these diverse projects – housing for people with learning disabilities in Ilkley, an environmental action initiative in Roundhay, Leeds, and Street Angels in Halifax – have become so successful that they have become independent charities in their own right.

In the best Churches Together groups, it is not necessary for all activity to be undertaken by all churches. In these places, the whole group 'owns' that which each is contributing to the total Christian witness within a town or suburb. So whereas street-preaching may not be to everyone's taste, there will be others content to pray – perhaps at Catholic Mass – for the witness of the street-preachers. Inevitably there are times when a subgroup of two or three churches can work closely together on a particular project, so within Leeds City Centre an Anglican church's homeless centre provides the Nurture Cafe at the nearby Methodist Mission.

In some places there are 'umbrella' Churches Together groups, which encourage and communicate the work of smaller groups in their area. It seems there is a particular size of town / small city for which this works best: Halifax, Wakefield, Harrogate, but also Leeds Churches Together in Mission (LCTiM) undertakes a similar role. In recent years, LCTiM has also produced professional Advent Calendars, DVDs and Lent Prayer Diaries promoting a varied set of ecumenical mission groups across the city, and made well-researched submissions to the local authority on the future vision for the city.

Sometimes relations between a subgroup of local churches are strong enough to lead to a local covenant, a form of Local Ecumenical Partnership (LEP) which does not require the merger of congregations. The Church in the Dale (Nidderdale, North Yorkshire) is one example, and Newsome, Huddersfield is another. In these covenant partnerships there are greater opportunities for shared life, such as joint baptism preparation or joint wedding preparation. In Newsome, the partnership has led to a shared community mission project based around a second-hand shop (a good place to drop-in for a chat), which raised funds to employ a community worker who coordinates a whole range of local services including gardening for the elderly, a pastoral visiting scheme and grants to other local charities, altogether a highly practical and visible outpouring of Christ's love.

The Covenant concept has within it the potential to transform much larger regions. This is currently being pursued by the churches in Cumbria and practical possibilities are being explored in Leeds. Anglicans and Methodists together are asking how far it may be possible to go, within existing constraints, in sharing ministry, appointments, and especially mission together. (See Liz Smith's chapter in this volume for more details of this.)

Other formal ecumenical partnerships include institutional chaplaincies where the institution may be the employer, as is – in part – generally the case in hospitals and prisons, and where denominational chaplains have chosen to work together. The impressive eight-way partnership at the Universities in Leeds Chaplaincy Trust was the fruit of the relationship between chaplains initially symbolized by personal covenants between them in the early 1990s. Other models of ecumenical chaplaincy include workplace / industrial chaplaincy, which has waned with industrial decline, but is still evident in airports and shopping centres.

It is but a small jump from traditional chaplaincy to what has become known as Fresh Expressions of Church. There are many ways of 'doing church' with people who come together from similar backgrounds, age groups, culture or interests, which are not necessarily geographically rooted (as in a local church building) and who may well have little or no previous Christian experience, let alone denominational tradition. Many areas – Greater Manchester is one region which is strong on this – have set up an ecumenical Fresh Expressions Area Strategy Team (FEAST), which brings together practitioners, 'champions' and 'permission-givers' from a range of denominations to explore ways of promoting Fresh Expressions. Pioneer ministries, community cafés, art projects and youth missions abound, all reaching out to people otherwise not connected to Christian life. A Mission Shaped Ministry training course leading in to Fresh Expressions would also be run ecumenically.

Beyond Churches Together

Not all mission activity is formally linked to Churches Together groups. There are Christian ecumenical residential communities: Focolare, Scargill (Wharfedale), Holy Rood House (Thirsk). A superb Hope for the Nations festival in Leeds, linked to the Global Day of Prayer, takes over the main shopping street one summer Saturday each year in a celebration of Christian life among the dozens of nationalities and cultures in the city. A ground-breaking Chaplaincy for Bradford courts is another independent initiative. Bradford Ecumenical Asylum Concern (BEACON) is one of many groups across the country supporting the claims for sanctuary of people fleeing persecution. The biggest example of trans-denominational activity is also in Bradford: Inn Churches coordinates people from over sixty churches who collaborate to provide overnight accommodation during the three harshest winter months for the most difficult-to-house homeless people who fall through the statutory services' safety net. It has proved so valuable and so successful that a similar project has now been held in Halifax too. The Bradford operation connects with Prayer for Bradford, a non-denominational evangelical network of local church leaders and church project leaders meeting fortnightly to pray for the city, and, through the relationships, to see their prayer lead into action. Later in this volume, Mike Love writes about a whole range of mission projects in and around Leeds which know no denominational constraints.

Relationships with statutory bodies and local authorities are best pursued in an ecumenical way, or, at the very least, with ecumenical ownership of the church which is best placed to conduct such relationships. The social responsibility officers in Leeds provide a *de facto* ecumenical reference group for one member who is immersed in local authority decision-making 'on behalf of the churches'. In the recent past, the Churches Regional Commission not only related to previous regional government structures but also established a successful rural project and a religious heritage scheme ('Treasures Revealed') across West Yorkshire.

That is not to say that those employed within denominational structures cannot produce good ecumenical mission work. Faith in Young People is the handle for denominational youth workers, mapping and supporting church youth work across Yorkshire; similarly, those with education responsibilities combine to market each other's courses under the heading Christians Learning Across Yorkshire (CLAY); a more formal institution for ministerial education for a subset of denominations is the Regional Training Partnership; in Leeds, social responsibility, Justice and Peace, and similar workers meet together to support each other and initiate common campaigning. As an example of the affective leading to the effective, strong relationships between Anglican and Catholic bishops in Wakefield and its environs led to a joint assembly and the production of a powerful and well-supported joint Lent course. Within denominational structures there is also recognition of the contribution of ministers of other denominations, not least in the appointment of Ecumenical Canons by Anglican cathedrals.

All this mission work requires more people and skills than individual churches could find on their own, gifts which they discover, collectively, are distributed around the churches. By pooling talents and resources, a hitherto unthought of scale of mission activity is possible. As I once heard Rowan Williams say, 'Your neighbouring church is God's gift to you'. You may not think you have the talents and resources (human or otherwise) to make a difference to your area. That does not mean God has not given you those resources; they may be in the church down the road. Only by building ecumenical relationships and trust will possibilities become apparent. In our unity is our mission.

Trust is an essential feature, especially when it comes to trusting another church to take the lead in a particular field to which you would aspire yourself. Churches Together in England has two simple ecumenical house-group suggestions for building up understanding and trust. 'Sharing

Spiritual Treasures' involves discovering which objects, photos, hymns, or Bible verses make each other's faith and tradition come alive. 'Gifts from the Treasure Trove' uses the methods of Receptive Ecumenism to the same ends. Without this trust it can be hard to admit, for example, that the few precious children and young people who are linked with one church might be better served by a neighbouring church. This isn't about 'poaching', but ensuring that those young people's experience of church is positive, encouraging and faith-building, something they want more of, something that will nurture them far more than isolation at their home church. Their present, and all the churches' futures, depend on us taking the risk of ecumenical trust today.

Single Congregation Local Ecumenical Partnerships

On occasion, levels of trust are high enough for churches of different traditions to contemplate moving in with each other as a Single Congregation Local Ecumenical Partnership (SCLEP). These are the descendants of the Areas of Ecumenical Experiment advocated by the Nottingham Faith and Order Conference of 1964. In some ways, SCLEPs may be thought of as representing an old approach to ecumenism, of the merging of structures into a single institution, very different to the Churches Together models discussed above. Viewed with suspicion by some, especially those with responsibility for maintaining denominational structures – SCLEPs can be notoriously messy – SCLEPs are still a valuable tool in the ecumenical toolbox. In the WYEC area we have 30 such churches, and this number has been increasing by a couple each year. Sometimes, it must be admitted, congregations come together for mutual support in a time of falling numbers, sometimes the congregational life is healthy but failing buildings lead to a pooling of resources and Christian living (in some cases, especially those involving a Catholic church, it is sufficient to have a Shared Building agreement and to continue to worship separately), sometimes a SCLEP is a church plant in a new housing estate, and sometimes, in the best examples, healthy churches take the positive decision to come together to equip themselves better for mission in their locality. In every case, the arrangement stands or falls on the prior quality of relationships between the churches. Where relationships are strong, the transition to shared use of a single building and shared worship within it can be managed with little discomfort.

SCLEPS can be found across the sociological strata: in rural communities (West Bretton, Wakefield) – though a single denomination church in a village can also show its awareness of other traditions by making a Declaration of Ecumenical Welcome and Commitment – and in suburbia (Eldwick, Bingley); in inner cities (Beeston Hill, Leeds), outer estates (Cottingley, Leeds) and town centres (Keighley). SCLEPs still have the potential to be prophetic, both by challenging church structures with their very awkwardness, and, in many cases, by their more outward looking mindset. Some of the best Single Congregation Local Ecumenical Partnerships are thoroughly engaged with their local community: Little Lane, Bradford holds street parties in a very multicultural part of the city; Wesley Road Chapel, Armley specializes in community lunches; St Andrew's Skipton and Christ Church Halton are packed with community events, while Christchurch Ilkley reaches out by providing one of the best cafés in town.

There are several issues faced by every SCLEP. Common gripes include duplication of administration and a lack of understanding by some denominational authorities. Ecumenical goodwill can vanish when property, finance and payments of Share or Assessment are concerned. The same words ('ordained' and 'deacon') have different meanings and are used differently. Other words ('elder', 'steward') can be used carelessly, interchangeably. SCLEPs are to be represented at meetings of deaneries and circuits, but how do those relate to each other, especially in terms of power, finance and authority? Indeed, where does power lie in the SCLEP? Central to the ecclesiology of some traditions is the authority of the local church, whereas to others the principal unit is the circuit, Parochial Church Council or diocese. And when it comes to appointment processes, one church's stationing is another church's scoping, and another church's 'Sections 11 and 12'. These diverse practices are long established, reflecting, but not – in general – essential to, the theology of the denominations. Where is the central willingness to embrace an ecumenical mindset in the practice of denominational operations? As things stand, membership of a SCLEP can require both patience and stamina. Indeed, membership itself is an issue, as it means different things to different denominations (and nothing at all to the Church of England!) In principle, a SCLEP is, at one and the same time, fully a church of each of the participating denominations, though members may belong to one or all of these. Questions may arise over personal and collective identity. Some churches thrive in absorbing the best of the distinctiveness of each partner tradition, while other SCLEPs pride themselves that 'you can't see the join, we're all "Christian" now', a post-denominational assessment not calculated to appeal to denominational authorities.

None of these issues, however, is insuperable, and, as has been indicated, there are many fine SCLEPs around, and the model continues to appeal to potential new partnerships. It helps, however, to have not only denominational but ecumenical oversight, support and promotion of such partnerships. This is a 'Sponsoring Body' role, fulfilled by most ecumenical intermediate bodies like WYEC.

The WYEC story

Almost every county in England, sometimes linking with a neighbouring county, has an 'intermediate' body like WYEC. Each has its own story. In the case of WYEC, we go back to the Leeds Council of Churches (LCC), which predated the 1942 founding of the British Council of Churches,[4] and which even in wartime organized 'Religion and Life' meetings. Post-war concerns included international order, the 'Colour Bar,' and what the new World Council of Churches might do to further world peace. By 1957, LCC was describing its aims as jointly 'to foster and express the spirit of Christian Unity [and] to awaken and inform the conscience of the community with a view to promoting social and international justice.' In practice, that meant promoting the Week of Prayer for Christian Unity and also Christian Aid Week, a recently-launched initiative of the Inter Church Aid and Refugee Service. In the 1960s there was a 'Coloured People's Committee,' and groups on a range of issues from 'Faith, Order and Mission' to 'Nuclear Deterrence'.[5] Some groups came in time to have an independent existence, such as Leeds Industrial Mission, a pioneer of industrial chaplaincy.[6]

Local Government boundary reorganization led to a morphing of LCC into Leeds Metropolitan Council of Churches (LMCC), which first met in 1975.[7] John Moorman, Bishop of Ripon, spoke to LMCC on 'Whither Ecumenism?' concluding that it was more about relationships than regulations. For him, regulations would not change significantly unless relationships were so strong that everyone wanted to change them.[8] By 1981,

LMCC's principal concerns were Christian Aid, Industrial Mission, Local Radio, Community Care and Hospital Chaplaincy.[9] Refusing to have their concerns constrained, LMCC developed close relations with the churches of Dortmund, one of Leeds' twin cities, beginning church exchanges in 1986, which still continue.[10]

As well as these activities, there was a separate development which pre-dated the 1985 national report of the Archbishop of Canterbury' Commission on Urban Priority Areas (ACUPA), otherwise known as *Faith in the City*. The Leeds Churches Community Involvement Project (LCCIP) produced its own parallel report *Faith in Leeds.* Back in 1973, in the aftermath of Vatican II, Gordon Wheeler, the Catholic Bishop of Leeds, formed the country's first diocesan Justice and Peace Commission.[11] This led to questions about what such phrases from South American theology as 'the Church of the poor' might mean for Leeds. Such questions, alongside the research of Archbishop of Canterbury' Commission on Urban Priority Areas (ACUPA) and the commitment of various senior church leaders in Leeds, led to the 1984 founding of Leeds Churches Community Involvement Project which quickly became known by the name of its significant 1985 publication, *Faith in Leeds* – which was revealed in the wake of the storm following ACUPA's own report that year, *Faith in the City.* Leeds was acknowledged to be the leader in such thinking nationally.

Alongside this innovative and rooted thought and action, there was a practical need to provide support for an increasing number of Local Ecumenical Partnerships. The model suggested nationally was for Sponsoring Bodies which would relate to a number of LEPs. Bradford Council of Churches, and especially the Bishop of Bradford and other regional church leaders, explored this in 1984–85, and came up with the concept of a West Yorkshire Ecumenical Council, which would both act as a Sponsoring Body, and also be a forum for the church leaders to 'promote and seek by prayer and other appropriate ways the fullness of unity in the Church founded by Christ'; to 'encourage effective and intelligent evangelism'; and to 'facilitate relations between the Christian Churches and the media' – responding together wherever possible. Note the importance of this media role from the outset.

The West Yorkshire area covered by the 'big five' denominations[12] included 1021 churches and 964 paid clergy. The five were joined by the

Moravian Church and the Salvation Army, before the official launch of WYEC on 14 October 1987 in St Anne's Cathedral, Leeds, which included the 'Church Leaders' Covenant and Commissioning of Ecumenical Officer.' That County Ecumenical Officer was a Methodist minister, Lewis Burton, former secretary to LCC. Future County Officers would be Bill Snelson (an Anglican priest who had been secretary to LMCC and who would become General Secretary of Churches Together in England), Stephanie Rybak (a Roman Catholic specializing in spirituality and organizing ecumenical pilgrimages), and Clive Barrett.[13]

The full WYEC Council consists of the senior church leaders and the denominational ecumenical officers of the seven denominations mentioned above, plus the Lutheran Church of Great Britain, the Religious Society of Friends (Quakers) and the West Yorkshire African Caribbean Council of Churches. The Sponsoring Body aspect of WYEC's role was initially carried out by six separate bodies, serving North Yorkshire and the five Metropolitan Districts of West Yorkshire. It is now performed by a single gathering of competent and committed denominational ecumenical officers.

Occasionally, though rarely, WYEC has organized public events, carol services for asylum seekers and their support networks, regional gatherings of Churches Together groups, regional unity services. Although this has not been the main focus for WYEC, the organization of a public forum for all the churches is a strength of some other county bodies, including Churches Together in South Yorkshire.

Unity among church leaders

One of the most important aspects of WYEC has been the provision of a forum for bringing together the senior church leaders: bishops, moderators, chairs, regional ministers. Each of the church leaders signs the WYEC Church Leaders' Covenant, usually at her or his initial licensing / induction service. This personal Covenant recognizes the similar responsibilities faced by leaders of each denomination, and acknowledges 'that we have much to offer and to receive from each other in the rich diversity of our traditions, which complement and challenge each other.'[14] After an echo of the Lund principle, the Covenant continues with the church leaders encouraging initiatives, conferring over appointments and acting on public issues. It is a powerful statement, the basis of the whole Council, made by those who 'rejoice in our growing partnership of trust as we share at a personal level in worship, friendship and consultation'. It is a prophetic model of encouragement to those in local churches to work together as closely themselves.

As well as attending formal Council meetings, WYEC Church Leaders take part in regular residentials, occasional pilgrimages and even Christmas dinners which build relationships, enhance the ecumenical mindset through greater awareness of each other, and develop the affective and hence the effective, with tangible results in pastoral and strategic cooperation.

One of the most visible outcomes of the relationship between church leaders, and an explicit aim of their Covenant, has been a growing tradition of public statements on matters of common concern, some of which have received considerable media coverage. These serve various purposes. An issue of pressing social need receives public profile, often enhanced by the scale of ecumenical cooperation. It is invariably a call to both those inside the churches (ourselves) and outside to take action to address this social need. It is an encouragement to local churches and Churches Together groups to do just that. (When I was in parish ministry, on an estate threatened by far-right extremism, a statement by senior church leaders encouraged our local Churches Together group to make its own public stand on this.) In this process, the unity of the church leaders is visible to all.

Early statements related to the Gulf War and the far right. In recent years, there has been public witness of senior church leaders concerning: the plight of asylum seekers in the UK; a positive response to 'A Common Word', an eirenic call from Muslim scholars; the crisis of debt; the far-right (again); inequality and community building; the victims of economic cuts; the City of Sanctuary movement for welcoming asylum seekers; the English Baccalaureate; the importance of local radio; and the plight of many young people and the pressures they face. More recently, there has been a move away from always denoting these concerns in a formal statement and towards a more prayerful expression. This is partly because WYEC has built up a tradition of senior church leaders coming together in public witness on Ash Wednesday each year, a time for the penitential acknowledgement that each of us directly or indirectly contributes to the social injustice being highlighted, giving a distinctive context to the call for personal and institutional reform.

The united expression of concern has gone beyond the press-release and photo-shoot. Deputations of church leaders have handed a local authority Chief Executive a prayer acknowledging the 'anger and angst' of those faced with the consequences of cuts to Council services. There has been lobbying of Home Office ministers and officials on the needs of asylum seekers, and a number of meetings held with UK Borders Agency officials to challenge failings in the asylum process.

In all this, there are some parallels with what is happening nationally with the Joint Public Issues Team of the Baptist, Methodist and United Reformed Churches. It all follows a long-established tradition of ecumenical cooperation by church leaders in making public statements. A Leeds Quaker wartime poster publicized a 1940 joint statement by the Archbishops of Canterbury and York, the Cardinal Archbishop of Westminster and the Moderator of the Free Church Council. At that time they were calling, inter alia, for 'extreme inequality' to be abolished, for a sense of vocation to be restored to daily work, and for the resources of the earth to be used for the whole human race with especial awareness of the needs of future generations.[15] Plus ça change ...

Personal endpiece

There is a lot of unity about! That much should be clear from the above. The sheer quantity of ecumenical work being undertaken at local level is staggering. The best mission and outreach is ecumenical. Admittedly, there is still some way to go in cultivating a universal ecumenical mindset, so that officials of all denominations – especially in the largest, who are most likely to be absorbed by their own institutions – automatically think in any new situation, 'How can we do this together?' One of the challenges, both for intermediate bodies and for local Churches Together groups, is to so educate and enthuse people of every tradition that the Lund principle is taken to heart at all levels of Church life.

It is part of the role of intermediate bodies both to interpret the national / international dimension of Church life to local churches and to proclaim the good practice of local Churches Together groups to those in national / international structures. The extraordinary mission of many local

Churches Together groups, so often ignored or understated, is worthy of such proclamation. Perhaps this model of local Churches Together mission is one which this country can offer to the world church.

There can be a freedom to Churches Together working which is not always found in heavy interdenominational negotiations which, aiming for consensus, can too easily focus on the negativities of difference. Many unity negotiations, for example, focus on issues of Eucharist and Orders. I was always taught that the Eucharist did not end when one left church; 'Ite missa est' – the Eucharist was for living. In living out the Eucharist side by side with Christians of other traditions, the question of the nature of the Orders of the President of the Eucharist is seen in a fuller context. In the vast majority of mission examples given above, such problems hardly arise. Catholics and Quakers, sacramentalists and Salvationists work and pray side by side. The more one is immersed in local ecumenical mission, the more one is open to re-interpreting, re-expressing, or re-considering one's own understandings of faith and order. Put into historical global ecumenical terms, Life and Work sets the context for consideration of Faith and Order. Immersion in shared ecumenical mission is a prerequisite for such consideration, which could not emerge in a vacuum. A living, local unity is a *sine qua non* for a fuller understanding of the meaning of unity. Unity is in the mission; unity is in the process.

14 *Local Mission and Unity*

Mike Love

This is a story about Leeds Christian Community Trust. Hebrew scripture scholar Walter Brueggemann describes the incarnation as 'the scandal of the particular'. What follows is a particular story – particular to its time and place – with no claim to any universal application. It's a good story to have been part of and, to the extent it has been good (I trust) a God story. Every story has to begin somewhere but inevitably is but a single thread in the fabric made of innumerable threads that only God can see to form. I apologize in advance to all those people to whom I should attribute so much of this story, but have no space to – you know who you are.

I was converted in my early twenties and taken to a Pentecostal congregation. Being Pentecostal meant having a lived and remembered history of rejection by other traditions. This led in turn to a rejection of those traditions, even when they began to be touched by Charismatic renewal in the 1960s and 1970s; 'if they truly had received the charisms of the Spirit, they'd be joining us'. Thus began my journey of Christian unity! The discovery that God did not dwell in our boxes began with my visit to David Watson's and Riding Lights' 'Whole Story' Mission in the late 1970s (about which I was warned to be careful). I was delighted by the freshness of worship, the use of creativity, and the evident presence of the Spirit. Thus began a lifetime of exploring what of God lay beyond my own experience. I used to say 'unity kills you'. Seeking unity seriously entails the deconstruction of all that separates us, and the application of a strong hermeneutic of suspicion to all – within and without – that is held in place by fear, exclusion, and vested interest. Throughout this chapter I use the word 'congregations' where the more usual word would be 'churches', based on my conviction there can only be one church if 'God was in Christ reconciling all things'.

In the early 1990s I was part of a team that brought 'March for Jesus' to Leeds. We were standing on the shoulders of a group of Christian ministers and lay people who had continued, with changing personnel, to meet since the 'Whole Story' mission, and who had then hosted the Luis Palau mission in the early 1980s. We managed to gridlock Leeds city centre with a march of 5,000 people and over 20 lorries, each bearing a music group; I'm not sure what contributed most to my headache that day – my responsibility for the logistics, or the unmusical cacophony of so many competing groups. March for Jesus did wonders for the imagination – it made unity visible and brought the gathered church out of its customary buildings into the city streets. We followed MfJ up with regular prayer gatherings for the unity of the church, and for the furtherance of God's kingdom in the city.

The early 1990s also saw Challenge 2000 adopted by nearly all the denominations. As the UK expression of the DAWN movement (Discipling A Whole Nation), Challenge 2000 aimed to promote strategic collaboration in church planting to reach the most unchurched parts of the UK. In Leeds we mapped the locations of worshipping congregations and began to see where there was an absence of Christian presence and witness. I'm not sure that we ever came close to strategic church planting but, once again, it was a good aid to the imagination to spur thinking about the whole city and the whole church.

In the Charismatic and Pentecostal world of the 1990s the key messages seemed to be about unity and cities, with prayer for both being top of the agenda. Starting in 1997 we started an annual fortnight of prayer for Leeds where we tried to uncover the spiritual foundations of the city and call it to its God given destiny. We started to meet with black majority church ministers and to hold joint meetings for prayer, reconciliation and celebration. We tried to discern what the Spirit was saying to the church in Leeds and what were the God inspired priorities for united mission. These were pivotal times, giving a new theological architecture to the imagination, and shaping many lives and ministries.

Several new cross-congregational initiatives began to emerge working with children, young people, and asylum seekers. A year-long training scheme involving practical experience and theological study began, as did a city wide communications platform for the Christian community. All of these were grass roots initiatives not instigated by, but supported by church leaders/ministers. But, two problems began to emerge common to all of them.

Beginnings of LCCT

All of these new initiatives were clear that they did not want to be 'para-church' organizations but as expressions of the unity of the church in Leeds in mission. They saw themselves as expressions of the unity of the 'church in Leeds' and wanted no existence independent of this. However, all life needs structure. To truly and transparently embody unity it wasn't appropriate that they should be hosted by a particular congregation or denomination. I worked as a solicitor and soon found myself looking at three applications to set up charitable trusts. Quite apart from not wanting the tedium of working through these applications, I felt that proceeding with them would leave to duplication and waste of effort, and each trust would end up chasing the same few willing people to be trustees and treasurers. I didn't see why we couldn't set up a single charitable trust out of which all these initiatives could operate, subject to the trustees having sufficient governance of them. I knew Ichthus in south east London, which had many congregations, were operating a similar trust running initiatives as diverse as a primary school and a laundrette. I talked to their chair of trustees (also a solicitor) and satisfied myself that we could do something similar in Leeds. The difference would be that the Leeds trust would not be run out of a single congregation of denomination.

The other problem was lack of money. Each of them had been started with lots of vision and commitment; having adequate funds to see them through a year was a long way down their list of priorities. And although there was a lot of goodwill from the various congregations which supported them, there wasn't a lot of money, with congregational budgets mostly allocated to their own projects and running costs. And then in one of the most wonderful serendipities of my life, I met a wealthy philanthropist who shared a commitment to Christian unity in his own home town (a long way from Leeds!) and had started to fund initiatives where people from more than one congregation were involved. He wanted to come to Leeds to meet some of the people I'd told him about and at the end of his day here he told me he wanted to give me £50,000. When I asked him what he wanted to see happen with it, he said it was entirely up to me! I felt it would put me in a difficult position were I to decide alone how to distribute the money so he suggested I find some people to help. Drawing on my ecumenical contacts a group came together including a Baptist, a Roman Catholic, two black Pentecostals, and a couple of 'new church' people. Most of us had hardly met previously, and it was important that none of us were ministers or clergy for the sake of transparency. This was one amazing group of people! Clearly our benefactor felt so too, because he immediately increased his offer to £250,000 over three years. So began Leeds Christian Community Trust, with its first meeting held in early 2003, but not before we had really tested the idea. We felt that the fragile new shoots of unity were precious and were concerned that money could be the tail that wagged the proverbial dog. We were also worried that the fluid, relational and organic nature of what was developing would be killed off in the act of organizing it and constituting it. A small group of us met with, and cross-examined the donor twice (he had a lot of patience!), and eventually discerned that this was indeed a gift from God and that we should take the risk of receiving it as such.

Learning from our donor's previous experience we agreed some very simple principles:

- We would initiate no projects of our own as LCCT but would be responsive to whatever came to us.
- We would support people from more than one congregation working together.
- We would support mission initiatives, and anything that enabled or stimulated the church in Leeds to united mission.
- We would give a project no more than £10,000 in any one year, up to a maximum of three years.
- We wanted to give money to existing projects but we would particularly support people with a missional dream or vision, however tentative.

- For these people we would fund them to give a day a week to begin to make their vision concrete. We would look after the legal, financial and charitable issues to enable them to 'run with their vision'.
- Because we would not be able to have the same 'hands on' management as a single project charity, we would require every project we supported to have its own support infrastructure – steering group, supporters' group, and so on.

Already queuing at the door were those projects I've mentioned. I'll describe three of these in some detail:

Leeds Youth Cell Network: based on cell church principles, this was a growing network of peer led cell groups (6–10 people) for young people. Building on the already existing strong relational foundation of the city's Christian youth workers – including Simon Hall, Duncan Stow, Lee Jackson, and Andy Lenton – it was a response to the loss of young people from church, particularly those congregations that had very few teenagers. LYCN supported these young people to become a cell with its own leadership focused on discipleship and mission, and linked them into city-wide, half-termly larger celebrations and days of hands-on social action mission. Many hundreds of young people have been part of this still growing network which has broken down denominational barriers. And many teenagers for whom normal congregational life was a turn-off, have found a context for finding and growing in faith and spiritual formation.

Transform: a small group of Christian Union students at Leeds University, some of whom had got involved in the city-wide prayer movement, felt called to give something back to the city by committing a year following graduation to mission with a commitment to unity. I'd seen all too many students feel called to do short term mission overseas and failing to see (or being helped to see) the mission on their own doorstep. Specifically several of this inspiring group felt called to live and work in Beeston, a low income, multi-racial area south of the river and definitely not an area of the city frequented by students. They did not want to start their own thing or to 'church plant' but to support the existing forms of church in mission and unity. They worked with Beeston Churches Together and, with the support of local ministers, Revs Peter Jackson and Tony Lee, they became a huge encouragement to many of the churches. We set about working with them to develop a year-long training year. We worked in conjunction with the Prayer for Bradford network chaired by Rev. Howard Astin in the belief that Transform could embody something of a much needed reconciliation between the two cities and provide an experience for trainees of two very different cities. We helped trainees discern their call and identified tailor-made placements for them. Each trainee had a major placement of 2–3 days, a contrasting minor placement of a day or so and, to counteract the sacred–secular dualism tendency of many year-out schemes, a 'proper job'. In fact, we described the year as a 'year-in' – an opportunity to get to know the cities of Leeds and Bradford and their churches, and to discover long-term calling. On Mondays trainees came together for a day of biblical and theological study, mutual support and learning from people who had pioneered new initiatives. Significant numbers of former trainees are still working in the settings they discovered through their placements, and in some cases they are now the leaders of those organizations. Several followed their dreams and visions and were supported by LCCT to turn them into reality. Throughout God always provided wonderful course coordinators, and Transform eventually came to an end in 2010 after nine fruitful years.

Network Leeds: If you start from an ecclesiology which seeks out what it means to be 'the church in Leeds', the body of Christ in and for the city, and the first-fruits of the reconciling work of God in Christ, it's not long before you want to see the 'communion of saints' translate into communication between saints. Organizations, and indeed relationships, are made or broken by the quality of communications within them. Our bodies cannot function effectively without the communication system that is our central nervous system. The church in Leeds has huge resources, and one has to assume it could be so much more effective in its life and mission were it not impaired in its functional communications. Suzie Hamlin, an award-winning industrial communications expert, began to apply her insights to communications within the Christian community in Leeds. In industry she had seen how communications were controlled by those with the power to do so, and how poor communications between the various functions of an organizations severely limited effectiveness, profitability, and morale. Communication in the church is typically hierarchical, with the flow of information through official channels controlled to reinforcing congregational or denominational messages and priorities. To see the ineffectiveness of communications in the church you only have to think of church notices. Suzie's experience was that effective communication starts with learning from the recipient what they want and need to know, and how they can best hear it. Could it be possible to 'de-regulate' communications to enable Christians to communicate with each other outside the silos of their own congregations, and to avoid the bottleneck of the church leadership (whatever form it may take)? Might people be enabled to discover others with similar callings outside of their own Christian tradition and, having found each other, begin to engage in mission together? How could a communications tool avoid being co-opted to the agenda of any one person or organization? There were concerns at the outset about who would have the power to censor contributions, but in practice this has hardly ever proved necessary. Network Leeds began to attempt to put some of Suzie's insights into practice, starting with an interactive website and a regular e-news bulletin; it has retained total editorial independence. Communications are an ever-changing flow responsive to changing conditions and so it has been with Network Leeds which continues to develop. Network Leeds has been the inspiration for many other towns and cities starting their own particular versions of it.

LCCT people

From the outset LCCT Trustees' meetings have been marked by an almost tangible unity which has continued through personnel changes (only two of the original Trustees remain – Hilary Wilmer and me). Current Trustees include three Anglicans, a Roman Catholic, a Baptist, a Black Majority Pentecostal, a member of the Salvation Army, and one non-aligned. We have been similarly blessed with outstanding paid staff. Starting with one part-time administrator, we soon employed Martin as a part-time finance officer; his remarkable gifts and skills enabled us to grow to over 30 in-house projects, most of which had their own idiosyncratic forms of keeping accounts (or not!). Four years in, we carried out an internal evaluation. We realized that as dreams and visions develop into initiatives, and initiatives into projects with independent funding, there are key developmental points at which they need help. This led to the recruitment and appointment of Rhoda who works sensitively and expertly with projects through those crunch transition times, which can be stages of growth, or of death. Latterly we saw the need to be more proactive in stimulating people to believe they might have a God-given dream or vision, and to support them in the early stages of forming it. Tim, who had developed Network Leeds from the outset, was appointed to do this outreach work. All LCCT staff are part-time and the wage bill is less than 7 per cent of the total charity expenditure. Given that a significant amount of the staff's work is with the actual projects, up to half of the wage bill can be apportioned out to the projects themselves, giving an incredibly low overhead cost for running the charity.

Diverse stories

I need to reiterate what I began with – the particularity of any story – and to stress that where I venture an opinion, or take a particular theological or ecclesiological standpoint, or weave facts into a narrative, it is mine alone and may or may not be shared by other LCCT Trustees, staff and project people. The particularity of story (which safeguards us from the hubris of thinking that our story is *the* story) was brought home to me early in LCCT's existence. Some of the LCCT Trustees met with some other people from other places where our donor was also giving money and I was invited to tell 'the story of Leeds'. Hilary Wilmer told another story of Leeds which pre-dated mine by at least ten years. Hers began in the 1980s with Christians from different traditions finding common cause in calling the church in Leeds to engage with issues of poverty, disadvantage, and marginalization and together to prioritize the city's 'Urban Priority Areas'. From this beginning several projects emerged including the Nightstop scheme, offering emergency hospitality to homeless teens; One City Projects, connecting suburban churches with the inner city; and the Church and Neighbourhood Action scheme at Barnados, which supported congregations in community engagement and development. The interweaving of Hilary's story with the one I told has greatly enriched my understanding of God's work in the city. The Christian unity I had looked for during the 1990s was unity with people not too different theologically from me. We didn't attempt to engage with the established ecumenical bodies, having a somewhat arrogant attitude towards them, believing them to be formalized, structural and lacking in life. Successive expressions of the Leeds-wide Churches Together had struggled and two had come to an end in fairly recent memory. In the early 2000s consultations took place which led to the formation of Leeds Churches Together in Mission (LCTiM). The addition of 'in mission' was, to my mind, crucial to giving content and purpose to ecumenism. It became apparent that the life in local Churches Together groups in and around Leeds was where there was a focus on joint mission initiatives. LCTiM saw the coming together of the two streams – the ecumenism of the major denominations, with the 'new ecumenism' of the charismatic congregations – to mutual and lasting benefit.

And finally, in this brief look at the wider context in which LCCT came into being, two other major mission initiatives deserve mention. The first, Leeds Faith in Schools was formed in 1994 to support Christian youth workers to work in schools. LFIS had the support of a wide range of congregations and Christians and continues to do so. The second is Kidz Klub that began in 2000 as a partnership of four congregations, and now reaches out to well over 1,500 children through weekly events and home visits to every child, and to many more through school assemblies in over 30 primary schools.

Growth

The original offer of funding from our benefactor was for three years but we are very blessed to have received funding every year. The Trust's income in 2010 was £1.1 million, approximately two thirds of which was raised by the member projects themselves.

Currently over twenty projects are member projects of the trust; some of the bigger projects have been transplanted from the seedbed of LCCT to become their own organizations. From the outset projects have had their own identity and individuality with the wording – 'part of LCCT' – in very small print at the bottom of the page. LCCT has also given grants to well over 100 external initiatives.

Initially LCCT was known at the Charismatic, Pentecostal, evangelical end of the church spectrum and the majority of projects came from those kind of congregations. The strong hope and intention was always that it should serve the whole church in Leeds but we were only too well aware of the lack of trust that blights relationships between different types of Christian. We knew that we would have to earn trust. The first indication that was happening was when LCCT was asked to 'house' the Three Churches Project carrying out community development work in the Miles Hill area of Leeds 7. And when LCTiM needed to incorporate, it made sense for it to come under LCCT's wing.

A list of projects supported by LCCT since 2003 can be found on our website, www.lcct.org.uk . It would be impossible to do them justice by describing their work in a few words, but generic areas of work include: youth and children's work; sport; communications and media; befriending prostituted women; community development and community relations; international students; coaching and training; refugees and people seeking asylum; Christian unity; mental health; the arts; excluded pupils; and social and economic justice.

Despite the clear economies of scale LCCT offers, some of the larger funders have been unwilling to support more than one LCCT project, with Comic Relief being a welcome exception, as they explain:

> 'Comic Relief has recently funded the Manuel Bravo Project, under the umbrella of Leeds Christian Community Trust. Manuel Bravo is a very small project which offers legal advice to refugees and asylum seekers in Leeds. It operates on a modest budget and benefits greatly from the central services and subsidized office space offered by LCCT. We were impressed by LCCT's community development approach to nurturing new ideas, offering central services and seed funding, helping them grow into sound projects and eventually move towards independence. With this secure base Manuel Bravo can build its service and management committee autonomously and at the same time get good support with financial management. It makes good sense to us; we can be confident that our grant is well-managed, restricted to that project and accounted for separately within the overall LCCT accounts.'

Fred Shed, Sky Shed and beyond ...

Many of the projects were being run out of people's own homes with the LCCT administrator and finance officer working in a cramped room in my house. Leeds Faith in Schools' office was in premises that had been a garment factory and they told us the floor above them had been empty for a long time. This became the Fred Shed which for 6 years housed 12–15 projects, not all of them LCCT projects. Why Fred Shed? I work with a Leeds based charity 'Together for Peace' and for one of our pieces of publicity we collected as many languages' words for 'peace' as we could; we found out that it is 'fred' in Danish, Norwegian and Swedish. 'Shed' is an Anglo Saxon word meaning rudimentary shelter or dwelling. The name stuck, though few visitors made the connection with the Scandinavian design motif of our signboard outside! And the occasional letters that came addressed to Mr F Shed showed that some people were just confused. The name was fun but true. LCCT is no more than a rudimentary shelter and has no pretensions to become a large influential organization. What it exists is for is the promotion of *shalom* – justice, peace, reconciliation with God and people, the healing of all that is broken, and the unity that is in God. With one large room divided by head height partitioning, Fred Shed was an easy place to hear about what was going on with the various projects housed or hot-desking there. Christians from many different denominational backgrounds worked or met there alongside people of no, or other, faith. As our lease was coming to an end and we began to think about where we should move to we were told about a scheme whereby landlords of empty office buildings were seeking charity tenants to which they could give free space, thus reducing the rates bill by 80 per cent. Although it meant having no security of tenure, in the economic context of 2011 it made sense for LCCT to become nomadic, move into rent-free offices and to manage space for other projects that were in desperate need of making whatever savings they could. Over thirty projects took up residence in the seventeenth and eighteenth floors of a city centre office block ('Sky Shed') with unique views of the city. LCCT has been uniquely placed to be able to serve other projects – explicitly Christian or not – by taking on the management of the space. In 2012 we will be moving again to 'Fred the third' on the same basis as Sky Shed. By a fine coincidence LCCT's administrator Richard also works for Voluntary Action Leeds.

Reflections

Shortly we will be receiving the report of our first external evaluation. Up against the end of year deadline for submitting this chapter, I have found the Christmas break to be a good time to personally reflect on nearly ten years work.

Money and power are inextricably linked. Having a significant amount of money to distribute has given power to LCCT and so we have endeavoured to keep our 'power footprint' as light as possible. The value judgements we make are not based on our preferred theological or ecclesiological positions (which are by intention extremely diverse), but on criteria such as avoidance of duplication and competition. We have sought to release and not control, giving as much freedom to projects as is possible while complying with good charity governance standards.

LCCT is criticized by some for not supporting the work of individual congregations. I suspect others still believe it supports only evangelical projects. Because we operate outside of the authority structures of denominations and congregations, some may consider LCCT unaccountable.

LCCT exists to promote others and therefore has been ambivalent about promoting itself. We held a 'launch event' several years after we began, and we have published a handful of newsletters. Many of the projects are well supported by the Leeds church – individuals and congregations – but LCCT has been largely unsuccessful in attracting local funding. This inevitably raises questions about its long-term viability. By limiting the amount of annual grant we have tried to counteract a dependency culture. Our funding from our donor has always been on a year-to-year basis and we are healthily aware it could come to an end at any time. And we never commit to funding projects beyond the coming year.

This helps to give LCCT a lightness of being which I believe the work of unity requires. Working between strong organizational silos (as true of the church as any other organization) necessitates a weakness of being and a resistance to the temptations of using power over against other power structures.

LCCT staff operate as a flat team without hierarchy and with considerable delegated authority, and play a full part in Trustee meetings discussions (though obviously not decisions). And it works! Our hope – not always realized – is that this can be a releasing model for the way projects organize themselves.

I have a nagging question. It seems that the vast majority of the Leeds church's money goes to maintaining congregational life. Why is it that missional initiatives always struggle for funding, and few could have any certainty of existence beyond a couple of years, while congregational structures remain secure in their existence? I have no doubt that much good for very many people has been achieved by the projects LCCT has supported, but how successful has LCCT been in contributing to a change of culture in the church in Leeds? To what extent has it helped to promote an organic unity and prioritizing of mission?

15 *Unity and Inter Faith Relations*

Helen Reid and Celia Blackden

This chapter scopes inter faith relations in the context of Christian unity and mission. It outlines key points in the progression and development of inter faith relations in Britain, with a focus on West Yorkshire and the Mill Town Corridor, and the role of ecumenism in this. The perspective of the chapter engages with recent history and looks ahead to the future. It examines developments and attitudes, theology and mission, and asks where this takes us as Christians with our neighbours of different faiths. The thesis of this chapter is that Christian unity and inter faith relations have been on a journey, and that Christian ecumenism has strengthened Christian participation in inter faith relations, while being distinct from inter faith.

It is worth noting that this chapter is located centrally in the section on Unity and Mission and this highlights the connectedness of these aspects of the life of the Church. Inter faith relations today are linked to mission and mission history, both here and abroad. Attitudes to gender and the recognition of cultural and religious influences are key to inter faith relations. Racism can have an effect on inter faith issues when faith groupings coincide with ethnic differences in majority–minority contexts. In the context of 'mission and action' there is a new type of witness given to a secularized society by believers of different religions acting together. So it is clear that each chapter should not be read in isolation.

Britain is home to a unique variety of peoples, cultures, ethnicities and faiths. The legacy of an international empire, various waves of migration and the experiences of conversion have joined together to make a complex mix. According to the 2001 Census (Office for National Statistics 2001), the majority of people have a faith identity and 72 per cent self declared as Christian. Analysis enabled the religious make up of geographic areas to be mapped and detailed work at parish level was undertaken by the Church of England (Mission and Public Affairs Council 2002). This showed that minority faith communities exist throughout the country, although there are higher densities in certain cities and conurbations. Minority faiths are also present in some rural areas, for example Skipton in North Yorkshire is the English market town with the highest proportion of Muslim residents.

West Yorkshire and the Mill Town Corridor is a stretch of land with a unique multi faith dynamic. Each of the nine world faiths is present here: sizeable Christian, Jewish, Hindu, Muslim and Sikh communities, and smaller numbers of Baha'is, Buddhists, Jains and Zoroastrians. There is a numerical predominance of Muslims among minority faith communities, and this community has a distinctive demographic. In Bradford, for example, there are 86 mosques, half of all births are 'Asian', and 60 per cent of the Muslim population is under 25.

Consequently the Northern Mill Town landscape is predominantly Christian and Muslim with an intergenerational spread that emphasizes the older and younger extremes respectively. Although the Christian majority remains, there is a changing proportion in the balance of faith towards Islam. Mill Towns can be places that are segregated with distinct faith and ethnic groups living in separate residential areas with their children attending different schools. In the Cantle Report (Home Office 2002) on responses to the riots in Bradford, Burnley and Oldham, this was referred to as 'living parallel lives'. Understandings of segregation are contested (Joseph Rowntree Foundation 2010) but certainly communities can exist independently to a significant degree.

1. Inter faith friendship and exchange

Hospitality

Christians have been responding to the presence of people of different faiths for over fifty years. There are wonderful stories from the sixties about hospitality shared with newly arrived migrants and the friendships that were built between individuals, families and communities. The starting point was often sharing meals and conversation, or practical help with completing forms or learning how to get round town. Sewa Singh Khalsi, a member of Leeds Concord, remembers the welcome offered to Sikhs by members of the local Methodist Church. Once the Sikh community was a little more established, they wanted to offer hospitality too, and the tradition of a 'Sikh Christmas Dinner' began.

The motivation for dialogue and friendship, from a Christian point of view, was often compassion for those who were newly arrived, and especially for those in difficult circumstances like Hindu, Muslim and Sikh Asians expelled from Uganda in 1972. A commitment to the well-being of people of different faiths continues to this day and research has shown that social action and service provision continue to be key aspects of Christian links with different faith communities (Reid 2004). For example, there are many Christian projects that focus on English language acquisition and this can become a basis for talking about faith and culture.

Today practical collaboration amongst the faithful of different religions has grown. At a national level, aid agencies like CAFOD, Christian Aid and Islamic Relief work together. At local level, for example, St George's Crypt, a charity for the homeless in Leeds, receives frequent gifts of food from people of different religions, as well as from a gurdwara and a mosque on the occasion of events or festivals. There is multi faith and ecumenical collaboration on the spiritual care of the elderly in the Methodist Care Home initiative in South Leeds. There have been multi faith clean ups in local areas in Leeds following a multi faith conference on care for the environment.

Interest in religions

Since the earliest days of inter faith relations there have been people with a conscious interest in the faith and religious practices of others. Local groups, like Leeds Concord founded by Peter Bell in 1976, were established where people come together to talk about their faith and to share their distinctive understandings of, for example, pilgrimage, peace or fasting. This often takes the form of panel discussions, guest speakers and visits to one another's place of worship. Active civic inter faith groups continue to be central to all that is understood by 'inter faith relations'.

The early development of Bradford Concord Inter Faith Society took place alongside the growth of 'multi-faith' Religious Education in schools.

There was mutual strengthening in terms of promoting an ethos of understanding and support for members of Concord and the Standing Advisory Council for Religious Education in schools. This shows the commonality between the educational theme of inter faith groups and religious studies in educational institutions.

This aspect of inter faith that embraces a curiosity and a willingness to learn about different faiths continues to stimulate relations. For example, Kirklees Faiths Forum recently ran events that included the opportunity to join in a traditional Jewish circle dance and to learn basic Arabic calligraphy. Since 2009 there has been an annual national Inter Faith Week in England. In the last full week of November, groups celebrate faith diversity and inter faith relationships. Communities take this opportunity to promote their work in a variety of ways. In 2011, for example, seventeen inter faith groups in Greater Manchester organized an event 'Inspiration of Faith, Influence of Faith, Impact of Faith' that was attended by the Deputy Leader of the Council.

Justice and peace

A further factor that has drawn Christians into engagement with people of different faiths has been a commitment to equality and inclusion both in local communities and nationally. In the 1970s much of this endeavour was called 'race relations'. However, in the 1980s there was a re-orientation in 'race relations' to recognize the primacy of faith identity as asserted by some groups. Consequently, promoting equality included a shared commitment to a society that enables those of minority faiths to live their faith fully and freely. Christians, therefore, who began with a concern for racial justice, then met with those of other faiths out of a concern for religious freedoms.

In both practice and in theory, however, it can be difficult to separate 'race' and 'faith' because aspects of each are interwoven. Exploring the influence of faith, ethnicity and culture is a helpful tool to understanding the internal dynamics of communities and the ways they interact. This in turn helps us all to build more effective relationships and ways of working.

Personal perspectives

For decades there have been inter faith marriages and families and this is a particular strand in inter faith relations that is both personal and intimate.

Mixed marriages may be inter faith, intercultural or international, and sometimes a combination of these. Some faith groups may teach that such marriages should not happen. Other groups within faith communities offer support to help couples and families be more confident and reflective (Inter-faith Marriage Network 2012).

Today there is a greater number than ever of inter faith marriages, relationships and personal friendships. One challenge this offers to the broad scheme of inter faith relations is that the boundaries of faith and personal identity can be and often are more complex. As faith communities, we need to be sensitive to the inter personal and family dynamics while appreciating the contribution people in inter faith families can make to inter faith relations more broadly .

Sharing the good news of Christ

A Christian commitment to witness and evangelism among people of different faiths has been part of inter faith friendships and church based mission initiatives. It must be acknowledged, however, that within the range of Christian traditions, if not denominations, there have always been significant differences concerning the meaning and motivations in 'sharing the good news of Christ'. For some this means an emphasis on relationships and the common good, for other it also focuses on an explicit invitation to become a disciple of Christ.

These differences are expressed in the language used, such as 'evangelism or dialogue', 'mission or inter faith relations', and 'dialogue or proclamation'. There have been concerns that these different approaches might undermine each other, for example, that evangelism might make people of different faiths suspect that all Christian engagement aims for conversion. Alternatively, that dialogue is simply watering down the faith and renders witness meaningless.

Given these concerns some Christians have made a conscious effort to learn from the 'other' Christian perspective. Some helpfully acknowledge the continuum between evangelism and dialogue approaches (Sudworth 2007). Those involved in evangelism recognize that they are intrinsically involved in dialogue and in striving to live well together. Those involved in dialogue understand the need for a clear Christian identity and theology.

The Methodist Church progressed this sharing by bringing together people with 'evangelist' and 'dialogue' approaches to produce a study guide for local groups. They produced an educational resource called 'May I Call You Friend? – Sharing our faith with people of other faiths' (The Methodist Church 2006). This was widely used in local churches by people with different perspectives and both its production and use could be described as a form of intra Christian ecumenism.

There is now a maturity in ecumenical relationships that acknowledges diverse approaches and continues both relationships and distinctiveness. For example, in Bradford people of different faiths meet on the 11th of every month to pray for peace according to their distinct traditions, and to share a meal together. There is also an ecumenical group of churches involved in a project where they offer a DVD telling the story of Jesus' life, death and resurrection to homes in a Muslim majority area. While these projects run separately, there is a sense that each contributes to the city, to the spiritual life of individuals, and each is a sincere and indeed welcome witness to Christian faith commitment. Our witness as Christians in a multi-faith context, either in dialogue or evangelism, is strengthened by our visible love for one another and our cooperation.

II. National perspectives

The churches independently and ecumenically have reflected on the presence of people of different faiths and offered guidance on how to respond with Christian integrity. The United Reformed Church was the first denomination to establish a Mission and Other Faiths Committee in 1972. Development was gradual, but by 1987 almost all the denominations had inter faith committees or consultative groups (Harris 2007). Further, it is notable that the URC and the Methodist Church now share a joint committee for Inter Faith Relations. This commitment of resources has been, and still is, a support and stimulant for localized participation in inter faith relations.

In 1984 the then British Council of Churches, through its 'Committee for Relations with People of Other Faiths' (CROPOF) agreed guidelines on dialogue as follows:

- Dialogue begins when people meet each other
- Dialogue depends on mutual understanding and trust
- Dialogue makes it possible to share in service to the community
- Dialogue becomes the medium of authentic witness

These guidelines helpfully encompassed the range of actions and motivations present in inter faith relations. They affirmed the importance of an approach to people of different faiths that was consistent with Christian theology and practice and that could be shared with people of different faiths.

The ecumenical conversations about approaches to different faiths also contributed directly to the development of national multi faith collaboration. Brian Pearce OBE, who worked tirelessly towards the establishment of the Inter Faith Network for the United Kingdom, was a member of the British Council of Churches Committee for Relations with People of Other Faiths. Interestingly the Network was founded in 1987 and it too celebrates 25 years in 2012. The Network raises the profile of inter faith relations in society at national, regional and local level and engages people of different faiths with policy makers and government. Its influence derives from representation of the range of faiths present in the UK and the commitment of each to promoting understanding, joint action and greater community cohesion.

The Catholic Church, whose teaching on inter religious relations is rooted in the Second Vatican Council document *Nostra Aetate* (translates as *In Our Age*), gave further guidance in 1984 (Secretariat for Non-Christians) outlining four types of dialogue:

- The dialogue of life, when people try to live in harmony, sharing their joys and sorrows, their problems and preoccupations
- The dialogue of action, when people of different faiths work together for human development and liberation
- The dialogue of theological exchange, when specialists seek to understand each others' religious heritage and appreciate each other's spiritual values
- The dialogue of religious experience, when people, rooted in their own religious tradition, share their spiritual riches with people of other faiths

This teaching, and subsequent texts, have been appreciated by different denominations and different faiths. More recently the visit of Pope Benedict XVI to Great Britain in September 2010 included a significant meeting with representatives of other religions. The occasion brought together men and women eminent in their fields, including, amongst others, academia, business, public service and the voluntary sector. This highlighted the contribution that people of faith, grounded in their religious principles and working side by side, can make to society. At the end of the visit the Pope also encouraged the Catholic Church in England and Wales to continue along the path of both ecumenical and interreligious dialogue.

Within unity and inter faith relations there is a clear role for Churches to develop and share their own understanding.

The Church of England and successive Archbishops of Canterbury have played a key role in developing inter faith relations and enabling broader ecumenical involvement. Whether we consider the early establishment of the Council of Christians and Jews in 1942 or the effort put in to the more recently founded Christian Muslim Forum (2006) and Christian Hindu Forum (2011), the landscape of inter faith relations has evolved with a significant contribution from the Church of England.

The Council of Christians and Jews has been a role model for dialogue and other bilateral inter faith groups. It is committed to addressing anti-Semitism and promoting Jewish–Christian relations. Given the unique nature of Jewish–Christian relations, other groups cannot be identical, but do recognize its pioneering work and breakthrough in dialogical relationships.

The Christian Muslim Forum stemmed from a Lambeth Palace initiative in the form of a listening exercise, when Christians and Muslims joined together to hear the concerns of their respective communities in their local context. From this there was an expressed desire for the leadership in each faith to model good relationships in order to stimulate and authenticate Christian Muslim relations at local and regional levels. The Forum was established comprising leadership from within different Christian denominations and Muslim groups endeavouring to promote unity within and between communities. It has shown leadership on issues such as the ethics of mutual witness and the debate on public celebrations of Christmas in England.

Many of the Free Churches have been actively engaged in inter faith relations over a long period, for example the Joppa Group within the Baptist Union of Great Britain. In addition to many activities and publications, ecumenical and inter faith engagement occurs notably in the fields of Educational, Healthcare and Prison Chaplaincy through the work of the Free Churches Group.

We have seen the work of the Churches growing over several decades of involvement and commitment at every level. Today that work is coordinated through the Churches Inter Religious Network of Churches Together in Britain and Ireland.

III. Challenges and resources

Conflictual events on the world stage, nationally and locally, have impacted on unity and inter faith relations. These have included the Honeyford Affair in Bradford schools, the Satanic Verses' controversy in many towns and cities, and the impact of the destruction of the Babri Masjid in Ayodyah. Such events have signposted some of the socio-political and justice implications of living in a religiously diverse society. On 11 September 2001, the attacks symbolized by the destruction of the Twin Towers of the World Trade Centre in New York highlighted powerfully the imperative for peace between faiths which is not politically naive. Four years later, it was a shock to the nation that it was British Muslims who took bombs onto public transport in London. It was particularly disturbing for the people of Beeston in Leeds and Dewsbury to discover that it was home to the bombers, and to the people of the Hyde Park area of Leeds that there was a local home with bomb-making equipment.

Many faith leaders spoke clearly rejecting violence as an expression of true religion and affirming the commitment of religions to peace. They saw the importance of a joint commitment for understanding and action that went broader and deeper than had previously been achieved. People of faith responded in many ways. While in the last 15 years, the number of inter faith groups in the UK has tripled to over 250 today, growth was most significant in 2001 following 9/11 and again in 2005 following 7/7 (Crabtree 2011).

In this context it must be acknowledged that there has also been a general trend of Islamophobia in the UK. Islamophobia can be defined as fear or hatred of Islam (Commission on British Muslims and Islamophobia 1997) and experiences of hatred and discrimination have been shaped by extreme responses to the events of 9/11 and 7/7. Christians and people of other non-Muslim faiths are not immune to the pressures that lead to

Islamophobia and people of goodwill actively seek to oppose it. In particular, there has been public Christian opposition to Islamophobic elements in far right political movements which has included repudiation of Islamophobia as un-Christian.

The last ten years have seen increasing government involvement in inter faith relations nationally and in many cases locally. The present government has recognized the role of individual communities within inter faith relations. An outcome is the Near Neighbours project launched in 2011 and funded by a grant of £5m from the Department for Communities and Local Government. This Programme directs funding and resources to grassroots inter faith action through the network of the Church of England parish system. The implementation of Near Neighbours requires further development of the existing ecumenical and inter faith cooperation. It will, perhaps be a good test of the thesis of this chapter – that we have come a long way in trust and cooperation.

IV. Looking to the Future

We have seen that the landscape of Christian relations with people of different faiths has changed radically in recent times, and more swiftly still in the first decade of the Third Millennium. Continuing this metaphor, we have moved from an empty moorland to moorland still, but with fields, some parks and gardens and even the occasional 'hot house' where Christian relationships and collaboration with our neighbours of other religions are deeper and more effective.

Factors that will determine how this landscape evolves in future include: faith communities responding together to the economic crisis and meeting people's immediate needs; collaboration in seeking justice for refugees, asylum seekers and migrant workers; our shared action for the environment; and spontaneous multi faith responses in compassion to those caught up in natural disasters. Through these channels, and others, there is likely to be a broadening and strengthening of friendship, understanding and joint action locally at neighbourhood level in our cities and towns, while not neglecting an ongoing and improving collaboration at civic level among leaders.

There is a growing awareness of inter faith relations that go 'beyond the nine'. This phrase is used to acknowledge the wider range of faiths and beliefs beyond the currently acknowledged nine world faiths mentioned earlier. These groups include those known sometimes as new religious movements (NRMs), which already are or wish to be involved in inter faith relations locally and nationally. This demands of Christians great clarity of identity and purpose while creating modes of engagement which do not undermine the good achieved so far.

There is increasing dialogue and involvement with people who do not have a formal faith but who share our concerns for a healthy society. The 2001 Census revealed that about a fifth of the population was included in the categories of 'no religion' or 'not stated'. Indicators of growing mutual esteem include the involvement of agnostics in the 2011 Pilgrims of Peace event in Assisi. As Christians we need to develop our capacity for engagement in respectful and constructive dialogue with ever growing circles of diversity. We must recognize however that within non religious groups there can be a perspective that wishes to marginalize faiths and exclude them from the public sphere. In this context a respectful and constructive dialogue may also need to be radically challenging.

Part of our mission as Christians on the path to unity is a continuing concern for religious freedom. Religious freedom is to be secured for all, including those who convert or those who live as a minority, either in Britain or elsewhere. This process of commitment to religious freedom is required of people of all faiths and of good will. It is not something that can be achieved by one faith group alone.

These growing issues and challenges for the future will be faced in the context of an ecumenical movement that is enlarging itself to include many new churches and new expressions of church. There is a need for deep trust and dialogue among Christians of different standpoints regarding both theological and practical approaches to inter faith relations. This will lead to a Christian witness to people of different faiths and those without formal faith that expresses our journey towards the unity Christ wants of us.

References

Commission on British Muslims and Islamophobia (1997) *Islamophobia: A Challenge for Us All.*

Crabtree, Harriet (2006) quoted in *The Times*, 19 November 2011.

Harris, Elizabeth (2006) Historical Notes on the Committee for Relations with People of Other Faiths (CROPOF) and the Churches Commission for Inter Faith Relations (CCIFR) 1997–2003 (can be accessed via http://www.ctbi.org.uk/)

Home Office (2002) *The Cantle Report – Community Cohesion: a report of the Independent Review Team.*

Inter-faith Marriage Network (2012) www.interfaithmarriage.org.uk.

Joseph Rowntree Foundation (2010) *Muslims and Community Cohesion in Bradford* (can be accessed via http://www.jrf.org.uk/publications/muslims-cohesion-bradford)

Mission and Public Affairs Council (2002) *Presence and Engagement. The churches' task in a multi Faith society*, paper to the Church of England General Synod.

Office for National Statistics (2001) *Census of Population and Housing* (can be accessed via www.statistics.gov.uk)

Reid, Helen (2004) 'Evangelism in a multi faith society – what is really going on?' in *Faith to Faith Newsletter 16*, April 2004

Secretariat for Non Christians (1984) *The attitude of the Church towards the followers of other religions: reflections and orientations on dialogue and mission.*

Sudworth, Richard (2007) *Distinctly Welcoming. Christian Presence in a multifaith society*, Milton Keynes: Scripture Union.

The Methodist Church (2006) *May I Call You Friend? Sharing our faith with people of other faiths* (available as a download from http://www.methodist.org.uk/)

V The Challenges of Unity

16 *Unity in the Face of Racism*

Anthony G. Reddie

In this essay I will be addressing the issue of how 'Black Christianity' in Britain has attempted to effect unity within the 'Body of Christ' by challenging the fracturing realities of racism within the church. The notion of the church as a body that is united under the Lordship of Jesus Christ is nothing new – this concept has been invoked by other authors in this volume. And yet, the unity that is so boldly proclaimed as central to the self-understanding of the church itself has often proved more illusory than real.

While the Body of Christ has been fractured by arguments over doctrine, ecclesiology, issues of class, gender and sexuality, perhaps the most ongoing challenge and indeed the most persistent scourge has been that of racism. Black Christianity in Britain has constantly sought to challenge oppressive realities within the Body of Christ. In using the term 'Black Christianity in Britain', I am speaking of the broad phenomenon of Black people of African and Caribbean descent who are domiciled in Britain, and within this context, can be said to believe in the God revealed in Jesus Christ and seek to give expression to the central tenets of the Christian faith in myriad forms of social-cultural practices. I have chosen to use the term 'Black Christianity in Britain', as opposed to defining my intent on simply an articulation of different paradigms of churches, because the latter is fraught with innumerable difficulties. The difficulties to which I am referring pertain to questions such as 'What is a Black Church?' let alone, what percentage of Black people do you need within a church to render it a Black one?[1]

I would much prefer to look at the broader phenomenon of Black Christianity, which incorporates all taxonomies, manifestations, expressions and articulations of the faith, which emerges from or is an expression of the myriad cultures and experiences of Black people of African and Caribbean descent, living in this country. This expression might mean Roman Catholic, or Anglican (liberal, catholic or evangelical), Methodist, Baptist, Reformed or the fastest growing trajectory, Pentecostal; let alone other manifestations, such as Seventh Day Adventist.[2]

My subjective background

The author of this piece is a Black Theologian and Christian educator born in Britain. I was born in Bradford West Yorkshire to Jamaican parents who came to this country from the Caribbean in the late 1950s. As such, I am a second generation Black Caribbean British subject. I was born into and nurtured within the Christian faith from the Wesleyan Methodist tradition. I ply my trade as a Black Liberation Theologian and educator in Birmingham, where I have lived for approaching the past thirty years of my life.

I have shared these bare details of my life with you because it is my firm belief that all knowledge, and the writing that emerges from it, is embodied. By this, I mean, there is always a relationship between the experiences that have shaped one's life and the resulting ideas and theories that emerge in any subsequent writing. Namely, that all knowledge and truth is contextual; it emerges from, and is shaped by, specific and particular times and spaces.

Many of the enduring values in my life can be traced back to my formative years growing up in a Black Christian home, but living within the predominantly White working class, trade union and Independent Labour Party stronghold of East Bowling. In this context, non-conformist Christianity, trade unions and labour party politics went hand-in-hand.

While my formative years were largely pleasant and affirming, what could not be disguised about our existence was the persistent reality of racism that affected the lives of all non-White people in the city of Bradford. I would argue that the consistent and persistent challenge that has faced Black people of Christian faith in Britain has been that of trying to get White Christianity to give expression to a non-racist articulation of the gospel. In using the term 'White Christianity' I am talking about people of European extraction and descent, who form the majority of the population, who believe in the God revealed in Jesus Christ and seek to give expression to the central tenets of the Christian faith in myriad forms of social-cultural practices.

Racism in Britain and the Black Christian experience

The existence of racism in Britain today and in many parts of the so-called developed West, as we speak, is testament to the continuance of an underlying Eurocentric Judeo-Christian framework. This framework was one that invariably caricatured Africans as 'less than' and 'the other' and often placed White Euro-Americans as the apex of human civilization. The notion that human beings can be categorized into a fixed set of identities, which characterize human potential and capability, often effected in notions of morality and ethics, can be traced back to the first four centuries of the 'Common Era' (CE). It was during this epoch that negative connotations pertaining to Black people as the 'other' begin to surface in Christian thinking.[3]

The scourge of racism in Britain is nothing new for Black people. As Beckford has demonstrated, one can chart a genealogy of racism in European intellectual thought that has exerted a disproportionately negative hold on the life experiences of Black people.[4] Scholars, such as Eze, have shown the extent to which the allegedly enlightened thinking of such 'luminaries' as Hume and Kant was infected with the stain of White supremacist thought.[5] The construction of the binary of Blackness (as bestial and less than) and Whiteness (as the personification of goodness and the opposite of Blackness) is a product of modernity.[6]

The chief legacy of transatlantic slavery was the unleashing of the rampageous and ravenous animal that is racism. The construction of racialized notions of fixed identity and restricted perspectives on Black human selfhood were the dangerous offspring of the chattel slavery of the 'Black' Atlantic.[7] The outworking of an immutable hierarchical manipulation of humanity did not disappear when the Act to abolish the British slave trade was passed in Britain in 1807. The act brought the making of slaves to an end, but racism and the notion of White supremacist norms, most certainly did not end.

Anthony Pinn has written extensively on the nature of the fixed identity constructions that have plagued the Black self since the dawn of modernity.[8] Pinn argues that the strictures of fixed identity (in effect, the ideas of 'race') are ones that seek to limit the repertoire of Black agency within a racialized framework in which Black people are essentially stereotypes who are base human beings distinct from and less than the normalcy and correctitude of Christian White Eurocentric norms.[9] Black Christianity in Britain can be said to have emerged via the mass migratory movement of Black people from Africa and the Caribbean in the years following the end of the Second War. This epoch is has often been termed the 'Windrush'.[10] The 1945 post-war presence of Black people within inner cities in Britain and the churches to be found there is a phenomenon that has been described by a great many sociologists and historians.[11] This influx is perceived as commencing with the arrival of 492 Caribbean people at Tilbury dock on the *Empire Windrush*, 22 June 1948. While there has been a Black presence in Britain since the times of the Romans, the birth of Black Christianity, in the form that we recognize today, for the most part, dates from the influx of these Caribbean migrants in the post Second World War epoch.

Yet, prior to the wholesale migration of Black people from the New Commonwealth, between 1948 and 1965, there is within British history the often submerged presence of Black people such as Mary Prince,[12] Olaudah Equiano[13] and Ignatius Sancho.[14] The experiences of these and other similar individuals speak to an experience that is characterized by an indomitable spirit that yearned for freedom. These pioneering individuals belonged to a community of Black slaves, many of whom were Christians, who resided at some point in their lives in London, and were key figures in the abolition movement, and yet for the most part they have been written out of British history.[15]

The earliest manifestations of Black Christianity in Britain, can be traced to the struggle of Black slaves in the seventeenth and eighteenth centuries in their fight for emancipation. Black Christianity in Britain has *always* had to respond to the realities of racism. The struggles of these Black slaves in Britain speak to the corruption and the biased self-serving nature of English Christianity at that time. The pioneering work of such luminaries as Sancho[16] and Prince[17] were valiant attempts to remind the

English establishment of the basic tenets of Christianity, which they had so regally exported to their empire throughout this era.

The story of how Black people came to Britain, many as communicant members of historic churches of the Protestant tradition, and were often summarily rejected by their White brothers and sisters in Christ has been documented by scholars such as Wilkinson.[18] I have argued that the genealogy of racism to which Robert Beckford makes reference represents the causal link between the virulent expressions of racism in the slave trade era of the seventeenth and eighteenth centuries in Britain, and the no less demoralizing polarizing experiences of rejection of Black migrants in the mid-part of the last century.[19]

In the next part of this essay, I want to highlight the three dominant approaches that Black Christianity in Britain has adopted in order to counter racism and so promote a sense of unity within the Body of Christ.

Different typologies for countering racism in Black Christianity in Britain

The first typology: the Colour Blind Approach

One means of countering racism has been a retreat into a 'Colour Blind' interpretation of the Christian faith. This approach is the first of the three typologies to which mention will be made in this essay. The colour blind approach accords with the very words in the title; i.e. that the adherents to this approach do not see colour in their hermeneutical engagement with the Christian faith. This particular typology works from the basis that God is spirit and that 'in Christ' there are no discernible differences in terms of identity and the embodied selfhood of Christian believers. (Galatians 3: vv. 28). As African American Black theologians Pinn and Hopkins[20] have demonstrated, and more latterly, Womanist theologian[21] Kelly Brown Douglas, Black Christianity, drawing on the dualistic modes of thinking developed by Greek antiquity and largely propagated through Pauline theology, has encouraged many Black people to downplay or even despise the physical reality of their Black bodies. In short, the finite nature of Black bodies does not matter as much as that of the infinite and transcendent soul that resides within. And thankfully, for many in this typology, the soul, unlike their Black body, has no colour.

By drawing upon notions of abstract theology, which seek to downplay the physical and psychological reality of their Blackness, conservative Black Christians are able to talk about Christian identity and unity in the Body of Christ by appealing to the supremacy of their spiritual identity as opposed to their physical one.

This colour blind notion is, in my opinion, one of the least successful attempts to deal with the reality of Blackness. The basic premise behind notions of colour blind theologies is the sense that it is our very Blackness or the more generic realities of physical difference (based on skin pigmentation and phenotypes) that are the cause of ructions and disruptions in the body Christ;[22] i.e., if we can only move beyond the immediacies of our restricted and sinful bodies towards the transcendent spirit and the soul that are the true essence of what it is to be human, then we will be better able to deal with racism and other forms of discrimination and prejudice. The problem with this notion is that it does not challenge the demonization of Blackness itself; i.e., being Black remains problematic, but one seeks to transcend Blackness, by ignoring it.

It is important to note, of course, that I am not asserting that only conservative Black Christians adhere to this particular form of theological construction. Many liberal and conservative White people will also make recourse to this form of thinking, but as this essay is largely concerned with Black people, the latter is not my primary concern in this work.

Although undoubtedly on the conservative end of the fight against racism, Colour Blind approaches, nevertheless, have offered Black Christians a means of continuing to argue for their innate sense of self-worth and dignity. The Colour Blind approach is one that exists in a variety of Black Christian approaches and practices, although I think it is fair to say it is perhaps over-represented in newer, more African Neo-Pentecostal churches. Although conservative in its overall posture, the Colour Blind approach still asserts a kind of resistance to racism.

In fact one can argue that *all forms of Black Christianity in Britain* represent a particular model of resistance to racism. At the more conservative end we have what some Black religious scholars such Valentina Alexander[23] and Robert Beckford[24] have termed as 'Passive Resistance'. This mode of anti-racist struggle is one that is based on a form of a pneumatologically-inspired connection with the Divine, whom Black Christians come to believe has created them to be free, through the power of the spirit and spirit-filled forms of religious-cultural practices. This form of assertion is an expression of an innate belief that it is a fundamental right of all people to claim their freedom in Christ, in and through the power, of the Holy Spirit.

The freedom these Black Christians claim is one that asserts their innate connection with a loving God. The love and concern of God for the believer might not give rise to any concrete or material change in their existential realities, but nonetheless, it bolsters their thinking and imagination to resist the racialized imposition of others. In effect, this is an internalized form of resistance, where the essence of Black humanity is preserved from the contaminating stain of racism. Passive radicalism has tended to be most visible and operative within the Black Pentecostal movement within Britain, although evidence of it can be found in other Black Christians, particular those older individuals of the 'Windrush' generation.[25]

The Second Typology: Black Christian Experience

The second typology that exists in Black Christianity in Britain in terms of countering racism is that which falls within the realms of 'Black Christian experience'. When speaking of Black Christian experience, this term refers to a religious-cultural orientated approach to Christian tradition, which arise out of Black experiences, but does *not necessarily* have an overtly political or an explicitly progressive and liberationist agenda. Neither, does this approach necessarily see Blackness as being a primary hermeneutical lens for re-interpreting the Christian faith, nor is it the case that one necessarily begins with Black experience as the normative source for doing theology.

This particular approach is more radical than the colour blind formulation as it recognizes the material reality of ethnicity and embodied difference in our understanding of what it means to be human. This typology is significant because it has sought to give expression to the nature and identity of Black Christian experience in Britain.

There is a wealth of material written and edited by Black authors who have expressed the important insights into the experiential articulation of Black Christian faith in Britain. The most significant examples of this work can be seen the scholarship of the likes of Mark Sturge[26] and Joe Aldred.[27] Both of these authors have added to the sum of knowledge regarding the

Black Christian religious experience in Britain. Their work highlights the important contributions Black Christianity has made in the fight against racism in Britain.

The Black Christian experience typology (within Black Christianity in Britain) has both critiqued and challenged racism. It has done so by asserting the importance of Black cultural life and its concomitant expressions as a means of challenging notions of Black inferiority. By seeking to outline the rich variety and expression of Black Christian life in Britain, this typology has sought to disprove the notion that Christianity is essentially best understood, as a White religion.

The likes of Aldred, in his work in *Respect*,[28] and also in his more recent edited work,[29] has provided an important and compelling framework for articulating the contextual, African and Caribbean basis of Black Christianity in Britain. This work has exploded the myths concerning Black inferiority and the belief that African and Caribbean cultures are not worthy receptacles in which the redemptive power of the gospel can be incubated. In the salient words of the renowned African American Church historian, Robert E. Hood, *Must God Remain Greek?*[30] (a synonym for White European articulations of the faith).

The Third Typology: Black Theology in Britain

When speaking of Black Theology in Britain, I am referring to the specific self-named enterprise of re-interpreting the meaning of God as revealed in Jesus Christ, in light of the ongoing struggles of Black people in Britain. This approach to engaging with the Christian tradition is not unlike Black Theology in differing arenas like the US or South Africa, where one's point of departure is the lived experience and reality of being Black and the hardship and suffering that are often synonyms with this identity. This lived experience is then placed in dialogue with 'Holy Scripture' and the Christian tradition.[31]

Black Theology in Britain, like all 'theologies of liberation', is governed by the necessity of ortho-praxis (righteous action) rather than orthodoxy (right belief). In using this statement, what I mean to suggest, is that one's starting point in talking about God is governed by the necessity to find a basis for acting and resisting in response to very real struggles of life. The need to respond to the realities of life as it is lived in postcolonial Britain,[32] is one that has challenged many Black British Christians to seek in God a means of making sense of situations that often seem inherently senseless.[33]

In seeking to make sense of the Black condition in Britain, Black Theology has been inspired by the work of, predominantly, North American scholars, most notably James Cone,[34] Delores Williams[35] and Jackie Grant.[36] Black Theology in Britain continues to offer a radical form of thinking and contextual praxis that simultaneously seeks to empower marginalized and disenfranchized Black people alongside the need to challenge and inspire White power to act differently. This continues to be the prophetic work of Black Theology in the British context.

Black Theology has been the most radical development within Black Christianity in Britain, in terms of its challenge to racism, and the question of church unity in this context. Whereas the Colour Blind Approach has resorted to a form of disembodied spirituality as a means of handling conflicts in terms of 'race' (i.e., we move 'beyond' the visible materialism of the Black body) and Black Christian Experience has offered a Black cultural, contextual reading of the Christian faith, Black Theology, provides a systemic, liberationist re-reading of the Black presence in Britain. The Black Theology approach mounts a direct critique of White hypocrisy as its primary means of critiquing White-led, dominated models of Christian unity.

Whereas the Colour Blind Approach has adopted 'passive resistance' as its mode of engaging with racism, conversely, Black Theology has utilized a notion of 'active radicalism' in its riposte to race based notions of oppression. Active radicalism is where those who are marginalized and oppressed seek to confront the oppressive and dehumanizing structures in a more deliberate and explicit manner. Black Theology in Britain has exhibited active radicalism when it critiques the very construction of Christian theology itself.[37] Active radicalism is the form of resistance fiercely advocated by James Cone, in the very first self-articulated book on Black Theology.[38]

The challenge to White Christianity in Britain

Black Christianity in Britain has challenged the scourge of racism as it has sought to effect unity within the Body of Christ. At the heart of this challenge has been the challenge posed to White Christianity to live out the gospel imperative to love one another as the whole of humanity has been loved by Christ. The challenges of John 13: 21–35 are real and have bedevilled White Christianity in Britain for centuries. This new commandment from Jesus sits at the heart of the Christian message and has implications for those inside and outside the community of faith.

Inside the faith, the followers of Christ are asked to love one another for 'by this, everyone will know that you are my disciples' (v. 35). The way in which the followers love one another will be a sign of their commitment to and belonging within the common life of faith in Christ Jesus.

Sadly, looking back on the events of 2007, a year in which we remembered the bicentenary of the abolition of the slave trade, the ancestors of Diasporan Black peoples – the ones who were themselves enslaved Africans – many of these people would no doubt have reflected ruefully on this text.[39] For many Black Christians, our becoming members of the Body Christ did not change how significant numbers of White Christians saw us or treated us.

Even when Black people became Christians there was little evidence of this love ethic displayed in the actions of many White Christians.[40] When many Black people travelled to the UK in the post Second World War migration of the 1950s and 1960s, where was the outpouring of love for one another upon their arrival in Britain?

It is no wonder, then, that many Black Christians have questioned the alleged nature of so-called White, English Christianity.[41] Looking from the outside in, some older Black Christians of the 'Windrush' generation have wondered whether many 'good White English Christians' have ever read and understood this passage at all?[42]

White English Christianity must be committed to a ruthless and fiercely argued critique of its Whiteness, in a manner that accords with the existential struggling for truth that Black people have been obliged and sometimes forced to undertake since the creation of modernity.[43] In critiquing Whiteness, I am talking about a thorough deconstruction of toxic relationship between Christianity, Empire and notions of White-British superiority.[44]

The quest for equity, liberation and justice is one that requires the committed determined action of all peoples, irrespective of faith commitment (plus those who profess to hold no such notions). But it also requires truth telling and a retreat from all forms of obfuscation that blind us to the structural and systematic forms of racism that continue to oppress Black people and other minority ethnic people in Britain. Whether we wish to acknowledge it or not, privilege and notions of who is important, have a colour. Similarly, systemic power and notions of belonging and what is deemed acceptable also have a colour. The failure to name and unmask these forms of unearned privilege has been, for me, the most telling indictment of White Christianity in Britain. The days of Black people having to struggle with the pernicious patterns of socio-cultural and religious 'double jeopardy' (we have to solve our own problems and those of White people also who, for the most part, have to failed to address their own Whiteness) should be at an end.

The task of unmasking the privileged construct of Whiteness is not a task for Black theologians alone. Conversely, the task of effecting the systemic and structural changes that better reflect the Kingdom of God within the urban context is a task for us all.

The future can be remade! Let us have faith in the light of the Spirit of God to banish the darkness of racism and oppressive, bad practice that so often litters our past and our present. The light awaits! Let us bask in the light!

17 Unity and Healing

Barbara Glasson

Travelling to morning worship in our Ford Cortina our childhood game was to 'spot the Anglicans'. The rules of this game were easy to learn, it was segregation by hat! While the Methodist congregation, of which we were a part, were distinguishable by their sensible felt top gear with occasional feather, the Anglicans of the 1960s were much more flamboyant, with wide brims and colourful ribbons. When you got really good at this new form of I Spy you could graduate to Catholics, with small black creations adorned with net, and you got bonus points if you could pick out a Strict and Particular Baptist! It was in this way that my small childhood world was invaded with the idea that there were other sorts of Christians apart from the homely gathering at the Methodist church on the High Street. I viewed these other manifestations as odd but probably harmless, provided I held my breath when exposed to incense at the once a year Christian Unity service.

For me then, the concept of 'home' and 'denomination' are inextricably linked, I was a Methodist, so were my mother and grandparents, so were my aunts and uncles, and so were the friends with whom I sang fervently about pennies dropping, expecting Jesus to hear the total clank of all our combined offering with grateful thanksgiving. Two things then happened to me which began to change this Methodist default position. The first was a trip to Taizé, and the second was an encounter with a Bishop with a fetish for blue flowers.

The trip to Taizé was also combined with being part of a youth fellowship which encouraged us to take faith seriously. We were at the stage in life where passion for God and for each other was mysteriously intertwined. Taizé took on a new intensity, a sense that my faith had been let out to explore. I learned that the *Cross and the Switchblade* was not the only avenue into believing and I sensed for the first time the power of silence to transform worship into a feast of otherness – an influence that I continue to cherish today. I realized that it was not necessary to give God ear-ache by dropping pennies or fervent petition or singing very loudly about the overflowing blood of Jesus but that stillness and inner peace were to be cherished too.

My encounter with the blue flower bishop some few years later was not so positive. My fiancé was intending to be an Anglican priest and to train at Lincoln Theological College. He was due to attend his selection conference when the focus of everything suddenly turned on me. He was, it transpired, not allowed to candidate if I was a Methodist. It was a rather curious dilemma as it was seemingly not an issue should I have been a Buddhist or even an atheist. According to the Bishop it was easy to solve if I was 're-confirmed' an Anglican. I was already theologically savvy enough to know that it was not possible to be 're-confirmed'. I had already been confirmed and made a Methodist member in a ceremony that may have marked immature faith, but was certainly sincere. We went to see the Bishop, who talked only to my partner and 'of' me. When I asked him a direct question, he walked me into his garden and told me how much he loved blue flowers. On that day, I developed a lifelong allergy to both blue flowers, and bishops! The next Sunday in a 'private' ceremony in the Methodist Church Hall, he laid hands on my head and there I was, a signed up member of the Church of England. As far as I recall I had my fingers crossed behind my back in the hope that my Methodism was fairly Teflon coated. Years later, I can still feel the outrage that anyone, least of all a Bishop, should lay hands on anybody without their express permission.

At Lincoln, Methodists (because I really thought I still was one) were definitely *persona non grata*. The Methodist member of staff regularly presided at the college eucharist but many of the students boycotted the occasions considering him 'not a real priest'. Although my husband was obliged to eat all his meals in college, I was not always welcome. I went to work as a nursing auxiliary at the hospital and on Sunday evenings escaped to the Methodist Church for a dose of home. Here I found my lifelong friend Alison, who was also being pursued by a Bishop as her husband was also a student, but she was putting up a fiercer resistance. My daughter was baptized by a Minister of the Uniting Church of Australia, in an Anglican Church with an ecumenical certificate!

At the end of our second year, my husband left me for another student. The anger and frustration, the sense of exclusion, the hurt and confusion of these years were very deeply imprinted on my sense of identity, and still occasionally catch me out. I had dreams about setting cathedrals on fire, of trying to preach to congregations that wouldn't stop talking, of being shut in vestries. But anger can be turned to creativity and I took it upon myself to begin my Local Preacher's training. Some years, another family and two sons later, I candidated for the Methodist Ministry.

I trained on EMMTC, an ecumenical course based in Lincoln but operating across the East of England. It was a part-time course, with people who were exploring vocation, either for ordained or lay ministries. There were Catholics and Anglicans together in my year and, although I was at that time the only Methodist, I sensed the rich source of the ecumenical river that washed over my soul. It was a deep and blessed time, full of earnest conversation and light-hearted friendship. I began to realize that ecumenism was not simply about healing separations but being able to draw at a deep well of wisdom and tradition. I began to appreciate the communion of saints, both dead and very much alive, that surrounded me. On Easter Sunday 1993, a blackbird heralding the dawn reminded me once again of the grace that I had known in my childhood, but this time poured out on the whole of creation, not just those with Methodist hats! When I was ordained in Tewkesbury Abbey in 1995 it was as if God gifted to me a sense of being Methodist in the midst of all the hurt and heartache of the Church of England. I did not have my fingers crossed on this occasion!

This overwhelming sense of God's grace amongst the brokenness and fragility of the church has been a hallmark of the rather curious ministry that has subsequently unfurled. As a Probationer Minister in Crosby, in the Liverpool Methodist District, I began to learn my trade. And because it was rather a grand church with a tasteful façade, I was called upon to take any number of weddings and baptisms. After a while, a troubling trend began to emerge that began to challenge me. It seemed that I had any number of divorced couples coming to me for re-marriage. The local Anglican vicar was refusing them and the Catholic priest was apparently saying to couples 'Go to the Methodist Church to get married and then come back'. I lost count of the number of people who said to me 'I was baptized a Catholic' and to whom I responded 'No you weren't, you were baptized a Christian!' In a post-sectarian city such as Liverpool, the matter of ecumenism is a living challenge, not just an optional extra. The fissures between churches tangibly impact on people's lives, on their sense of worth, on their feeling of being accepted before God. Divisions in doctrine cause lasting damage and there is often a tension between statutes and pastoral compassion. This is not to say that we should have an 'anything goes' approach to faith, but a mutual respect between viewpoints that doesn't compound pain or underscore guilt seems a pre-requisite of being Christians together. I learned that Ministers often take the brunt of this tension and that to maintain integrity within ourselves and across denominations there needs to be space for open and honest dialogue. Saying 'The Methodists will do it, and then come back' is neither honest nor fair.

Having taken five years to learn something of negotiating the challenges and delights of Circuit ministry, it came time for me to move and a strange set of circumstances which I put down to the perversity and humour of the Holy Spirit found me lobbed in the city centre of Liverpool without a church or a congregation, the Methodist Central Hall having closed some years previously. Having spent so much of my life endeavouring to be an ordinary Methodist and included in the mainstream of the church, it seemed ironic to be set loose once again to work on the edge. A year of walking and wondering amongst the troubled and turbulent people of Liverpool One, brought me to a new conversation with God, one in which the starting point would always have to be community rather than church.

During this time I was more than grateful to Canon Nick Frayling at Liverpool Parish Church for his deep-hearted ecumenical commitment. I remember being crammed into a taxi with him and his colleagues as we took the Good Friday cross up to the Cathedral for the procession through the city, one in which it was common to be shouted at or spat upon. Nick has unity engraved on his Anglo-Catholic heart. He taught me that stereotypes of ourselves or others are never acceptable and he also unknowingly healed many memories for me. We had an ecumenical confidence at that time which was emboldening.

What emerged around me over the next ten years was a community that met together to bake, break and share bread. Known as ' Somewhere Else' a community met each Tuesday and Thursday around ovens in an upstairs room above the bookshop called News from Nowhere. (See Glasson, B., *I am Somewhere Else*, DLT, 2009.) While the bread makers found their voices to express faith journeys amongst the rising dough, the community downstairs in the bookshop provided reading material for those on the margins – in particular the LGBT community, survivors, Green activists, anarchists and those with alternative spiritualities. There was a symbiotic relationship between the bakers and the booksellers and ideas and people passed between us as if by osmosis. My first wedding at Somewhere Else happened to be a couple that came into the bookshop, and my books travelled downstairs to be sold. We offered rooms to the Stop the War Coalition while the Big Issue vendors took shelter in the shop until the baking began at 10 o'clock. I learned, amongst many things during my time at Somewhere Else that to live life in all its fullness, means engaging with the perverse, the troubled and the unlikely and finding within our shared humanity a sense of otherness and connection that I would want to describe as 'of God'. I realized during this time that ecumenism is not simply a crossover between denominations but a call to engage with the whole of life and to be challenged by people of alternative or no faith.

I began to hear stories of people who had survived far bigger hardships than my own. In particular I listened to adult survivors of childhood abuses, from within and outside the church. Their implicit and explicit naming of the place of God in their lives, was humbling and challenging, not least because their experiences ran through all the denominations. Their stories indicted the churches in tales of complicity and neglect and, in hearing them, I was brought up once again against the need for the churches to act honestly, openly and with integrity. There is no excuse for the games that give one set of people malicious power over another and no excuse for hiding abusers or silencing the abused. The bread broken amongst the gatherings at Somewhere Else became a symbol of both our unity and our need for honest dialogue. Many will testify that bread is too often an instrument of exclusion.

While at Somewhere Else, I completed my PhD, which rejoices in the title of *Bastards and Nonconformists*. It was my effort to look at how the

Methodist Church had related to lone parents since Victorian times and to endeavour to name and honour good practice. I will acknowledge that this study was both therapy and academic challenge and brought me to converse with theology in a new way. I was able to fill in some of the gaps between giving up RE pre-'O' level and lurching through a degree in Agriculture before going on EMMTC. During my reading and studying, I engaged with theologies from Barth to Bonhoeffer, got myself up to speed with Feminist Theology and had a whole summer reading Moltmann's complete works from cover to cover. I realized afresh that when we study theology, we study it ecumenically, and we are able to soak ourselves in the insight and wisdom of the thinkers from all traditions. Thoughts about God are not limited to denomination, otherwise I would be holed up with John Wesley for far too long! On the contrary, in the academic world the denominations are able to speak across the barriers of church divisions and enter a new territory, one in which it is possible to roam into unchartered territory. My PhD viva was conducted by an Anglican Priest and Mary Grey, the Roman Catholic theologian who has brought me to the most profound insights into what it means to be a woman of faith, a humble and profound human being. Although the viva was not necessarily my finest hour, the conversation in a small seminar room at Nottingham University that it engendered, was a curiously healing experience. I was, at last, able to converse across the table of faith with those who were different from me but able to listen. Study has always been a source of healing for me, it has taken me to a safe place in which I could articulate my faith without fear of reproach. I believe that everyone should have the chance to study ecumenically, it is a great gift to the soul.

And so, here I sit in Bradford, having left the bread church two years ago. I am in a community that is predominantly Muslim and, as I write, I hear people speaking in Urdu outside the window. I am asked to reflect on what ecumenism means to me and how it has brought healing into my life. I need to distil the insights of my own life journey and convey something of the essence of what it means to be ecumenical, a person of the whole earth and the people of the earth. So, like a good Methodist I will say three things!

Firstly I want to say that healing is not about fixing things but about integrity. When we break a bone we can steady it by putting the arm into plaster. This fixes the fracture and enables the other parts to function. But if the limb is to be healed, then the ragged part of the bone must knit together again. If I think of my own experiences of ecumenism, I can see that the times when things fragmented or disintegrated were devastating in their consequences. There was an inner and outer meltdown that caused a paradigm shift of the soul. I learned, and continue to learn, that where things fall apart between us, then we need time and safe space in order to reintegrate the ragged edges so that new and stronger bonds can be formed. I believe this is true both of individuals and of institutions. The fissures between denominations will not be healed by plastering over the cracks, but rather by a knitting together of the places where the break has occurred. In the case of pastoral damage or abuse, then there is no shortcut to honest conversation in which the hurts can be expressed. Too often, our ecumenical conversations skit across the surface of our shared reality in a polite fashion, not acknowledging the exclusions and isolation that is the pastoral outfall of such behaviour. Such institutional dishonesty can only lead to damaging outcomes.

We all realize that if the gay priests were taken out of the churches, the structures would dissolve. We are all aware that abuse has been covered up or individuals scapegoated at the expense of the institution's face. We all know that many of the priests that swear allegiance to the Queen or the 39 articles or the Bishop, only make these oaths in the hope that they are never called to enact them. While we continue to be institutions predicated on half-truths then we forfeit our integrity before God and the earth. The breaks between us cannot heal, unless we find the honest encounters and tell the truth. I know that I am a Methodist, and I believe that a Bishop putting his hands on my head makes not an iota of difference to the ontological reality of God within me. I have had to work my ecclesiastical socks off to be able to maintain wholesome relationships with my brothers and sisters of other parts of the Christian communion. And so I come barefoot to this ecumenical table, saying 'this is who I am before God'. I believe that until we all take off our shoes before the mysterious God of love, then the church is sunk.

We are intended, I believe, to be knit together in the creative possibilities of God. We are fearfully and wonderfully made. There is nowhere we can flee from God's presence, we are known through and through. So let's stop crossing our fingers when we make vows and start living openly in the light of the God who sees us anyway. We cannot go on playing one denomination off against the other for pastoral convenience, the outfall is too great. To find our integrity within the community that is the Trinity is not to become identical Christians, but to realize that we only have the strength to carry the load, when we are united in purpose and mutual respect.

Secondly, I want to suggest that healing is not about saying things but about listening. The churches have pontificated for far too long about unity. What they have failed to do is open up the safe places to listen to human experience, its hurts and struggles, and to be transformed by it. Yes, we must be attentive to the hermeneutic of Scripture, tradition and reason, but we must not do so at the expense of human experience. And that is all experience, not just the acceptable bits. If the faith is a living thing, then it will be shaped and moulded by the experiences of the people that are living it out. And how will we know what these experiences are if we are not prepared to sit and listen? What we will hear will be mightily troubling. You only have to go to a gathering of LGBT Christians or abuse survivors to know that experience challenges dogma to the core. But these prophetic communities, full of individuals who have clung onto faith through thick and thin, have insights into what makes a new community, insights that the church ignores at its peril.

Listening is no easy task, it is an intentional calling, yet I believe more and more that it is the mission of the church. We have been far too intent on being busy, on running around, on calling meetings or having campaigns, and we have failed to attend to the voiceless, the confused and the lost. Not only are these people the focus of the gospel, they are at the heart of what will bring about a new creation. Ecumenism is not neat, it is not about tying the bow on a signed and sealed legal document, but rather it is the result of a passion for the earth and the people of the earth for which we are prepared to give our lives. We must listen, and continue to listen, and let what we hear seep into our souls so that, together, we rise up to transform the world.

And all this because God listens to us, not just as individuals but also as movements and communities. God attends to the heart of the matter, and if we can do the same then we are part of the missio dei, the longing of God for the integrity of creation.

And lastly I want to suggest that healing comes about not by forgetting things, but about remembering differently. If I think of my own skirmishes with life and faith, then I can see that there have been many occasions when things have gone horribly wrong. But throughout all of that there has been a sense of the God of love having hold of me by the collar. Reminding myself that I am, and always have been, part of God's story, enables a different kind of remembering. A remembering that is not all remorse or anger, but rather is fired up with changing what happens next. It is annoying to be tripped up by memories and can cause me to be a pain in the neck when I see things differently from others. But in the remembering, there is also a putting back together of those things that were shattered by ridiculous demands of protocol or dogma. I am a Methodist, I will always have nonconformist blood, I make no apology for that. I have been blessed and challenged by the Catholics, the Anglicans and all the others who have brought a wealth of spirituality and wisdom along with the things that have dismembered my sense of being. For this I will continually be thankful to God.

Healing is not about being fixed, it is about finding integrity and insight amongst people who are different from ourselves. It is not about blind forgiveness, but more about the passion to find a better way. It is not so much about a consistent life journey as about finding God in the cracks, and amongst the struggling who carry the pain of exclusion and loss.

I happened to be at a felt-making workshop the other day. The challenge was to make a felt hat by forming it on a ball. When I took mine off the mould I decided it wasn't a hat at all, but more like a bowl! When I think about those Methodist churchgoers of my childhood in their felt hats, I wish now that they had taken them off and used them as bowls. Imagine all the wisdom and insights we could have gathered if we had turned all those hats upside down, the Catholic hats, the Anglican hats, even the Strict and Particular Baptist hats, and collected the pearls of great price that are the inheritance of the searching, digging, foraging people of God!

VI The Prayer of Unity

18 Unity and Prayer

Kathryn Turner and Catherine McElhinney

Before embarking on this chapter, it might be a useful exercise to look back over ecumenical services you have attended in the past. The chances are that some will have been excellent – some boring – others confusing – a few positively embarrassing – and that you sang, probably with a fair degree of predictability, 'Bind us together'. Some services could have been seen almost as a showcase of a denomination's rich traditions, which had the advantage of being offered by people who were able leaders but who may well have unwittingly excluded others. Some services may have been filled with explanations of what we are going to do and why, which allowed people to be involved but focused more on practicalities than prayer. And yet, having experienced the highs and the lows, Christians have still felt called to come together to pray in response to Christ's call that we be one.

As we look back at our efforts we need to bear in mind how relatively new it is for Christians from different denominations to come together to pray. Kathryn, for example, can remember that, for the Diamond Jubilee of the Girl Guides, simultaneous services took place at Westminster Abbey and Westminster Cathedral: in 1970, it did not seem to occur to anyone that a joint service might be possible. Catherine recalls her mother's fear of excommunication if she went into a church that was not Catholic – even for a wedding! It highlights God's power at work that within the next generation, we would be creating liturgies that have been used around the world by Christians of all denominations. Before looking at our work as Wellspring (www.wellsprings.org.uk), we will explore some of the developments in shared worship amongst Christians over recent years.

One of the first and most startling realizations as Christians came together was probably that 'not everyone prays like us'! Over the centuries, the different denominations developed ways of praying that fed their people – some very focused on the Word – others on song – others on sacrament and ritual – some with space for silence – others with emphasis on words and preaching. Some denominations, Roman Catholics in particular, had services that were carefully prescribed and so were very similar whichever church someone went into; others were more flexible and reflected the styles of minister and congregation. When Christians from such varied traditions came together to pray, the differences were highlighted – how could our desire to find unity in prayer be expressed amidst such diversity?

From the earliest days of praying together, there has been a keen awareness of what we cannot do together. The differing theologies of what Jesus intended at the Last Supper has meant that shared communion is not possible and so eucharistic services, though central to the catholic traditions, are problematic in ecumenical settings. There is now greater sensitivity at the time of communion with an almost standard invitation to those who cannot receive to come forward for a blessing: a sign, perhaps, of the late Cardinal Hume's suggestion at the 1987 Swanwick Conference that we are in a real but, as yet, incomplete communion. Where a highly significant Mass is celebrated, for a major anniversary, for example, there are also attempts to include people from other denominations in such roles as reading and leading intercessions. This sometimes raises the eyebrows of liturgical purists but indicates a desire at grassroots level to include fellow-Christians in the liturgical dimension of the celebration as much as in the social.

An interesting attempt to make the best of the divisions of Christians concerning the Eucharist is to be found in Taizé. The Community there is internationally known for its work in reconciliation which began during the Second World War with the vision of Br Roger Schutz and a small group of like-minded men. The founding brothers were, in the main, from Protestant traditions but sought to establish a monastic way of life combining prayer, study and work. From its earliest years, young people have been drawn to the Community, and today thousands of them spend a week or more creating a community such as exists nowhere else. The brothers deliberately set out to bring together people from different backgrounds and provide a place where they can meet, converse, work and, crucially, pray together. The prayer centres on the three prayer times of the Community – morning, lunchtime and evening. The brothers do not propose intercommunion as such, but try to respect the rules of the different Churches. A Catholic Mass is celebrated every Sunday morning in the main church; there is also an early morning celebration daily in a smaller chapel. Every day at the Morning Prayer, there is the opportunity to receive communion, and the distribution is done in the same way as at the Sunday Mass with hosts that have been consecrated at the early-morning celebration. This communion is distributed by brothers of the Community; and at the same time, in a certain part of the church, holy communion from the Lord's Supper is offered (distributed by young lay people) for those from the Reformation Churches who wish to receive it. There is also a third option, proposed for 'those who do not feel ready to receive the presence of Christ in the Eucharist, those who are not baptized, little children, those who for different reasons do not receive communion'. At communion time, in various parts of the Church young people stand offering bread that has been blessed with a formula recalling Christ's blessing of the bread at the feeding of the five thousand. The communion is accompanied by the singing of one of the Taizé chants and the atmosphere is one of deepening unity. The Orthodox liturgy is also celebrated occasionally, when an Orthodox priest is present.

Community prayer in Taizé originally centred on the psalms in French. As the numbers of people from an increasing range of countries grew, the Community responded by taking the risk of selecting short phrases from psalms or spiritual writings and setting them to music. As well as French and Latin, songs emerged in other European languages. This continues to this day with songs produced in Eastern European languages, reflecting increasing numbers from those countries but also songs in Swahili, Malayalam and Chinese. The style is well known, but is devised so that the prayer becomes like a mantra and the words go deep into the soul – the Word making its home in the person who prays. It is proof of Augustine's dictum that those who sing pray twice as, after stumbling over the words of chants in foreign languages, a person finds they become embedded in the heart and mind and often recognizable months or even years later.

The element of prayer most frequently commented on by visitors to Taizé is the silence. Each prayer session has, at its heart, a period of silence roughly seven to ten minutes long. At the start of the week, many people feel uncomfortable with such an extended time but, usually, by the end of the week, it has become the most valued part of the prayer. While there are enormous lessons to be learned in struggling to communicate with people who have no common tongue – to work alongside them – and to sing prayers in their language – there is something very powerful in being in silence with several thousand other people, aware that the Spirit is communicating with each individual and that all are united in that experience.

The experience of praying in Taizé was profound and developed for us an appreciation of what was possible when praying with people of other traditions, or none. Taizé-style services are quite popular and do bring people together in prayer but it can be hard to convey fully the atmosphere of contemplative stillness of Taizé itself. Their reflective style does not always provide a framework in which common reasons for ecumenical prayer can be set. People coming together for events such as a town Carnival Service or other civil services would probably expect something more interactive or even entertaining!

This highlights another important aspect of ecumenical services. Most services in the churches of the various denominations will be attended by regular worshippers and visitors accompanying family and friends. By contrast, those who come to ecumenical services will often be made up of regular worshippers but also, on occasion, people who are there because they have to be (the local mayor and Carnival Queen, for example). Others may come because the service is touching a chord – for example, at a time of crisis or tragedy. Still others may come at certain seasons, such as Christmas or Easter, where something deep within them tells them that it is a time to go to church. This offers a challenge to those preparing the worship – particularly when some of our 'churchy' language is all but incomprehensible to those who may be joining us: it is not unknown for people to come having only the vaguest idea of who Jesus is, other than the baby they remember from school Nativity plays. Like Jesus, Paul and missionaries throughout the ages, we may have to lay aside our assumptions about what people know of the Christian faith and explore ways of enabling a diverse range of people to pray and worship a God who they are not sure they believe in.

Although many Christians had long been praying together during the Week of Prayer for Christian Unity and Women's World Day of Prayer, the 1980s saw many churches forming local covenants and exploring ways of praying together. Around that time, the Wild Goose Worship Group was formed by members of the Iona Community who provided – and continue to provide – resources for common worship. These are characterized by language that is both poetic but also accessible to people from many different backgrounds – giving people words through which they can pray. They acknowledge the painful realities of people's lives and the need for a spirituality that is both engaged and earthed in human experience – reflective of the incarnation ... Because Jesus became human, all human experience is valid in prayer – not just the comfortable or holy bits. This led to many challenges when liturgies were prepared for protests against nuclear submarines at Faslane and naming the economic structures that led to poverty. For some this seemed shocking but many of the words and images were drawn directly from Scripture and for many people, this juxtaposition of the Word of God with the situations they were in was startling and revelatory. Faith was speaking to life, a faith that did not fear 'to face the world around.'[1] Shared human experience crossed denominational boundaries; people encountered the Christ who makes of his friends a 'Touching Place'[2] for the broken and marginalized. The Wild Goose books and music cover the range of the year's times and seasons as well as some dedicated to particular themes such as *When Grief is Raw* – a book of songs for times of sorrow and bereavement.

The Wild Goose Worship Group highlighted one particular area in which Christians often come together in prayer – that of social concern and justice and peace. As Christians work more closely together in supporting people in the developing world, or more locally in initiatives such as Street Pastors, ways of praying about these together become ever more significant. We are not doing these things purely out of altruism but because of a gospel imperative and it is important that they are seen to be rooted in prayer, which, of course, brings added power to our action. Where, for example, the Street Pastor initiative has been established, Prayer Pastors play that crucial role of praying for them and for the people they will meet which many of those walking the streets on Friday and Saturday evenings will attest to having been a source of strength and support.

Devising worship and prayer that can be shared ecumenically can still be problematic. Although there are many traditional prayers that can be used, one significant disadvantage in ecumenical services is that they are often led by just one person. Obviously, there are times when a prayer spoken by an individual on behalf of others is appropriate but, where people from different denominations have come together, it can be preferable to include the gifts of others in leading prayers or proclaiming the Word of God. This also gives visible witness to the fact that all the churches are making a vital contribution to the service and are not there simply as observers. Another way of including others is the use of responses which allow everyone to become involved. In practical terms, all of this highlights the need for preparation. While the Holy Spirit often works in spontaneity, good planning also has its part to play, particularly for people who do not normally worship together. It can be as simple as distributing reading parts to the various churches and asking them to nominate a reader or arranging a meeting to pray through the service in advance and to decide who will do what. This also ensures that, during the service itself, the prayer is allowed to flow with few hiatuses as people try to work out what comes next!

Meeting beforehand can address another issue that can beset ecumenical services – music! Just as we discover that 'not everyone prays like us', we often discover that we are literally 'not singing from the same hymn sheet'. While there is plenty of music we have in common, it is very easy to make the mistaken assumption that 'everyone will know this' simply because it is familiar to 'us'. Meeting beforehand or circulating suggestions via email can help to avoid situations where few know the hymns and we are faced with the rather embarrassing situation of one voice singing what should be a rousing chorus from everyone! The Iona community has several hymns set to well-known folk tunes and these enable people to participate because the melodies are familiar even if not from Church! A useful book called *Common Ground* (published by St Andrews Press) brings together a collection of words and music which are both accessible and biblically based.

Finding ways to pray and to meet God in the worship of Taizé and Wild Goose Worship brought a new dimension to our own personal prayer. It enabled us to engage deeply with real things and offered a way to pray with others in our own community that was informal and differed from the more traditional forms of Catholic prayer available to lay people. We encountered the God of the psalms – the God who is big enough to contain anger, grief and pain as well as joy in Creation, with a freshness of expression for the contemporary world. Although the psalms were part of the Prayer of the Church, they were not part of the prayer-book of the ordinary Catholic until comparatively recently.

In our first efforts, we made considerable use of the music and prayer resources of both Taizé and Wild Goose Worship Group but increasingly found ourselves writing our own material for a regular Sunday evening prayer in the parish and for other groups. As our resources grew, we wondered if they might be of use to others outside our own community. Our parish priest at the time was very supportive of what we were creating and when it was our church's turn to lead a Churches Together service, recognized that what we were doing would readily lend itself to use in an ecumenical setting. One of the first offerings was for a One World Week service in 1996 with a theme of 'Bringing the Edges Together'. It was interesting that, to illustrate the theme, we were able to use the breaking of bread in a way that united us in concern for the broken body of Christ in the world without causing confusion about a Eucharistic dimension.

Here, for example, are the reflections for the 'edges' facing our own area at the time:

Reader 1 We break the bread of ....(name of town/city):
our young people living on a knife-edge
of unemployment
and exploitation by drug dealers;
our old folk living in fear
of crime and violence;
Christians afraid of our voices.

Reader 2 We break the bread of ....:
people living on the leading-edge of the care of the user,

> the care of the weak and the frail;
> people living the prophecy of the Kingdom
> the life of the good neighbour;
> people prepared to risk insult and misunderstanding
> in following their Lord.

Different breads to represent the different countries and continents were made (or bought!) by people from the various denominations and became part of an agape meal which concluded with a commitment to go and live out the concern – to work together to be those on the leading edges.

By way of contrast, we were later asked to devise a Carnival Service – without any clear idea as to what this should include. We did know that the funfair on the recreation ground outside the church would not be in full swing at the time but thought that it could somehow be included. Reflecting on what struck us about Carnival Week in the town we came up with the funfair – the dressing-up competitions for the children and window displays in the shops all speaking of colour and fun. This led to the idea of rainbows and the realization that humans often accept the drab and mundane despite having been given the eyes to see more – and to savour it. The idea of creating a rainbow of different coloured net stretched between the balconies of the church was therefore obvious, if not easy to execute! The service opened with responses celebrating the gift of creation and went into the story of what happened shortly afterwards …

Reader In the beginning God saw all that was made
Reader And indeed it was very good
Reader And God wanted to share it all with human beings
Reader And indeed …
Readers God had a problem!
Reader Human beings stopped gazing in wonder –
and forgot to see God in the majesty of Creation
Reader They stopped seeing a thousand shades of green
Reader and blue
Reader and yellow
Reader and red …
Reader and became content with drabness.
Readers God's beloved human creatures lost the plot!

Reader And God looked at his beloved human creatures and wondered:

God What was I thinking of?
My beloved people have eyes – but they do not see.
My beloved people have ears – but they do not hear.
Could I have been so mistaken?

Reader And God was sad because his dream for humanity seemed just to be fading into a puff of grey cloud ...
Reader and the grey cloud seemed to be getting larger ...
Reader and larger
Reader as it filled with God's tears
Readers And God realized what was going to happen!

God If all my tears fall, there's going to be a flood!
I must warn my people!

After recounting the story of Noah in a fairly light-hearted way, the service took people through some of the words from the prophets which spoke of the love of God for humanity, culminating in the gift of his Son. Although few people in the congregation could have put it into words themselves, they had explored the great themes of Creation, Incarnation and Redemption and seen them as expressive of God's love for humanity. For many, the abiding memory of the service would probably have been the Carnival Court and the Mayor leading the congregation out to the funfair where they released coloured balloons. However, the Mayor returned afterwards to say that it had been the most inclusive and meaningful service he had attended in his role.

The theme of the prophets and the story of God's love also appear in one of the most popular of our online liturgies: 'Passing on the Light'. With the approach of the new millennium in Advent 1999, Catherine's school wanted something very special to mark this momentous event. There did not seem to be anything ready-made that quite did the job so we set ourselves the task of creating something that would actively involve over 100 children and their families. The breakdown of a coach on a Christmas shopping trip to Lille offered an unlooked-for window of opportunity to give thought to this! Clackett's Lane service station on the M25 may not know it but it has to be acknowledged as the place where a liturgy was born that has now been used in South Africa, several American States and Australia – as well as in the UK and Ireland. The 'Passing on of Light' refers to the whole of salvation history as expressed in the lighting of one candle from another as the names of some of those entrusted with God's promise were announced – leading to the heart of the service:

Reader 1 Then an angel appeared to Mary
and passed a new light to her …
Creation held its breath

Reader 2 And an angel appeared in a dream to Joseph
and passed a new light to him …
Creation held its breath …

Reader 3 And in the dark of a stable in the town of Bethlehem
a new light was given to the world:
the one who was there in the beginning came into the world
in him was life – and the life was the light of peoples.
The Word became flesh and lived among us.

The light continued to pass from generation by generation to our own with a candle given to everyone present and the challenge was laid before the children and their families – who would now pass on the light if we did not? Many carried their lit candles out into the local streets with the words of 'Christ be our Light' ringing in their ears. The service was simple and inclusive and has proved to be adaptable to other settings and sizes of congregation.

The use of ritual and symbol has been a hallmark of the liturgies Wellspring has produced. For some in the reformed traditions, these can be viewed with some suspicion but most people understand that there are things that cannot be expressed in words. Lighting a candle is an almost universal symbol for the conquest of light over the dark. During a Good Friday service leading to the Walk of Witness, over 150 Christians willingly lit a candle to place at the foot of a cross to witness to their faith that through the Cross comes resurrection and hope for the world. It was for another Good Friday morning service that we decided to draw on a Catholic tradition – the Stations of the Cross. It seemed important to explain the background to the Way of the Cross as being a way that people used to express their desire to share that last journey of Jesus with him at a time when travel to Jerusalem was impossible for the vast majority of people. The service took the form of a series of guided reflections using paintings of the Stations as portrayed by great artists. We acknowledged that some had no scriptural basis but were rooted in Catholic tradition and expressed something of the reality of what must have happened or we wish would have happened. For example, for the Station illustrating Veronica wiping the face of Jesus, would we not wish that someone would have done so in the face of such suffering? At the end, a Baptist came to us and spoke of his wonder that, as the stations unfolded, the skies outside had grown steadily darker until the time came for the Walk of Witness when the sun came out – he had been taken into the account of Jesus' Passion in a way that was entirely new and, in a way, more real.

Easter and Christmas often attract more people than usual to churches and this gives an opportunity to reach out and engage them. One service that has spoken particularly to people from different Christian traditions, even those with the most tenuous of links, is the Blue Christmas service. The idea originated in the USA as a way of offering something to people for whom Christmas was not a season of peace or joy because of bereavement or loss. In the Wellspring Blue Christmas service, we draw on shared traditions such as the Advent Wreath and Nativity story and allow people to name the pain they suffer but also, hopefully, offer them hope and strength to face the festivities. The service begins with the lighting of the Advent Wreath – and includes the following:

Reader 1 We light our third candle
recalling nights of watching and waiting –
sleepless – anxious
when dawn seemed to ebb further from the horizon
and hope seemed forlorn.

Reader 2 Let it speak to us of the sureness of morning –
of the passing of darkness

of suffering –
and the promise of an eternal sunrise
dawning for those we have loved and lost
and dawning too for us –
though we may yet be in that darkest hour before the dawn.

The ritual suggested is very simple – the names of loved ones or the situation causing pain are written on strips of cloth. These are then brought together to form a sort of blanket on which the Christ-child is laid. The love of God expressed in the Incarnation is experienced with no need for explanation.

Although there are things that separate Christians, there is far more that is shared. By being confident about our own traditions and respectful of others, it is possible to devise services that are inclusive. Perhaps even more importantly, by seeking to welcome each other, we can also open the door to the stranger. To the words of the Old English Rune of Hospitality

I met a stranger yest'-er'en.
I put food in the eating place,
drink in the drinking place,
music in the listening place,
we might add ...
  and prayer in praying space
in the hope that ...
... in the name of the Triune,
the stranger will bless us and our churches.
...
for often, often, often goes
the Christ in the stranger's guise.

19 'For God's sake – get on with it'

Mary Tanner

(*Based on a sermon preached in Bradford Cathedral, Week of Prayer for Christian Unity, 2010*)

Here we are once more at the beginning of the Week of Prayer for Christian Unity. It all began in 1908, when an American, Paul Watson, suggested keeping an octave of prayer for the re-union of Christendom between the Feast of St Peter on 18 January and the Feast of St Paul on 25 January. Christians together all over the world have kept this week ever since.

You might well ask – 'Where has all this praying year by year got us?' That's the question that the Archbishop of Canterbury asked at the time of the centenary of the Week of Prayer. If an Archbishop can ask that, it's not surprising if we do too. It's so easy, isn't it, to forget just how far we have come? So much has happened that the pioneers of Christian unity, those in the mission field, could hardly have begun to imagine. It's so easy for us to take for granted what has been accomplished by God's grace.

Who would have believed that a Pope would take off his episcopal ring and put it on the finger of an Archbishop of Canterbury, as Pope Paul VI did to Archbishop Michael Ramsey when the Archbishop visited Rome in 1967? Who would have thought a century ago that Lutherans and Roman Catholics would have reached agreement on the doctrine of justification which lay at the heart of the Reformation divide, enabling them to move beyond the condemnations they each made of the other? Who would have thought that many churches – Pentecostal, Roman Catholic, Orthodox, Methodist, Reformed, Anglican – could have reached such convergences in understanding baptism, eucharist and ministry as is expressed in what is surely the most important ecumenical document of the twentieth century – *Baptism, Eucharist and Ministry?* Who would have thought that 349 churches from many different cultural contexts would have acted together for justice and peace in a Decade to Overcome Violence, or that Christians from different traditions would act together as ecumenical accompaniers in areas of tension and violence around the world? Who would have thought that a Pope would invite Christians of other traditions to help him think about his ministry in the service of unity, as Pope John Paul II did in his Encyclical Letter, *Ut Unum Sint?* Who would have thought that Christians in this country would act together in so many places – in Cockermouth to help those whose homes were flooded; in Bradford to care for the homeless and asylum seekers; in Stamford to fill in the gaps together in caring for the elderly?

Who would have thought that new, formally celebrated relationships between churches would have changed the ecclesial map in Europe, and in other parts of the world: the Leuenberg Agreement, establishing pulpit and altar fellowship between Lutherans, Reformed and Methodists; the Meissen Agreement between Anglicans in Britain and Ireland and the Evangelical Church in Germany; the Reuilly Agreement between the French Lutheran and Protestant churches and Anglicans; the Porvoo Agreement bringing Anglicans and Nordic and Baltic Lutheran churches into communion? All these agreements are motivated by a desire to be one and a determination to share more effectively in mission and ministry. Whether we recognize it or not, we do live 'beyond the limits of the landscape' that those who celebrated the Week of Prayer for Christian Unity a century ago would have dared to imagine possible.

I could go on and on with stories of positive signs of changed relations that have taken place over the last 100 years. These are the fruits of fervent prayer and the conviction of many Christians that God desires us to be one and to be open to receive the gifts of the Holy Spirit through the life and witness of others. We have come out of our denominational corners. We have come to understand the causes of our divisions better, we do act together in serving local communities, we do often witness together for peace and justice – or at least we do when we remember that it is more effective together. In a world where we are more and more aware of globalization, with instant communication as a result of the internet, facebook, and twitter, we are beginning to understand the necessity of being Christians together, not just in the very local situations, or even national situations, but of being together in facing the economic and social challenges in our interconnected world. We are growing in awareness of a wider sense of belonging and the relation of the local and universal dimensions of the Church's life.

We have learned together insights about unity that were hardly in the conversation a century ago. Unity is not about knocking divided churches together in some sort of ecumenical joinery, or some sort of life of the lowest common denominator. We could all come together, sign innumerable declarations and covenants, but without a deep and lasting transformation we should not be united in the way Christ desires. We have, through the ecumenical movement, thank God, learnt something of what it means that we must be renewed into unity, renewed in the deepest fabric of our life together, renewed in the human community of the Church. We have not only to overcome our doctrinal differences but together overcome those things that are causes of deep divisions in the life of the Church – the division between women and men, between those of different cultures, between rich and poor, between those who have power and influence and those who have none.

We have come a long way in an ecumenical century. Perhaps this is far enough. Perhaps it's time to put an end to this annual Week of Prayer for Christian Unity. I know that's what many of my friends think. They tell me that it's enough to be polite to one another and to cooperate when it suits us. Our energies ought to be put to mission and evangelism and not into unity. To spend time on unity is to waste resources, human and financial.

If you are tempted to think that then remember what St Paul wrote in I Corinthians – there is one Body – with a rich diversity of gifts, yes, of course – but one Body. Ask yourselves – is that what the world sees when it looks at us? Is that what it is like for me when I am unable to receive the sacrament of the Lord's Table with the Roman Catholic members of my own family, or when we can't even stay together in our own Anglican family and work through our differences over issues of sexuality, or the consecration of women as bishops, but seem to say so easily, 'I have no need of you – I will go it alone'? Are we really faithful to the prayer of Jesus? Do we offer to the world a model of life together where we can live together with, and through, our differences really believing that we shall be led into all truth?

The most obvious outward signs of our continuing failure to make visible the unity God wills is the scandal that even when we offer hospitality to one another and receive from one another bread and wine, there is no full eucharistic communion which then extends into a united life, the eucharist after the eucharist. There is no single, interchangeable ministry that leads us in mission together, there are no common structures of communication and mutual accountability which enable us to wrestle and respond together to the problems of today's world – moral, ethical, economic problems. Instead, our continuing divisions mean that we squander precious resources of manpower, buildings and money. Our witness in the world is weakened. And worst of all, by our continuing divisions, we fail to witness credibly to the God who, in Christ, broke down all dividing walls and reconciled all in one Body on the Cross. It is hard to convince the world of the Christian message of reconciliation offered to all in, and through, Christ if we deny it by the way we go on living in separation, not sharing our insights and our gifts, not being ready to receive gifts from others, not discovering that rich diversity of which St Paul speaks in Corinthians. Unity is not uniformity.

If we have understood the message of Paul in Corinthians about the one Body, or been drawn into the High Priestly Prayer of Jesus, then how can we give up on the search for Christian unity, how can we fail to pray with Jesus, in the power of the Spirit, to the Father – 'May we all be one ...'?

When I get despondent – all those tough theological conversations, all those tedious meetings; when I'm unsettled by the jibes of friends – you are wasting your time and wasting valuable resources, you are chasing after some will o'the wisp; when I am tempted to think – all this prayer and still we are not one – it's then that I remember a particular moment that was for me a moment of disclosure, a moment of re-affirmation that there is no other way than the way of seeking the unity for which Christ prayed, for God's sake and the world's sake.

I was staying in a very large Roman Catholic Seminary, built when Ireland had many, many priestly vocations. Numerous doors led off wide, long corridors, each door looked the same as the next. In one room a group of about twenty theologians from different countries and different churches were meeting to prepare a World Conference on the unity of the Church. An excitable French Canadian Roman Catholic theologian was in full flight explaining his vision of Church unity. Everyone was concentrating on the picture he was painting. The door opened and in shuffled a dishevelled, unshaven man. The speaker continued without seeming to notice the stranger. The man sat down in an empty chair in the circle. He listened intently. Who was this strange man? Perhaps someone new to our group, from an Eastern European country, now able to travel as the Wall had just come down. Perhaps his flight had been delayed or was suffering from jet lag. When the speaker finished talking all eyes were on the stranger. No one dared break the silence. It was the dishevelled stranger who broke the silence. He barked, 'Do you know what's happening out there', he pointed to the window. 'People get drunk, they take drugs, they fight in denominational gangs, they shoot to kill, and family is against family'. The stranger went on, 'He came to bring unity and peace. For God's sake get on with it'. The stranger got up and shuffled out of the room.

We asked at the reception desk who the man was, how did he know we were meeting in that room at that time? But no one could tell us. They hadn't seen anyone come in or go out. For us our stranger was a messenger. Get on with it – get on with working for unity, that was what he, Jesus, wanted, what he Jesus died for, and that is what the world with all its brokenness and division, desperately needs, the sign that a better way of living together is possible, a way of living as one reconciled people, concerned for the needs of others, a way of unity.

'Get on with it for Christ's sake and for the world's sake' – for Gaza, for Iraq, for Afghanistan, for Zimbabwe, for Sudan, for Dafur, for Haiti, for all the broken places and all the broken people that need the message of reconciliation that we have been entrusted with. 'Get on with it, for Christ's sake and the world's sake'. Go on praying for unity as Jesus did. Get on with it, recognize Christ in one another, offer your gifts to one another and be open to receive gifts from the other, and discover that the ecumenical agenda is an 'agenda for joy'. Go on working for unity. This is what Jesus died for – the one Body made visible and audible, attentive and active – so that the world, through us, might believe. And go on praying:

> O God, holy and eternal Trinity,
> We pray for your Church in all the world.

Sanctify its life; renew its worship;
empower its witness; heal its divisions;
make visible its unity.
Lead us, with all our brothers and sisters,
towards communion in faith, life and witness
so that, united in one body by the one Spirit,
we may together witness to the perfect unity of your love.
Amen

A prayer written for the Fifth World Conference on Faith and Order, 1993, Santiago de Compostela, Spain, with its theme –'Towards *koiononia* (communion) in faith, life and witness'.

Notes

Ecumenism: an Overview *Clive Barrett*

1 GS Misc. 191, May 1984. *The Consultative Committee for Local Ecumenical Projects in England: A Pattern for Local Ecumenism*, A2.
2 A product of the Nottingham Faith and Order Conference, 1964; by 1984 these were known as Local Ecumenical Projects (LEPs), today's Local Ecumenical Partnerships.
3 For the full story of the Swanwick Declaration, see David Cornick's comprehensive history in this volume.
4 It is also the 350th anniversary of the 'Great Ejection' – see Val Morrison's introduction to this volume – and the 400th anniversary of the first Baptist Church in Spitalfields, London.
5 See Liz Smith's comments on the formational character of ecumenical engagement.
6 Charta Oecumenica, I.1
7 Charta Oecumenica, III.8
8 Charta Oecumenica, III.8
9 Essentially a Gandhian concept, 'Peace is the Way' is attributed to A J. Muste, *New York Times*, 16 November 1967.

Chistian Unity in Scripture *Neil Richardson*

1 1 and 2 Timothy and Titus (the 'Pastoral' Epistles) are thought by many scholars to be largely the work of a later interpreter of Paul. Scholars are more divided about the authorship of Ephesians, Colossians and 2 Thessalonians. There is a similar lack of agreement about whether Peter was the author of 1 Peter, but there are few advocates for the Petrine authorship of 2 Peter.
2 James 1:1 and 2:1 are the only references in James to 'Jesus Christ', though numerous echoes of Jesus' teaching occur in this letter.
3 There is a difference of emphasis, rather than contradiction between, e.g. Galatians 2:11–21 and James 2:14–26.

4 Galatians 2:1–11 and Acts 15:1–33 are not easily matched. On this see the later discussion in section III.
5 See especially J. D. G. Dunn *Unity and Diversity in the New Testament* (London, SCM, 1977).
6 R. Brown's *The Community of the Beloved Disciple* (New York, Paulist Press, 1979) may be somewhat speculative, but draws attention to a possible ecclesial history behind the relationship between Simon Peter and 'the disciple whom Jesus loved' in John's Gospel.
7 I owe this phrase to C. K. Barrett, who uses it to describe the author's use of the Old Testament in John's Gospel.
8 See my *John For Today* (London, SCM, 2010), pp. 112–13 and 116.
9 On John's distinctive 'voice', see, for example, P. Duke, *Irony in the Fourth Gospel* (Atlanta, John Knox 1985), and, more critically, A. Reinhartz, *Befriending the Beloved Disciple: a Jewish Reading of the Gospel of John* (New York, Continuum, 2001).
10 The *consensus fidelium* played an important role in the formation of the New Testament canon.
11 'Reconciliation' language occurs largely in Pauline writings: Romans 5:10–11, 11:15, 2 Cor. 5:18–20 (cf. 1 Cor. 7:11), Eph. 2:16 and Col. 1:20, 22; otherwise only at Matthew 5:24.
12 See John T. Fitzgerald, 'Paul and Paradigm Shifts: Reconciliation and its Linkage Group' in *Paul Beyond the Judaism/Hellenism Divide* (Louisville, Westminster John Knox Press, 2001) ed. Troels Engberg Pedersen (pp. 241–62).
13 John 1:14, 3:16, 12:32, 1 Cor. 8:6, 2 Cor. 8:9, etc.
14 Quoted in Arland J. Hultgren's *Paul's Letter to the Romans. A Commentary* (Grand Rapids MI, Eerdmans, 2011), p. 232.
15 K. Barth, *Church Dogmatics* II.1 (Edinburgh, T. & T. Clark, 1957) p. 353.
16 Only at Acts 11:26, 26:28 and 1 Peter 4:16.
17 J. D. G. Dunn *Did the First Christians Worship Jesus? The New Testament Evidence* (London, SPCK, 2010), p. 47. See now also Gary M. Burge's important discussion of theological geography in *Jesus and the Land* (London, SPCK, 2010).
18 In Paul's writings, 'in Christ' tends to denote Christian identity and roots, 'in the Spirit' is usually contrasted with life 'in the flesh' or 'under the law', while 'in the Lord' normally occurs in the context of ethical instruction.
19 See, for example, J. Lieu *The Gospel of Luke* (London, Epworth, 1997), p.141.
20 See *John For Today* (pp. 84–90).
21 So-called because the fundamental issue was whether Gentile converts to Christian faith should 'Judaize' (Gal. 2:14) – i.e., become practising Jews.
22 Scholars have long debated why Luke mentions the so-called 'Apostolic Decree (Acts 15:23–9), and Paul nowhere does.
23 This seems the majority view amongst commentators, even though 'Jew' and 'Gentile' are not specifically mentioned here.
24 N. Richardson, *Paul For Today* (London, Epworth, 2008), pp. 133–44.
25 On 'the weak' in Paul's letters, see (most recently) B. Longenecker, *Remember the Poor. Paul, Poverty and the Graeco-Roman World* (Grand Rapids MI, Eerdmans, 2010) who notes 'the wide semantic domain' of the word in Paul, including 'an economic dimension' (p. 143).

26 Such adaptability is rooted in the gospel itself: '... to live and act in solidarity with every kind of person in every kind of situation is to have a *share* in *the nature of the gospel'*, Anthony C. Thiselton, *The First Epistle to the Corinthians* (Grand Rapids MI, Eerdmans, 2000), p.707. I have italicized his translation of Paul's words. As Professor Morna Hooker has demonstrated, Paul does not refer here to the 'blessings' of the gospel, as so many translations imply. I am very grateful to Professor Morna Hooker and the Rev. Dr Brian Beck for their willingness to read an earlier draft of this chapter, and for their helpful comments on it.
27 'Each other' in the New Testament must be seen in the light of the gospel as indefinitely extendable.
28 The foundational mission, of course, is the Father's sending of the Son.
29 Ian M. Fraser, *The Fire Runs* (London, SCM, 1975), p.134. On 'politeness' versus honesty, Galatians 2:11–14 is worth noting; we have only Paul's side of the argument, but we are addressing ourselves to what is in Scripture, not what is missing from Scripture. And was the Jerusalem conference (Acts 15) as polite and statesmanlike as Luke makes it sound?
30 Rom. 1:8, 1 Cor. 1:4, etc.
31 I do not by that contrast imply an invidious comparison with contemporary Judaism.
32 Other occurrences of *koinonia* illustrate its 'vertical' and 'horizontal' dimensions: e.g., 'the *koinonia* of God's Son' (1 Cor. 1:9; cf. 10:16, 2 Cor.1:7, Philipp. 3:10 and 1 John 1:3, 6–7) and – simply – 'sharing' (e.g., Heb. 13:16) (if that is its meaning here).
33 Titus 2:9–10 and 1 Peter 2:18–22 are more one sided, with their instructions to slaves to be submissive.
34 There are a number of female names in Romans 16. On this see especially Peter Lampe, *From Paul to Valentinus: Christians at Rome in the First Two Centuries* (Minneapolis, Fortress, 2003).
35 *John For Today*, pp. 63–8.
36 T. Merton, *Contemplation in a World of Action* (London, Unwin Paperbacks, 1980) pp. 144–5.
37 The obverse of this saying – Matthew 12:30, Luke 11:23 – complements rather than contradicts the saying.
38 Outgoing grace suggests that inter faith encounters are an integral part of Christian ecumenism. 'Christianity will never realize its full stature as a genuine Catholicism, that is, as the universal religion of mankind, until it has incorporated into itself all that is valid and true in all the different religious traditions', Bede Griffiths, *The Golden String. An Autobiography* (latest edition, London, Medio Media, 2003), p. 151.
39 The sequel to this third story is the telling contrast between the disciples and blind Bartimaeus, who follows Jesus 'in the Way' (Mark 10:52; compare, perhaps, Acts 9:2, 19:23 and 24:22).
40 Galatians 6:14; compare Romans 5:2–3 with 5:11.
41 I owe this analogy to Professor Morna Hooker of Cambridge.
42 Brian P. Flanagan, 'Communion Ecclesiology and Otherness: Resources for Inner-Denominational Otherness' in Gesa Elsbeth Theissen (ed.) *Ecumenical Ecclesiology* (Edinburgh, T. & T. Clark, 2009), pp. 143–60.

43 Philip Zeigler, 'Stumbling Upon Peter? The Question of the Church in Ecumenical Dialogue' in Murphy and Asprey, op. cit., pp. 25–6.

The Story of British Ecumenical Endeavour *David Cornick*

1 Quoted in Adrian Hastings, *A History of English Christianity 1920–1985* (London, Collins, 1986) p. 307
2 John Kent, *William Temple: Church, State and Society in England 1880–1950* (Cambridge, Cambridge University Press, 1992) pp. 15–16.
3 John Munsey Turner 'Temple, William' in N. Lossky *et al.* (eds) *Dictionary of the Ecumenical Movement* (Geneva, WCC, 1991) pp. 976–7.
4 Hastings, op. cit., p. 307.
5 David Thompson 'The unity of the church in twentieth-century England: pleasing dream of common calling?' in R.W. Swanson (ed.) *Unity and Diversity in the Church* (Oxford, Studies in Church History 32, 1996), pp. 507–31.
6 Resolution 9, www.lambethconference.org/resolutions/downloads/1920, accessed 13.10.11.
7 Hastings, op. cit., p. 466.
8 Hastings op. cit., p. 392 goes so far as to claim that its foundation in 1942 marks the true division between the pre- and post-war ecclesiastical worlds.
9 Hastings, op. cit., p. 394.
10 David Thompson, 'Ecumenism' in Hugh McLeod (ed.) *World Christianities c.1914–c.2000* (Cambridge, Cambridge University Press) Cambridge Histories Online, 03 Jan 2012, at p. 64.
11 Eliot's pamphlet was *Reunion by Destruction* (1943); for discussion about it, Barry Spurr *'Anglo-Catholic in religion': T. S. Eliot and Religion* (Cambridge, Lutterworth Press, 2010), pp. 165f; for an Indian perspective, J. Jayakiran Sebastian '… not hurrying on to a receding future, nor hankering after an imagined past': Edinburgh 1910, T. S. Eliot, postcolonial missiology, and our mission to God' *Journal of Postcolonial Theory and Theology,* vol. 2, issue 1.4 (March 2011).
12 Spurr, op. cit., pp. 74–5.
13 Hastings, op. cit., p. 469.
14 The judgement is Keith Robbins, op. cit., p. 351, a view partially echoed by Adrian Hastings, op. cit., p. 565.
15 Hastings, op. cit., p. 562.
16 Mary Reath, *Rome and Canterbury: the Elusive Search for Unity* (Plymouth, Rowan and Littlefield, 2007) p. 40, relying on William Purcell's *Fisher of Lambeth.*
17 Hastings, op. cit. p. 541.
18 'Church unity talks on a wide front' *The Times,* 8 September 1964, accessed via the digital archive.
19 'Taking the lid off the problems of church unity' *The Times,* 14 September 1964, accessed via the digital archive.
20 See the accounts in *The Times* and Adrian Hastings, *Oliver Tomkins: the Ecumenical Enterprise* (London, SPCK, 2001) pp. 127–8 for Moorman and his diary.
21 Hastings, *A History of English Christianity 1920–1985* (London, Collins, 1986), p. 392.

22 Keith Clements, 'Free Church, national church.' *Theology*, vol. CXIII, no. 876, Nov–Dec 2010, pp. 421–8, at p. 424.
23 Hugh McLeod *The Religious Crisis of the 1960s* (Oxford, Oxford University Press, 2007) pp. 38–9 and 62–7.
24 McLeod, op. cit., p. 261.
25 Hastings, *A History of English Christianity*, p. 610.
26 Mary Reath, op. cit., pp. 46f.
27 'Primate prays for miracle but unity plan fails', *The Times,* 4 May 1972, p. 4. Accessed Times online 14.11.11.
28 John Huxtable *As it Seemed to Me* (London, United Reformed Church, 1980) p. 70.
29 http://www.ctbi.org.uk/pdf_view.php?id=100 , Colin Davey, *The Story of the BCC*, accessed 18.11.11.
30 http://www.ewtn.com/library/papaldoc/jp2seven.htm (accessed 18.11.11), echoing *Unitatis Redintegratio*, n. 8.
31 Colin Davey and Martin Reardon, ' "Not Strangers but Pilgrims". The 1980s Inter-church Process: from Councils of Churches to Churches Together', paper given at Cambridge Centre for Ecumenical Studies in 2004. Available via the Methodist Church website at http://www.methodist.org.uk/downloads/ec-not-strangers-but-pilgrims.pdf.
32 Churches Together in England *Called to Be One* (London, CTE, 2002) pp. 9–10; John Reardon, *The Council of Churches for Britain and Ireland 1990–1999* (London, CTBI, 2000) pp. 1–2; see also the accounts in Anthony Howard, *Basil Hume: the Monk Cardinal* (London, Headline, 2005) pp. 202–9 and Adrian Hastings, *Robert Runcie* (London, Mowbray, 1991) pp. 124–37.
33 Howard, op. cit., p. 209.
34 Davey and Reardon, op. cit.
35 John Reardon, op. cit., sets out the difficulties with clarity and charity, pp. 3–10 and 35f.
36 *Called to Be One* (London, CTE, 1996 and 2002; 2002 edn cited) p. 62.
37 Robbins, op. cit., p. 469.
38 Joe Aldred 'The Holy Spirit and the Black Church' in Joe Aldred and Keno Ogbo (eds) *The Black Church in the Twenty-first Century* (London, Darton Longman and Todd, 2010) pp. 45–62, at pp. 46–7.
39 Interestingly those who show most interest in ecumenism belong to what Andrew Walker called the 'Restoration 2' stream which is associated with leaders such as Gerald Coates and Roger Forster, which was more open to wider culture than the 'Restoration 1' stream – see Andrew Walker, *Restoring the Kingdom: the Radical Christianity of the House Church Movement* (Guildford, Eagle, 1998).
40 Walter Kasper, *Harvesting the Fruits: Basic Aspects of Christian Faith in Ecumenical Dialogue* (London, Continuum, 2009), p. 8.
41 Paul Murray, 'Hands across the Tiber: ecumenism in the wake of Anglicanorum Coetibus,' *The Tablet,* 1 January 2011, pp. 14–15.
42 *An Anglican-Methodist Covenant* (London, Church House Publishing and the Methodist Publishing House, 2001) p. v.
43 Hooker and Young, op. cit., p. 93.
44 Hastings, *A History of English Christianity*, p. 629.

45 Colin Davey *The Story of the BCC: Notes* (on Churches Together in England website http://cte.churchinsight.com/Articles/110744/Churches_Together_in/About_us_Directories/Why_Unity_Matters/The_Route_We.aspx.
46 http://www.vatican.va/holy_father/john_paul_ii/encyclicals/documents/hf_jp-ii_enc_25051995_ut-unum-sint_en.html para 9. Accessed 23.05.10.
47 Sermon before the University of Cambridge, 6 November 2007, edited text available on www.bishopoflondon.org.

The Roots, Range and Reach of Receptive Ecumenism *Paul D. Murray and Andrea L. Murray*

1 See Paul D. Murray (ed.), *Receptive Ecumenism and the Call to Catholic Learning: Exploring a Way for Contemporary Ecumenism* (Oxford: Oxford University Press, 2008), particularly Murray, 'Receptive Ecumenism and Catholic Learning: Establishing the Agenda', pp. 5–25; and Murray, 'Receptive Ecumenism and Ecclesial Learning: Receiving Gifts for Our Needs', *Louvain Studies*, 33 (2008), 30–45; and Murray, 'ARCIC III: Recognising the Need for an Ecumenical Gear-Change', *One in Christ*, 45 (2011), 200–11. Also in preparation is Murray and Marcus J. Pound (eds), *Receptive Ecumenism and Ecclesial Learning: Learning to Be Church Together*, deriving from the 2nd Receptive Ecumenism International Conference in January 2009 at Ushaw College, Durham.
2 On something of the forerunners to Receptive Ecumenism, see Murray, 'Receptive Ecumenism and Catholic Learning', op. cit., pp. 12–14; and Murray, 'Receptive Ecumenism and Ecclesial Learning', op. cit., pp. 32, 38–41; also Murray, 'Expanding Catholicity through Ecumenicity in the Work of Yves Congar: *Ressourcement*, Receptive Ecumenism and Catholic Reform', *International Journal of Systematic Theology*, 13 (2011), 272–302.
3 See Murray (ed.), *Receptive Ecumenism and the Call to Catholic Learning.*
4 A related volume is in preparation: Paul D. Murray & Marcus J Pound (eds), *Receptive Ecumenism and Ecclesial Learning: Learning to Be Church Together*.
5 This phase of the work will issue in a range of publications, including a further major volume: Paul D. Murray & Marcus J. Pound (eds), *Receptive Ecumenism and the Local Church: An Exercise in Transformative Practical Ecclesiology*.
6 It is anticipated that this will issue in a fourth major volume: Paul D. Murray, Marcus J. Pound and Paul Lakeland (eds), *Receptive Ecumenism in International Perspective: Contextual Ecumenical Learning*.
7 See Murray, *Reason, Truth and Theology in Pragmatist Perspective* (Leuven: Peeters, 2004), particularly pp. 131–61 & 196–7.
8 Daniel W. Hardy, 'Acceptance Speech on the Occasion of Being Awarded an Honorary DD by General Theological Seminary, New York. Delivered in *Absentia* by Deborah Hardy Ford' (18th October 2007), in Daniel W. Hardy, with Deborah Hardy Ford, Peter Ochs and David F. Ford, *Wording a Radiance: Parting Conversations on God and the Church* (London, SCM, 2010), pp. 10–13 (p. 12). For further on SR, see David F. Ford and Chad Pecknold (eds), *The Promise of Scriptural Reasoning* (Oxford, Blackwell, 2006), pp. 185–207; also http://www.interfaith.cam.ac.uk//index.php; http://etext.virginia.edu/journals/ssr; http://www.scripturalreasoning.org; http://etext.lib.virginia.edu/journals/jsrforum.

9 See Murray, 'Preface', in Murray (ed.), *Receptive Ecumenism and the Call to Catholic Learning*, op. cit., ix–xv (xi–xv).
10 See Philip Knights and Andrea L. Murray, *Evangelization in England and Wales: a report to the Catholic bishops* (London, Catholic Communications Service, 2002).
11 Significantly, more so than any of the other international bilateral dialogue processes – even ARCIC II's identification of outstanding issues for one side with the other at the end of *The Gift of Authority* – the then most recent document emerging from the Methodist–Roman Catholic International Commission, *The Grace Given You in Christ*, had already moved very close to asking what each could fruitfully learn from the other.
12 See *May They All Be One* ... But How? *Proceedings of the Conference Held in St Albans Cathedral on 17th May 2003* (St Albans, The St Albans Centre for Christian Studies, 2003). It is no accident that from the outset it was envisaged that the first two Receptive Ecumenism events would be held respectively in honour of Cardinal Kasper and Archbishop Williams.
13 The nine participant regional denominational groupings are: the Roman Catholic Diocese of Hexham and Newcastle; the Anglican Dioceses of Durham and Newcastle respectively; the Northern Synod of the United Reformed Church; the Methodist Districts of Darlington and Newcastle respectively; the Northern Baptist Association; the Northern Division of the Salvation Army; and the Assemblies of God.
14 See Murray, 'Searching the Living Truth of the Church: The Systematic Task of Ecclesiology in Practice', in Mike Higton and Jim Fodor (eds), *The Routledge Companion to the Practice of Christian Theology* (London & New York, Routledge, 2012), forthcoming.
15 The Third International Receptive Ecumenism Conference will take place from 8–11 July 2013 at Fairfield University, Connecticut, USA on the theme 'Receptive Ecumenism in International Perspective: Contextual Ecumenical Learning'. To register interest, contact ccs.admin@durham.ac.uk.
16 See Murray, 'Receptive Ecumenism and Faith and Order', *One in Christ*, 43 (2009), 189–94.
17 See the official communiqué released at the end of the May 2011 meeting: www.anglicancommunion.org/acns/news.cfm/2011/5/27/ACNS4874. What follows draws upon Murray, 'ARCIC III: Recognising the Need for an Ecumenical Gear-Change', op. cit., pp. 11–13.

Focusing a Vision: Affect and Effect in Ecumenical Dialogue *Stephen Platten*

1 cf. here Walter Kasper, *Harvesting the Fruits* (London, Continuum, 2009).
2 Personal letter to the author of this essay.
3 Alan C. Clark and Colin Davey (eds), *Anglican/Roman Catholic Dialogue: The Work of the Preparatory Commission* (London/New York/Toronto, Oxford University Press, 1974).
4 The present author is the current chairman of the governors of the Anglican Centre in Rome.
5 See the chapter on Receptive Ecumenism in this volume, by Paul and Andrea Murray. c f also Paul Murray, *Receptive Ecumenism and the Call to Catholic Learning* (Oxford, Oxford University Press, 2008)

6 Anglican–Roman Catholic International Commission, *The Final Report* (London, SPCK/CTS, 1982)
7 Catholic Response to the Final Report of ARCIC I, *L'Osservatore Romano* 50 (1220) 16 December 1991, 21f. and *Information Service* 82 (1993/I) 47–51.
8 Anglican–Roman Catholic International Commission, *Clarifications* (London, CHP/CTS, 1994)
9 cf. Colin Buchanan, *News of Liturgy*, May 1995, pp. 4–5; also same author in the editorial of *News of Liturgy*, April 1995; and C. O. Buchanan, *Taking the Long View*, July 2006, Church House Publishing.
10 Quoted in Edward Yarnold, *They are in Earnest* (Slough, St Paul Publications, 1982), p. 210.
11 Anglican–Roman Catholic International Commission, *Church as Communion* (London, CHP/CTS, 1991)
12 Anglican–Roman Catholic International Commission, *The Gift of Authority* (London, CTS/Toronto, Anglican Book Centre/New York, Church Publishing, 1999), para. 7, p. 13.
13 *Church as Communion*. op cit. para. 49, p. 31.
14 Apostolic Constitution, *Anglicanorum Coetibus*, 4 November 2009.
15 Anglican–Roman Catholic International Commission, *Life in Christ: Morals, Communion and the Church* (London, CHP/CTS, 1994), p. v.
16 op cit., para. 36, p. 13.
17 op cit., para., 103, p. 37.
18 *Growing Together in Unity and Mission* (London, SPCK, 2007).
19 *Together in Mission and Ministry*. (London, CHP, 1993).
20 cf. *Together*. op cit., p.53. 'Existing Agreements Between Our Churches', Christopher Hill.
21 Called to Common Mission available at http://www.elca.org/Who-We-Are/Our-Three-Expressions/Churchwide-Organization/Office-of-the-Presiding-Bishop/Ecumenical-and-Inter-Religious-Relations/Full-Communion-Partners/The-Episcopal-Church/Called-to-Common-Mission/Official-Text.aspx
22 This unity was required to happen by the then King of Prussia, Frederick William III in 1817.
23 *The Meissen Agreement*. Council for Christian Unity of the Church of England. London. 1992.
24 (1) the holy scriptures of the Old and New Testament as the revealed word of God; (2) the Nicene Creed as the sufficient statement of the Christian faith; (3) the two sacraments – baptism and the supper of the Lord – ministered with unfailing use of Christ's words of institution and of the elements ordained by him; (4) the historic episcopate locally adapted in the methods of its administration to the varying needs of the nations and peoples called of God into the unity of his church. 'This originated with the Episcopal Church in the USA as a means of setting out foundations for organic unity. It was adopted by the Anglican Communion at the 1888 Lambeth Conference.'
25 His presence at the Medellin conference in 1968 was but one example of his openness in this area.

The Priority of Local Ecumenism *Clive Barrett*

1 Charta Oecumenica, a joint 2001 statement of the Conference of European Churches and the Council of European Bishops' Conferences, expresses something similar in the signatories' commitment 'to overcome the feeling of self-sufficiency within each church.'
2 From the World Council of Churches Faith and Order Conference in Lund, Sweden, 1952.
3 See Christian Nightlife Initiatives, http://cninet.weebly.com.
4 Lewis Burton, *Ecumenical Relationships Across the Christian Denominations in Leeds, 1960–1993,* PhD thesis, University of Leeds Department of Theology and Religious Studies, March 1995, p. 13. The opening words of the thesis are, 'Leeds is a place where ecumenical things happen …'
5 Burton, p. 15.
6 Burton, p. 17.
7 Burton, p. 24.
8 Burton, p. 26.
9 Burton, p. 28.
10 Burton, pp. 30, 31. West Yorkshire has pioneered twinning. Leeds Peace Association twinned with Lille, France, in the 1850s. Keighley had sister towns of Suresnes and Puteaux, France, from 1905. There is, in effect, a regional twinning with the Ruhr, with several links: not only Dortmund–Leeds but also Hamm–Bradford, Unna–Kirklees and Herne–Wakefield. This latter is very much a live ecumenical link, with church groups from Herne regularly visiting Wakefield and its environs.
11 Burton, p. 54.
12 Church of England (three dioceses), Roman Catholic Church, Methodist Church (two districts), Baptist Church, United Reformed Church.
13 Valuable support during a long gap between appointments was provided by David Rowland, Baptist Ecumenical Officer. Sadly, David passed away during the preparation of this volume.
14 See wyec.co.uk for the full text. Accessed January 2012.
15 From the archive of the Northern Friends' Peace Board, West Yorkshire Archive, Leeds.

Unity in the Face of Racism *Anthony G. Reddie*

1 For a helpful sweep of the different types of 'Black Churches' in Britain see Joe D. Aldred, *Respect: A Caribbean British Theology* (Peterborough, Epworth Press, 2005) and Mark Sturge, *Look What The Lord Has Done!: An Exploration of Black Christian Faith in Britain* (London, Scripture Union, 2005). See also Arlington Trotman 'Black, Black-Led or What?' Joel Edwards (ed.) *'Let's Praise Him Again': An African Caribbean Perspective on Worship* (Eastbourne, Kingsway, 1992), pp. 12–35.
2 My apologies to any of the traditions I have overlooked in this brief descriptive sweep.
3 See Robert E. Hood, *Begrimed and Black: Christian Traditions on Blacks and Blackness* (Minneapoli, Fortress, 1994), pp. 23–43.

4 Robert Beckford, *Dread and Pentecostal* (London, SPCK, 2000) pp. 95–130.
5 See Emmanuel C. Eze, *'Race' and the Enlightenment* (Oxford, Blackwell, 1997).
6 See James W. Perkinson, *White Theology* (New York, Palgrave, 2004), pp. 154–84.
7 Dwight N. Hopkins, *Being Human: 'Race' Culture and Religion* (Minneapolis, Fortress, 2005), pp. 144–60.
8 See Anthony B. Pinn, *Terror and Triumph* (Minneapolis, Fortress, 2003).
9 Anthony B. Pinn, *Terror and Triumph*, pp. 1–80.
10 This term emanates from a pivotal event on the 22 June 1948, when 492 Jamaicans arrived at Tilbury docks on the *SS Empire Windrush*. These post-war pioneers ushered in a wave of Black migration to Britain from the Caribbean, which (for the most part) forms the basis for Black African and Caribbean communities in Britain. For further information see Mike Phillips and Trevor Phillips, *Windrush: the Irresistible Rise of Multi-racial Britain* (London, HarperCollins, 1999).
11 Selective literature includes R. B. Davidson *Black British* (Oxford, Oxford University Press, 1966). R. A. Easterlin, *Immigration* (Cambridge Mass, Harvard University Press, 1982). Paul Hartman and Charles Hubbard Charles, *Immigration and the Mass media* (London, Davis-Poynter, 1974). Edward Scobie, *Black Britannia: A History of Blacks in Britain* (Chicago, Johnson Publishing, 1972). Ken Pryce, *Endless Pressure* (Bristol, Bristol Classical Press, 1979). Winston James and Clive Harris, *Migration, Racism and Identity* (London, Verso, 1993).
12 Mary Prince was a Black slave woman in the nineteenth century who published her autobiography in 1831 detailing her experiences of hardship, struggle and emancipation. Her book was entitled *The History of Mary Prince, a West Indian Slave. Related by Herself. With a Supplement by the Editor. To Which Is Added, the Narrative of Asa-Asa, a Captured African* (London, published by F. Westley and A. H. Davis, 1831). Her book was a key text in the Abolitionary movement of the nineteenth century.
13 See Vincent Caretta (ed.), *Olaudah Equiano: The Interesting Narrative and other writings* (New York and London, Penguin Books, 1995).
14 See Vincent Caretta (ed.), *Letters of the Late Ignatius Sancho, an African* (New York and London, Penguin Books, 1998).
15 Peter Fryer, *Staying Power: The History of Black People in Britain* (London, Pluto Press, 2010), p.10.
16 See Vincent Caretta (ed.) *Letters of the Late Ignatius Sancho, an African* (New York and London, Penguin Books, 1998).
17 See Mary Prince, *The History of Mary Prince, a West Indian Slave. Related by Herself. With a Supplement by the Editor. To Which Is Added, the Narrative of Asa-Asa, a Captured African* (London, Published by F. Westley and A. H. Davis, 1831).
18 See John L. Wilkinson, *Church in Black and White: The Black Christian Tradition in 'Mainstream' Churches in England: A White Response and Testimony* (Edinburgh, St Andrews Press, 1993).
19 I address this causal link in theological terms in Anthony G. Reddie (ed.) *Black Theology, Slavery, and Contemporary Christianity* (Farnham, Ashgate, 2010), pp. 2–25.

20 See Anthony B. Pinn and Dwight N. Hopkins (eds) *Loving The Body: Black Religious Studies and The Erotic* (New York, Palgrave, 2005); Kelly Brown Douglas *What's Faith Got To Do With It?* (Maryknoll, NY, Orbis Books, 2005).

21 Womanist theology is the theological articulation of God as understood through the lens of the experiences of Black (predominantly African-American) women. It seeks to address the tripartite jeopardy of being Black, female and poor in the wealthiest nation in the world. Significant womanist theological texts include Delores Williams, *Sisters in the Wilderness: The Challenge of Womanist God-Talk* (Maryknoll, NY, Orbis Books, 1993). See also Kelly Brown Douglas, *The Black Christ* (Maryland, NY, Orbis Books, 1994); Emile Townes, *Womanist Justice, Womanist Hope* (Atlanta, GA, Scholars Press, 1993); Renita J. Weems, *Just a Sister Away: A Womanist Vision of Women's Relationships in the Bible* (Philadelphia, Innisfree Press, 1988); Katie G. Cannon, *Black Womanist Ethics* (Atlanta, GA, Scholars Press, 1988).

22 See Dwight N. Hopkins *Being Human* (Minneapolis, Fortress, 2005), pp. 118–159.

23 See Valentina Alexander, 'Passive and Active Radicalism in Black Led Churches' in Michael N. Jagessar and Anthony G. Reddie (eds) *Black Theology in Britain: A Reader* (London, Equinox, 2007), pp. 52–69.

24 See Robert Beckford *Dread and Pentecostalism* (London, SPCK, 2000), pp. 46–8.

25 See Anthony G. Reddie, *Faith, Stories and the Experience of Black Elders: Singing The Lord's Song in a Strange Land* (London, Jessica Kingsley, 2001).

26 See Mark Sturge, *Look What The Lord Has Done!* (London, Scripture Union, 2005).

27 See Joe D. Aldred, *Respect: Understanding Caribbean British Christianity* (Peterborough, Epworth Press, 2005). See also, Joe D. Aldred, *Preaching With Power* (London, Continuum, 1998), also Joe D. Aldred, *Praying With Power* (London, Continuum, 2000) and also Joe D. Aldred *Sisters With Power* (London, Continuum, 2000).

28 See Joe D. Aldred *Respect: Understanding Caribbean British Christianity* (Peterborough, Epworth Press, 2005).

29 See Joe Aldred and Keno Ogbo (eds) *The Black Church in the 21st Century* (London, DLT, 2010).

30 See Robert E. Hood, *Must God Remain Greek?: Afro-Cultures and God Talk* (Minneapolis, Augsburg-Fortress, 1990).

31 See Michael N. Jagessar and Anthony G. Reddie (eds) *Black Theology in Britain: A Reader* (London, Equinox, 2007), p. 1.

32 In using this term I am referring to the historic and continued frameworks of British life that have been shaped by and continue to respond to the theories and practices that arise from the phenomenon that was and is colonialism and neo-colonialism. For an explication of this in light of British life see R. S. Sugirtharajah, *Postcolonial Reconfigurations: An Alternative Way of Reading the Bible and Doing Theology* (London, SCM, 2003) and see also R. S. Sugirtharajah *The Bible and Empire* (Cambridge, Cambridge University Press, 2005), pp. 60–97.

33 These themes are explored to great effect by Robert Beckford in the third of his groundbreaking trilogy of work, *God of the Rahtid* (London, DLT, 2003), pp. 1–30.

34 See James H. Cone, *A Black Theology of Liberation* (Maryknoll, NY, Orbis Books, 1986).

35 See Delores Williams, *Sisters in the Wilderness: The Challenge of Womanist God-Talk* (Maryknoll, NY, Orbis Books, 1993).
36 See Jacqueline Grant, *White Women's Christ and Black Women's Jesus* (Atlanta, Scholar's Press, 1989).
37 The best collective articulation of Black Theology in Britain can be found in Michael N. Jagessar and Anthony G. Reddie (eds) *Black Theology in Britain: A Reader* (London, Equinox, 2007).
38 See James H. Cone, *Black Theology and Black Power* (Maryknoll, NY, Orbis Books, 1989).
39 See Anthony G. Reddie *Black Theology, Slavery and Contemporary Christianity* (Farnham, Ashgate, 2010), pp. 2–25.
40 It is important that I make the point that not all White Christians are guilty of this behaviour. Examples of alternative practices can be found in Kenneth Leech, *Through Our Long Exile* (London, Darton, Longman and Todd, 2001); Kenneth Leech, *Doing Theology in Altab-Ali Park* (London, Darton, Longman and Todd, 2005), Kenneth Leech, *Race: Changing Society and the churches* (London, SPCK, 2005), Kenneth Leech, *Struggle in Babylon: Racism in the Cities and Churches of Britain* (London, Sheldon Press, 1988). See also David Haslam, *Race for the Millennium: The Challenge to Church and Society* (London, Churches Commission for Racial Justice – CCRJ, 1996), John L. Wilkinson, *Church in Black and White* (Edinburgh, St Andrews Press, 1990) and Timothy J. Gorringe, *Furthering Humanity: A Theology of Culture* (Farnham, Ashgate, 2004).
41 See Michael N. Jagessar 'A Brief Con-version: A Caribbean and Black-British Postcolonial Scrutiny of Christian Conversion'. *Black Theology: An International Journal* (Vol.7, No. 3, 2009), pp. 300–24.
42 Anthony G. Reddie, *Faith, Stories and the Experience of Black Elders*, pp. 11–26.
43 Perhaps the best work that addresses issues of Whiteness and privilege in Christian theological terms is Alison Webster, *You Are Mine: Reflections on Who We Are* (London, SPCK, 2009).
44 I have addressed this issue in my most recent self-authored book. See Anthony G. Reddie, *Is God Colour Blind?: Insights from Black Theology for Christian Ministry* (London, SPCK, 2009), pp. 37–52.

Unity and Prayer *Kathryn Turner and Catherine McElhinney*

1 'Don't tell me of a faith that fears to face the world around' in John L. Bell and Graham Maule, *Love and Anger: Songs of Lively Faith and Social Justice,* Wild Goose Publications, 2004.
2 'A Touching Place' in John L. Bell and Graham Maule, *Wild Goose Songs: Love from Below*, Wild Goose Publications, 2004.

Acknowledgements

Every publication has its own story and this one is no exception. Thanks must go to West Yorkshire Ecumenical Council, for its encouragement of the concept, not least to Liz Smith and Stephen Platten; above all to John Packer, not only for practical sponsorship but more especially for his personal support, priorities and model of ministry.

My personal thanks to: Monseigneur Billy Steele, whose homilies are always inspiring; Peter Whittaker, who started me off on the County Officer road; Alex Waring, my WYEC colleague; Jenny Bond of Churches Together in England, whose influence is often understated; Virginia Hearn, who has safely steered us through any turbulence; and to all of the contributors, many of whom have been working under considerable personal pressures.

This is also an appropriate time to thank those who have been part of my own ecumenical journey, not least colleagues in the developing Chaplaincy team at the University of Leeds, 1987–97. I often ask Churches Together groups for their earliest ecumenical memories, prompting stories of long forgotten Whit Walks, for example. In my case, it's when I was a schoolboy helping to take the vicar's dog for a walk. We called on the local Roman Catholic priest, and with him and others became what I subsequently realized was a small circa 1970 demonstration along Southsea beach promenade for the Campaign for Nuclear Disarmament! It is hardly surprising that I have come to associate unity with mission, to see the transformation of the Church going hand in hand with the transformation of society, that reconciliation and peace in the Church and the world are intertwined. To the ecumenical giants of past generations – Nathan Söderblöm, Swedish ecumenist who won the Nobel Peace Prize, and George Bell, ecumenical pioneer who campaigned against obliteration bombing in the Second World War – this link would have been implicitly understood. Continuing thanks go to them all.

Contributors

Clive Barrett is County Ecumenical Development Officer for West Yorkshire Ecumenical Council, and a member of the Enabling Group of Churches Together in England. A visiting research fellow in Peace Studies at Bradford, he is chair of the Peace Museum, Bradford.

Celia Blackden is Inter faith Officer at Churches Together in England, fostering Christian awareness and ecumenical collaboration. She lives in Leeds and authored *Friendship and Exchange with People of Other Faiths: a context for witness and dialogue*, Grove Books EV91.

David Cornick is General Secretary of Churches Together in England.

Christopher Foster, Bishop of Portsmouth, is Vice Chair of the Enabling Group of Churches Together in England.

Barbara Glasson, an Ecumenical Canon of Bradford Cathedral, is the team leader of Touchstone, the Methodist Church's presence in Bradford city centre.

Kirsteen Kim is Professor of Theology and World Christianity at Leeds Trinity University College. Between 2009 and 2011 she worked as Research Coordinator for the Edinburgh 2010 project. She is Vice-moderator of the World Council of Churches' Commission on World Mission and Evangelism.

Mike Love is part of Together for Peace, 'a small charity with a big network' in Leeds. He chairs Leeds Christian Community Trust, the

BME Network advisory group, and is a trustee of Left Bank Leeds. He is vice-chair of the Stronger Leeds partnership board.

Catherine McElhinney is deputy head of a Catholic school in the Catholic Diocese of Portsmouth and **Kathryn Turner** is Coordinator for Spiritual Formation in the Diocese of Hexham and Newcastle. They have long worked together preparing prayer and worship resources. Seeing the possibilities offered by the internet for sharing what they created, they launched the Wellspring website (www.wellsprings.org.uk) in Advent 1998. It receives thousands of hits every year as people freely download some of the 1,000 pages there!

Val Morrison is the General Assembly Lay Moderator of the United Reformed Church.

Andrea L. Murray is the Ecumenical Officer for the Roman Catholic Diocese of Hexham and Newcastle, and an Associate Lecturer for the Open University. She is co-author, with Philip Knights, of *Evangelization in England and Wales: a Report to the Catholic Bishops* (London: Catholic Communications Service, 2002). Andrea has been a core member of the Receptive Ecumenism and the Local Church comparative regional research project in the North East of England.

Paul D. Murray is Professor of Systematic Theology within the Department of Theology and Religion at Durham University, where he is also Director of the Centre for Catholic Studies. He serves on the British Methodist–Roman Catholic Committee, and on the third phase of work of the Anglican–Roman Catholic International Commission (ARCIC III). He is editor of *Receptive Ecumenism and the Call to Catholic Learning: Exploring a Way for Contemporary Ecumenism* (2008), and co-editor (with Gabriel Flynn) of *Ressourcement: A Movement for Renewal in Twentieth Century Catholic Theology* (2012).

Vincent Nichols: the Most Revd Vincent Nichols is Archbishop of Westminster and a President of Churches Together in England.

Stephen Platten, Bishop of Wakefield, has been in ordained ministry since 1975. He taught Christian Ethics at Lincoln Theological College and has worked in cathedrals in Portsmouth and Norwich. For five years he was the Archbishop of Canterbury's Secretary for Ecumenical Affairs.

He is Chair of the Governors of the Anglican Centre in Rome and the Chair of the Church of England's Liturgical Commission. He has been a member of the House of Lords since June 2009.

Anthony G. Reddie is a Research Fellow in Black Theology at the Queen's Foundation for Ecumenical Theological Education in Birmingham. He is editor of *Black Theology: An International Journal*, the only academic periodical in Black Theology in the world.

Helen Reid is a Methodist and Programme Director at Bradford Churches for Dialogue and Diversity. BCDD is an ecumenical organization that works in the fields of training for religious literacy and community development in multi faith neighbourhoods.

Neil Richardson was Tutor in New Testament Studies and later Principal of Wesley College, Bristol. He served as President of the British Methodist Conference in 2003–4.

Liz Smith is currently Chair of the Leeds Methodist District. She is committed to developing healthy ecumenical relationships and she is delighted to be Chair of West Yorkshire Ecumenical Council in this Anniversary year. Her interests include feminist theology, walking and poetry.

Mary Tanner, DBE, is a President of the World Council of Churches, having been a member of its Faith and Order Commission since 1974, including being Moderator 1991–8.

Alison Tomlin is currently one of the Presidents of the Christian–Muslim Forum, having been Chair of a Methodist District and President of the Methodist Conference. 'I accompany people in prayer, leading quiet days and silent retreats. I work for justice and peace with people of all faiths and none.'

Ernie Whalley is President-designate of the Baptist Union of Great Britain, having been Regional Minister for Ministry with Yorkshire Baptist Association.

Index